PENSIONS:
MORE INFORMATION, LESS IDEOLOGY

# Pensions: More Information, Less Ideology

## Assessing the Long-Term Sustainability of European Pension Systems: Data Requirements, Analysis and Evaluations

edited by

**Tito Boeri**

*Fondazione Debenedetti and University of Bocconi, Italy*

**Axel Börsch-Supan**

*University of Mannheim, Germany*

**Agar Brugiavini**

*University of Venice, Italy*

**Richard Disney**

*University of Nottingham, United Kingdom*

**Arie Kapteyn**

*Tilburg University, The Netherlands*

**Franco Peracchi**

*University of Tor Vergata, Italy*

KLUWER ACADEMIC PUBLISHERS

BOSTON / DORDRECHT / LONDON

A C.I.P. Catalogue record for this book is available from the Library of Congress.

ISBN 978-1-4419-4916-5

Published by Kluwer Academic Publishers,
P.O. Box 17, 3300 AA Dordrecht, The Netherlands.

Sold and distributed in North, Central and South America
by Kluwer Academic Publishers,
101 Philip Drive, Norwell, MA 02061, U.S.A.

In all other countries, sold and distributed
by Kluwer Academic Publishers,
P.O. Box 322, 3300 AH Dordrecht, The Netherlands.

*Printed on acid-free paper*



Printed in the Netherlands.

# CONTENTS

# LIST OF CONTRIBUTORS

*Michael Anderson* is a research demographer at Mountain View Research. He holds a PhD in demography and a masters in statistics from the University of California at Berkeley.

*Tito Boeri* holds a Ph.D. in Economics from New York University; has been senior economist at the OECD from 1987 to 1996. In this position, he has co-ordinated the work carried out by the OECD in the field of human resource policies in the economies in transition since 1990. He is currently Professor of Economics at Bocconi University, Milan, where he teaches a course on the Economics of Transition.

*Axel Börsch-Supan* is Director of the Mannheim Research Institute for the Economics of Aging. He received a Ph.D. from MIT and taught at Harvard's Kennedy School of Government before he moved back to Germany. Börsch-Supan is a member of the Berlin-Brandenburg Academy of Sciences, the German Academy of Sciences Leopoldina, and the Council of Advisors to the Federal Ministry of Economics and Technology.

*Agar Brugiavini* is Professor in Economics at the University "Ca' Foscari" of Venice, Italy. She obtained a Ph.D. in Economics at the London School of Economics, UK and was recently awarded a Fulbright Fellowship at Northwestern University, USA. She is scientist in charge for a EU sponsored TMR (Training and Mobility of Researchers) programme on saving and pensions. Her research areas are in pensions and pension reforms, savings and insurance markets. She has done extensive empirical work on individuals' behaviour using micro data at individual level and household level for different European countries.

*Marco Buti* is in charge of public finances in the Euro area at the European Commission and has been visiting professor at the University of Florence and at the European University Institute. He has published several books and articles in the areas of fiscal and monetary policy, welfare state, European unemployment and Economic and Monetary Union.

*Declan Costello* is an economist in the public finances department of the Directorate General for Economic and Financial Affairs of the European Commission. He has been closely involved with the EMU project for several years including the arrangements for the practical changeover to the Euro and the establishment of the framework for the surveillance of Member States' budgetary positions (the Stability and Growth Pact). Since 1999, he has been responsible for assessing the long-term sustainability of public finances in EMU and the production of more comparable long-tem projections for public pension expenditures in EU Member States. He has also involved in steps to enhance co-operation in between Member States in the field of pension reform.

*Richard Disney* is Professor of Economics at the University of Nottingham, a Research Fellow of the Institute for Fiscal Studies, London, and a Director of Axia Economics. He has published widely on the issues of pensions, retirement and social security and has acted as a consultant to OECD and the World Bank.

*Arie Kapteyn* is a senior economist at RAND. Before that he was the director of CentER at Tilburg University and professor of economics. His research specialises in consumption, saving, labour supply, financial behaviour of households, retirement and ageing. He has published extensively in these areas.

*Nan Li* is a Research Demographer at MVR. He has a 1988 Ph.D. in economics and demography, and held a senior faculty position at China's Xi'an Jiatong University before joining MVR. Expertise: population dynamics, control theory, fertility and mortality of China and Asia, stochastic population forecasting, sex-ratio dynamics in Asia, immigration policy, old-age dynamics in the G7 countries

*Carole Maignan* is a Research Officer at the Fondazione Eni E. Mattei- Venice-Italy. She holds a Ph.D. in Economics and she works in the areas of economic consequences of an ageing population, risk behaviour, and, more recently, in the impact of the new economy.

*Michael Marmot*, Professor of Epidemiology and Public Health and Director of the International Centre for Health and Society at University College London, has been at the forefront of research into health inequalities for the past 20 years, as Principal Investigator of the Whitehall studies of British civil servants, investigating explanations for the social gradient in morbidity and mortality, and the English Longitudinal Study of Ageing. He was awarded a knighthood in 2000 for services to epidemiology and understanding health inequalities.

*James Nazroo*, Reader in Sociology and head of the Health and Social Surveys Research Group in the Department of Epidemiology and Public Health at UCL, is an investigator of the English Longitudinal Study of Ageing. His ageing related research also includes studies of ethnic inequalities in older ages and early retirement among British civil servants. His publications also cover work on ethnic inequalities in health and gender inequalities in mental illness.

*Cheti Nicoletti* is a post-doctoral researcher at the Tor Vergata University. She earned her Ph.D. in Statistics in Florence University and she holds a Master in economics from University of Louvain.

*Howard Oxley* is a senior economist in the Economics Department at the OECD. He has main area of interest and work is public sector economics and, in particular, public expenditure.

*Franco Peracchi* (Ph.D., Princeton U., 1987) is a Professor of Econometrics at Tor Vergata University in Rome. His research interests include econometric theory and methods, nonparametric and robust statistical method, and labour economics.

*Shipad Tuljapurkar* is the President of MVR and the chief scientist. He has a 1976 Ph.D., and held faculty positions at several universities, most recently at Stanford University. He is currently a Consulting Professor at Stanford, a Member of the Center for the Demography and Economics of Aging at the University of California, Berkeley, and a Member of the Science Board of the Santa Fe Institute. Tuljapurkar is author or co-author of numerous scientific papers and two books. Honors: 1990, elected Fellow of the American Association of Arts and Sciences; 1996, received the Mindel Sheps award from the Population Association of America; 1998, received the John Simon Guggenheim fellowship. He serves on the editorial boards of several scientific journals and on review panels for national scientific agencies.

BOERI, BÖRSCH-SUPAN, BRUGIAVINI, DISNEY, KAPTEYN, PERACCHI

# INTRODUCTION

The ageing of the population in the developed countries poses one of the major challenges in the 21st century. The population aged 60 and older is expected to rise in OECD countries: the demographic shift is explained by several factors, but the spectacular and largely unpredicted decline in mortality at older ages and lowering birth rates are major determinants of current trends in ageing. This challenge cannot be met by repeated and uninformed references to an incumbent disaster, but rather by providing timely and accurate information to citizens and policy makers and by carrying out research on the causes and effects of these changes.

In February 2000 a group of about 100 experts on pensions in Europe, prompted by the initiative of the Fondazione Rodolfo Debenedetti, issued an Appeal to the President of the European Commission, Romano Prodi, requesting that European citizens be better informed about the long-term sustainability of their pension systems and, more broadly, as to the implications of the ageing of the European population. In particular, the Appeal, which is reproduced in the Annex to this volume, asked for i) the *harmonisation of methodologies* used in the various countries to report pension outlays and forecast future pension liabilities; ii) a *definition of common standards* as to the frequency of expenditure forecasts and the length of the forecast horizons and iii) the development of a *European panel survey* of persons pre- and post retirement age, providing timely information on trends in contributors to the pension system, and on the determinants of retirement decisions.

The appeal was subscribed to by scholars having different views as to the ideal pension system that should accompany the demographic transition. It was signed also by professional economists advising policy-makers located sometimes at the polar extremes of the political spectrum. It called for more information and less ideology.

This volume is a natural follow-up to this Appeal. It broadens its perspective in that it involves contributions from different fields (and not only from economists) on the challenge that ageing poses to the developed world and to Europe in particular.

The implications of the ageing of the population can only be fully understood with a multidisciplinary perspective. The recent demographic trends have multiple dimensions. The first and most apparent change is the decline in mortality, and in particular the marked increase in the age at which death rates start to peak (one aspect of the so-called "rectangularisation" of the survival curve). Moreover, the



*T.Boeri, A.Börsch-Supan, A.Brugiavini, R.Disney, A.Kapteyn and F.Peracchi (eds.), Pensions: More Information, Less Ideology, 1—7.*

elderly are typically no longer active in the labour market and require more health care, and a shift in disability trends could also result from these demographic trends. More generally, household composition and household decisions, including labour supply, the demand for goods and services, and saving, will be affected by the demographic shift. Hence, the increase in the relative share of the elderly has major implications, which deserve attention from the scientific community and from policy makers. These implications should not be analysed in isolation but as a complex and simultaneous change in society.

## 1. ARE THE RECOMMENDATIONS PROVIDED IN THE APPEAL TO PRODI STILL VALID?

The simple truth emerging from the studies in this volume is that we still know too little about the impact that the demographic shift and increases in life expectancy will have on household behaviour, welfare arrangements and society as a whole. We can at this stage at best characterise the sources of this uncertainty. For example, in some cases we can quantify some of these risks by making use of general and flexible forecasting techniques which replace the usual High, Medium and Low scenarios adopted by actuaries (see the contribution to this volume by Anderson, Tuljapurkar and Li). The uncertainty is partly generated by the complexity of the ageing process, which this multidisciplinary volume tries to address, and by a lack of information that undermines any timely and scientific analysis. One aspect emerging from all the different dimensions of the problem analysed in this volume is that multidisciplinary research is needed and good quality data is the top priority.

A key area where we need to know more relates to the incentive structure of early retirement and the role of policy in affecting the retirement age. In several respects the ageing challenge will be bigger in Europe than in other parts of the world: compared to the rest of the developed countries Europeans *effectively* retire early. The projections of fiscal imbalances and financial concerns on unfunded health and old age provisions may even be too rosy, in the sense that many individuals under 60 have already retired and hence do not contribute to the productive base from which the consumption of the elderly has to be financed. On the contrary, the early retirees themselves need to be supported by the working population. The high percentage of non-labour force participants under the age of 60 is the result of developments that have taken place since the 1960s. This suggests that government and company policies (embedded both in social security and in company pension plan rules) may have contributed substantially to the decline in labour force participation (Gruber and Wise, 1999). Indeed, an important determinant of the decline in labour force participation before the age of 60 lies in the generous retirement benefits provided by the social security and welfare system of European countries, which introduced an "implicit tax" on continued work (see the contribution of Boeri, Brugiavini and Maignan to this volume). Measures of the cost of early retirement are hard to come by. However, building on the idea of "unused capacity" (i.e. the complement to labour force participation) one can provide a rough measure of the percentage of people, in each age group, who could potentially participate to the labour force but are not part of it. This is *prima facie* evidence of the resources available for production, which are not utilised. According to these estimates, the cost of early retirement, expressed as the share of potential GDP which is lost, peaked for all OECD countries during the 1980s and mildly declined in the 1990s (Herbertsson and Orszag, 2001). Hence early retirement is not just a cost to the public pension programme or to the company's pension plan, but has overall macroeconomic implications. Obviously, in a pay-as-you-go programme, these fast growing groups of early retirees have to be supported by an equally fast shrinking working force. Given the speed at which older men leave the labour force, it is not extreme to project that, around 2030 or so, in many European countries a quarter of the earnings of the working population may be needed just to support the elderly, if the present incentives and old age security systems persist (trends are described by Disney in this volume).

Governments have been trying to tackle mainly the financial problems related to ageing and a number of public pension reforms and health care reforms have taken place in recent years. These are mainly "parametric" reforms, in the sense that they often leave unaffected the unfunded nature of the welfare system (the terminology is that of Chand and Jaeger, 1996). One example is given by public pension reforms undertaken in the early 1990s in countries such as Italy, which have typically increased normal retirement ages and changed eligibility criteria and benefits with the objective to achieve fairness for all groups of workers. However these changes may have limited immediate impact on costs given the persistence of other early retirement "avenues" and the continued overall generosity of programmes. But even the political process of proposing and finalising welfare reforms has an overwhelming impact on the final outcome. In fact one observes that reforms in Europe have often been mild and time-inconsistent as a result. In a number of cases reforms done by one Government have been undone by the subsequent Government, in some cases within the same coalition. There are political reasons for the marginal nature of these reforms. A majority of citizens in the countries facing the most severe problems of sustainability of their pension systems – such as France, Germany, Italy and Spain – appear to be in favour of the status quo size of the welfare state and may therefore oppose radical reforms such as those frequently advocated in academic discussions (these surveys are described in Boeri, Börsch-Supan and Tabellini, 2001).

One major problem in even starting to think about financial problems and the reform process is a lack of a well specified framework for the analysis. Only in recent years have we seen a number of studies which provide attempts at characterising existing welfare systems on a common basis and measuring the impact of welfare reforms (for example OECD, 1998; OECD, 2000 and EC, 2000). In particular, Disney and Johnson (2001) have shown the value of providing cross-country measures of income provision in old age and more generally redistributional features of different pension systems existing in different countries. Even starting from a very precise and common methodological template, the study of Disney and Johnson had to consider only a reduced number of countries where calculations could be carried out and develop the analysis on the basis of cross-sectional data sets. But a more precise picture could be achieved by making use of longitudinal data for many countries, as one can track individuals (and households) to see if different cohorts and different individuals fare better after a policy change or under different welfare regimes. The lack of a valid framework is also apparent from the observation that EU countries have not agreed on a proper measure of public pension liabilities, i.e. the value of commitments already made to current and future retirees (Disney in this volume). This measure requires three ingredients: assumptions on the underlying trends of the economy, time horizon and forecasting procedures. If EU countries could agree on a common framework on these parameters, a clearer picture would emerge of the impact of the demographic shift on fiscal imbalances and the likely effect of reforms. This book documents the progress made recently in this respect, but also the long way to go before harmonising forecasting procedures. As discussed by Oxley in this volume, ongoing work at OECD involves the checking for mutual consistency of the key macroeconomic assumptions required in projecting age-related expenditure and the definition of common standards as to the length of the forecasting interval and the frequency of projections. Yet, there is still a high degree of heterogeneity and uncertainty surrounding pension liabilities projections. This makes it hard to evaluate social security programmes and leaves space for manipulation which interferes with the reform process and with policy co-ordination at the EU level. The agreement recently reached at the EU level on the multilateral surveillance of the long-term sustainability of public finance can only be applied broadening the scope of expenditure projections to include the multi-dimensional implications of ageing, when a common set of indicators is adopted to supplement and summarise the projections (Buti and Costello in this volume)

Better information to citizens as to the current and future costs of public pension systems can help garner consensus on reforms introducing a significant funded component in the pension systems (Boeri, Börsch-Supan and Tabellini, 2001). Citizens have also to be informed that piecemeal changes may appear like "ideal reforms" but they may be more costly than a fully-fledged and transparent move toward a "pension portfolio". To quote a few of these costs: actual cost of implementation of a parametric reform, the opportunity cost of policies subject to political manipulation and the negative externality created by the confusion surrounding a plethora of frequent changes, let alone the administrative costs involved by frequent and marginal reforms. A justification to proceed step by step with small, parametric reforms, is that we do not have a full picture of the impact of a more definite move toward a pension portfolio on household saving (see Börsch-Supan in this volume). Would workers be willing to provide self-finance for old age insurance if partial privatisation of the system occurs? Can we expect new saving and an increased capital stock as a result of a shift from unfunded to funded welfare provisions? If such a shift occurs, should governments mandate the purchase of old age insurance in private markets or let households decide for themselves?

The other major concern in the policy debate is on health programmes, as ageing could also imply a more expensive health care system. However, some authors point out (see Nazroo and Marmot in this volume) that the ageing process has not been clearly demarcated as yet. It cannot be described as an increasing physical and financial dependency of the elderly on their children or on society. The third age could be a period of self-fulfilment and financial independence if people have a forward looking behaviour and if distortions brought about by the wrong incentives are minimised. These considerations makes clear that each country will have to consider adjustments to the entire welfare state: it would be myopic and even dangerous to discuss the effect of the demographic changes on one aspect while neglecting the others. Thus, while pension systems and health care programmes are closely linked, more hard evidence is needed on whether increasing longevity is associated with an accelerating, proportional or decreasing health care budget. A further problem is that many welfare systems have been designed simultaneously, to the extent that in some countries one cannot even distinguish the part of the contribution which is paid in for health insurance or old age provision. Since different countries have adopted policies that are often very different both in terms of old age insurance and in terms of health care, there is considerable scope for learning from each other's experience. In order to be able to do so, it is generally insufficient to simply compare policies and outcomes across countries and across time. It is important to initiate the collection of comparable data in different countries. Only if data are similar in nature across countries can we learn from the differences observed in these countries.

## 2. WHAT KIND OF DATA WOULD THEN BE NEEDED?

This volume is a blueprint for a strategy of further development of comparable data, and an associated research programme, across Europe. The leading example is the Health and Retirement Survey (HRS) in the US, which is the focal point for a large multi-disciplinary group of prominent researchers in the area of ageing to address pressing policy questions. The scientific community has learnt a few stylised facts on household behaviour by making use of the existing data in Europe. For example it emerges that there is a wide spectrum of behavioural patterns in terms of saving and portfolio composition. But are there likely to be variations across countries due to differences in institutional arrangements, taste parameters or in attitudes toward risk? - only detailed comparative data at the household level can help answering this question. The English Longitudinal Survey of Ageing (ELSA), at the time of writing in the field, is the first major HRS-type research programme in Europe (funded by the US National Institute of Aging and co-financed by a number of UK government departments), but more surveys of this type are now needed in Europe. Such data does not come cheap. But it is worth reiterating that the basic problem with existing data sources is that they provide measures which are hardly comparable across countries (or even over time for the same country). Even the data collection experience of the European Community in this area has produced limited results because a large coordination effort is required at all levels, and underlying policy issues and resulting target populations have to be clearly defined (see Nicoletti and Peracchi in this volume).

In the strategy of the Appeal the common core of information to be collected from households should have the following three main features.

*1. Interdisciplinary*: Societal and individual aspects of ageing involve at least health, socio-economic, psychological, and demographic dimensions, which often cannot be studied in isolation.

*2. Longitudinal*: Each cohort is different. Younger cohorts will have very different experiences from today's elderly. Need to separate age and cohort effects for sensible statements about ageing processes.

*3. Accessible*: Need to have data investigated from diverse and sceptical points of view. Exploit creativity and control mechanisms of research community at large.

Moreover, as a fourth feature, the data should be comparable through the European Union. This provides an important added value in comparison to the single-nation US-American Health and Retirement Survey:

*4. Cross-nationally comparable*: Europe is a fascinating laboratory because it features so many different policy approaches. Cross-national comparability helps us enormously to understand what influence different policies have on human behaviour.

This volume is an attempt to explain why in all the different areas of research and policy making such data framework is becoming essential. We, the promoters of the Appeal to Commission President Romano Prodi, are currently involved in exploring the possibility of such a pan-European survey in different countries of the European Community and in Europe at large. We are aware that this is a major task that requires the support of many researchers as well as enlightened and responsible politicians. The advantages are clear: the scientific community would be able to carry out rigorous research and answer policy questions, but also European countries will be able to exchange ideas on a common basis and politicians take informed decisions. At the same time European citizens will be able to obtain more precise and timely information on the future of welfare systems. We hope that this volume strengthens the interest in studying the challenges of population ageing. We also hope that it contributes to extending the range of disciplines and countries involved in the initial steps to create a pan-European data base on ageing. Most importantly, we hope that we can convince our readers how important informed choices are for our future.

## REFERENCES

BOERI T., BÖRSCH-SUPAN A. and TABELLINI G. (2001), "Would you like to shrink the welfare state? A survey of European Citizens", in *Economic Policy*, April, 32.

CHAND S. and JAEGER A. (1996), Aging populations and public pension schemes, Occasional paper no.147, Washington D. C., International Monetary Fund.

DISNEY R. and JOHNSON P. (eds.) (2001), *Pension systems and retirement incomes across OECD countries*, Edward Elgar, Aldershot, London.

EUROPEAN COMMISSION (2000), *The contribution of public finances to growth and employment: quality and sustainability*, Communication of the Commission to the Council and the European Parliament, COM (2000),846

GRUBER, J. and WISE D. A. (eds.) (1999), *Social Security and Retirement around the World*, The University of Chicago Press, Chicago.

HERBERTSSON T. and ORSZAG M. (2001), The cost of early retirement in the OECD, Institute of Economic Studies Working Paper 1:02, University of Iceland.

OECD (1998), *Maintaining Prosperity in an Ageing Society*, Paris.

OECD (2000), *Reforms for an Ageing Society*, Paris.

MICHAEL ANDERSON, SHRIPAD TULJAPURKAR AND NAN LI

# HOW ACCURATE ARE DEMOGRAPHIC PROJECTIONS USED IN FORECASTING PENSION EXPENDITURE?

## 1. INTRODUCTION

This paper concerns the nature and role of uncertainty in long-range planning (50 to 75 year horizons) for systems such as public retirement programmes. The majority of such systems are evaluated on the basis of fiscal criteria for long-run sustainability, such as actuarial balance, or long-run adequacy, such as the ability of the system to meet defined obligations. To illustrate uncertainty in concrete terms we will use as an example public retirement systems which combine a pay-as-you-go element with a reserve fund: examples include the US Social Security System, the Canadian Pension Plan, and similar systems in many European countries. In such systems, the balance B(t) in the reserve fund in year t is determined by the interest earnings on existing balances, the inflow of funds into the system from taxes on wages, and the outflow of funds paid to beneficiaries. If we look forward from a particular starting time, the dynamics of the system depend on the future trajectories of wages, the numbers of wage earners and of beneficiaries, and the interest rate earned by the fund. Most people would agree that there is increasing uncertainty over time about all of these trajectories. Our goal here is to illustrate how this uncertainty may be quantified and projected through time, as well as to show how this quantitative assessment may be used by analysts to inform policy makers.

The traditional method used by most official agencies to quantify uncertainty is to develop at least three scenarios for the evolution of the demographic and economic variables that shape the system. We will refer to these as the High, Medium and Low scenarios. These scenarios are intended to span a reasonably broad range of outcomes, and thus to inform policy makers about what might happen. However there is no weighting among alternatives, and the individual alternatives are perfectly deterministic trajectories specified *a priori*.

In a series of papers, we have worked with Ronald Lee to develop methods for the use of stochastic models for the demographic and economic components of fiscal systems (Anderson *et al.*, 2000; Tuljapurkar *et al.*, 2000; Tuljapurkar and Lee, 1998; Lee and Tuljapurkar, 1997). It is important to note that our primary goal is not to develop "better" forecasts of the future. Rather our goal is to develop a systematic



*T.Boeri, A.Börsch-Supan, A.Brugiavini, R.Disney, A.Kapteyn and F.Peracchi (eds.), Pensions: More Information, Less Ideology*, 9—27.

procedure for incorporating historical variability into our projections. We are open to, and indeed encourage, the use of alternative forecast models, so long as there is reason to believe that they can do better than ones we have used before. But we insist that each forecasting component must include a dynamic stochastic model that captures historical deviations form the model. From this stochastic model we can then project probability distributions for the dynamics of the system under study, and also measures of risk that accompany particular goals of sustainability or adequacy.

We begin with two sections that describe the demographic and economic components that we have modelled in our studies of the populations of the G7 countries (US, UK, Germany, Italy, France, Japan, Canada), and the US Social Security system. Then we describe how these are integrated into a model of US Social Security, and illustrate the probabilistic information that the model yields.

## 2. SOURCES OF UNCERTAINTY

There are four rough categories of uncertainty faced by fiscal planners: Demographic uncertainty, economic uncertainty, behavioural uncertainty, and uncertainty arising from unknown structural complexities. The sections below describe in detail how we deal with the first two categories of uncertainty.

In short, we attempt to gauge demographic and economic uncertainty through the use of dynamic stochastic models for the underlying components of the system. For example, we model mortality rates by first using a nonlinear transformation of central death rates, and then identifying and selecting a parsimonious time series model that captures the trend and variation in the transformed rates. In practice we have used a variety of time series models as the stochastic drivers in our existing models. However there is no reason why more complex dynamic models, or models with stronger coupling between components, could not be used if they could be shown to have greater historical validity than the models we employ. The approach we advocate here is independent of the particular models used.

Essentially, the size of the variation in the historical time series, as estimated by the variances of the innovation terms in our models, provides a measure of uncertainty about the future behaviour of the series. By repeatedly simulating future trajectories of these time series models with independent, pseudo-random innovations, we can generate an entire distribution of fund balance trajectories over time, along with cost rates, income rates, and actuarial balances.

But first, a word is in order concerning the latter two sources of uncertainty. One significant source of uncertainty for fiscal planners is the behaviour of future workers and retirees. For example, if the age at normal retirement were raised an additional year, would workers work an extra year, or would they continue to take early retirement? It is also impossible to know exactly what labour force participation rates may be at other ages, or to what extent women will continue their advance into the labour force.

We treat the behaviour of retirees by allowing for the deterministic adjustment of various parameters in our model, such as hazard rates of retirement by age, in order to assess the impact of different modes of behaviour.

Fourth, there is a broad range of structural economic effects which could intervene in unpredictable ways. Examples include major technological innovations, the globalisation of trade and capital, feedback to or from other economic/demographic variables, or some other dynamic interaction with demographic or behavioural forces.

At present we do not consider any economic/demographic interactions, feedback, or dramatic structural economic changes, leaving aside these complexities for future modelling projects.

### *2.1 Demographic uncertainty*

One of the central sources of uncertainty in fiscal forecasts comes from the question of exactly how many taxpayers and beneficiaries will exist at each age and sex, since the answer question affects fiscal inflows and outflows in obvious ways. The size of the population at any future time and age depends in turn on future mortality, fertility and migration at each age and sex. We model mortality and fertility stochastically, and take migration rates to be deterministic, for reasons discussed below.

#### *2.1.1 Mortality*

Mortality is difficult to forecast for several reasons. Over the past half century, mortality rates in most industrialised countries have been characterised by a long-run decline, with some short-run variation around this trend. The specific structure of this decline, however, is not immediately obvious. Life expectancy (denoted $e_0$) has generally increased, but in a nonlinear way; the left side of Figure 1 shows $e_0$ in the United States from 1900 to 1996. Life expectancy has increased substantially, although the gains seem to be slowing over time. Also, there were years of dramatic variation around this trend (the influenza epidemic of 1917, for instance).

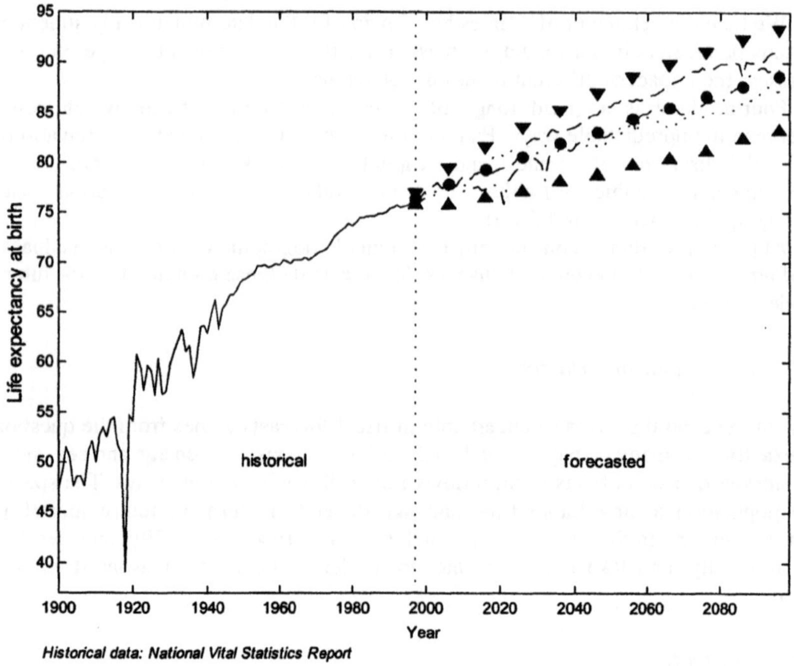


*Figure 1. Life expectancy at birth in the United States, 1900-2096*

Historically, forecasts of mortality have been unduly influenced by the most recently observed, short-run variations in rates. In the US during the 1960s, improvements in mortality appeared to slow down, and subsequent forecasts reflected this in their pessimism. Hence the substantial gains to life expectancy which began in the late 1970s were completely unanticipated.

Age-specific death rates have also declined non-linearly with substantial short-term variation, and rates at some ages have decreased more rapidly than rates at other ages.

Finally, the very nature of mortality in industrialised countries has also changed dramatically over the past century. The causes of death have largely shifted from infectious diseases to the chronic illnesses of old age. Also, infant mortality and its causes have decreased much more dramatically than mortality rates at other ages.

Thus, it is not surprising that it is difficult to find any simple patterns in these complex phenomena; yet one does exist. Ronald Lee and Lawrence Carter (1992) have constructed a model of mortality rates for the US which illustrates a remarkably elegant feature of death rates over the past century. The model describes how the death rate at age x and time t, m(x,t), evolves over time. The formula for the death rate is:

$$log(m(x,t)) = a(x) + b(x)k(t) + error(t)$$

where a(x) and b(x) are age-specific parameters which are constant over time, and k(t) is an index which indicates the overall level of mortality at time t. Given the constants a(x) and b(x), any value of k(t) implies an entire life table of death rates.

A decrease in mortality is reflected by a decrease in k(t), which in the model implies a decrease at death rates at *all* ages. Thus according to the model, all death rates move up or down each year depending on whether k(t) rises or falls, but the *amount* by which the log of each age-specific rate changes is proportional to b(x).

For the US, Lee and Carter observed that the value of k(t) has decreased linearly over the past century. This implies that in the long run, age-specific death rates have decreased *exponentially* at age-specific rates. Lee and Carter also found that the k(t) series is well modelled as a random walk with drift:

$$k(t+1) = k(t) - drift + innovation(t)$$

where the innovation term is an independent, identically distributed random variable.

The right side of Figure 1 shows the $e_0$ forecast derived from this fit for the years 1997-2096 (ignore the dashed lines for the moment). Notice that these are much more than simple extrapolations of the linear trend in the k(t) index. The forecast of $e_0$ has a 95% probability interval at each time point, reflecting an entire distribution of estimates. The circle in the middle is the median of this distribution, the upper triangle is the 97.5th percentile, and the lower triangle is the 2.5th percentile. These distributions are constructed by simulating the random walk model pseudo-randomly on a computer, repeated 1,000 times with independent innovations. Three random trajectories are plotted as dashed lines in the plot.

Each generated trajectory of k(t) varies randomly from year to year, just as the historical value of k(t) has fluctuated. Also, since the innovations in m(x,t) are exponentially declining in absolute magnitude, the variance in the corresponding life expectancy trajectories is constrained accordingly, even at very long horizons. Notice that the historical variance in life expectancy has also decreased quite substantially, so we should expect this sort of result.

The randomly-generated variation in the future k(t) trajectories also reflects our uncertainty in the estimate of the size of the drift term. Under the assumptions of the model, we can estimate this term as a sample mean, which is normally distributed. Hence for each trajectory in our simulation, we draw a random value for the drift term from a normal distribution having a standard deviation equal to the standard error of the estimate.

Ideally, the b(x) parameters of the model should also be generated stochastically in order to reflect uncertainty in their estimates. Unfortunately, the estimation of standard errors for these parameters is not so straightforward, so we have ignored this detail to date. However, for the purposes of life expectancy forecasts, it appears that the variance in the innovation term for k(t) dominates the distribution in the long run.

Recently Tuljapurkar *et al.* (2000) have demonstrated that this linear decline in k(t) is common to all the G7 countries (US, UK, Canada, France, Germany, Italy and Japan). Figure 2 shows the fitted values of b(x) for each country by age. The pattern for all countries is quite similar to that for the US, again reflecting the rapid pace of decline in mortality at the youngest ages.

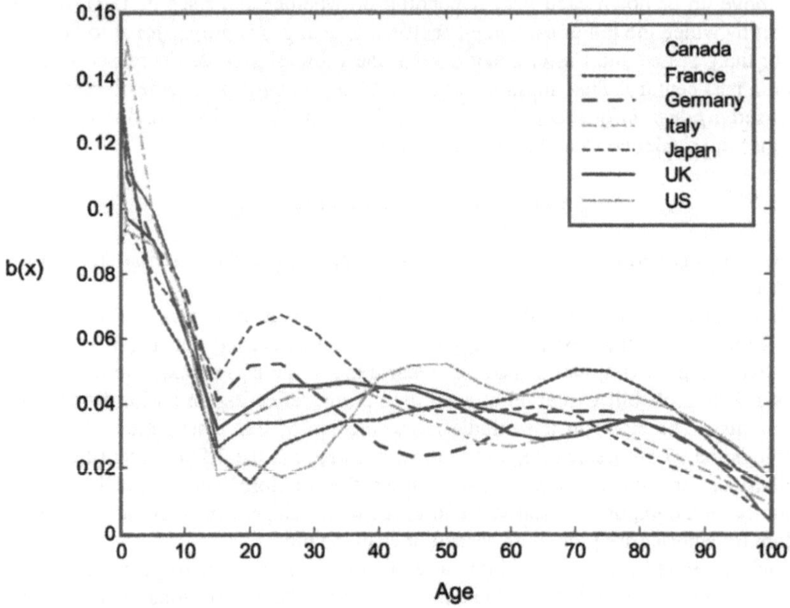


*Figure 2. Lee-Carter b(x) parameters for the G7 countries*

Figure 3 plots $e_0$ forecasts for the G7 countries, along with the official, government forecasts. In every country, the official medium forecast (the diamonds) is exceeded by the median of the stochastic forecasts (the circles). Triangles denote the 67% probability intervals. In Japan, the median $e_0$ forecast is approximately 8 years higher than the official medium forecast for 2050. In Canada, France and Italy the median of the stochastic forecasts lies above the official High forecast in 2050. These plots clearly demonstrate that if $e_0$ follows the official medium forecasts, it would mark a substantial (and in our view, improbable) departure from the historical trend.

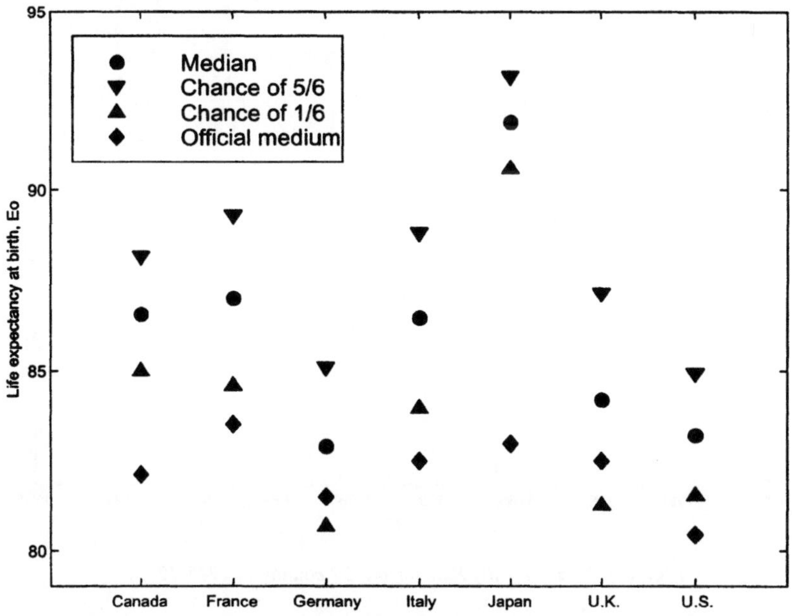


*Figure 3. Forecasts of life expectancy at birth for the G7 countries in 2050*

Tuljapurkar *et al.* suggest one possible explanation for the exponential decline in death rates. They start with the assumption that mortality decline in this century has resulted from a sustained application of resources and knowledge to public health and mortality reduction. Year-to-year mortality rates decline proportionately because society allocates resources in proportion to age-specific levels of observed mortality. The constant rate of change over time results from a long-run balance between the rising resources devoted to combating mortality and the increasing complexity and intractability of the predominant causal mechanisms behind death.

*2.1.2. Fertility*

Fertility is substantially more difficult to forecast than mortality. First, historical variation is greater in magnitude and less regular. Figure 4 plots the Total Fertility Rate for the G7 countries for 1950 to 1995. Except for Japan, the pattern for all countries over the past fifty years is quite similar, with post-war increases followed by dramatic decreases to less than 2 by the 1970s.

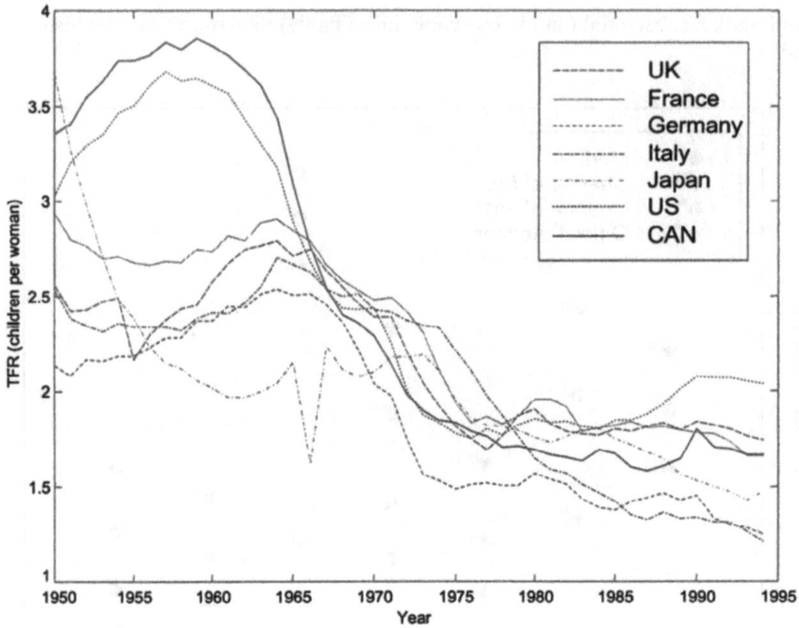


*Figure 4. Total Fertility Rate for the G7 countries, 1945-1995*

In fact fertility rates in the US have experienced several large swings over the past century. The period TFR was at 3.5 children per woman in 1910, declined to 2.2 by 1935, rose to over 3.5 again by 1955, and decreased yet again to less than 2 by 1975, where it has remained since. This confluence of events has seriously frustrated past forecasting attempts. Figure 5 shows how the Census Bureau's medium forecasts of the past (dotted lines) have completely misjudged future fertility rates (continous lines). Expert opinion simply cannot prevail in the face of such vast fluctuations.

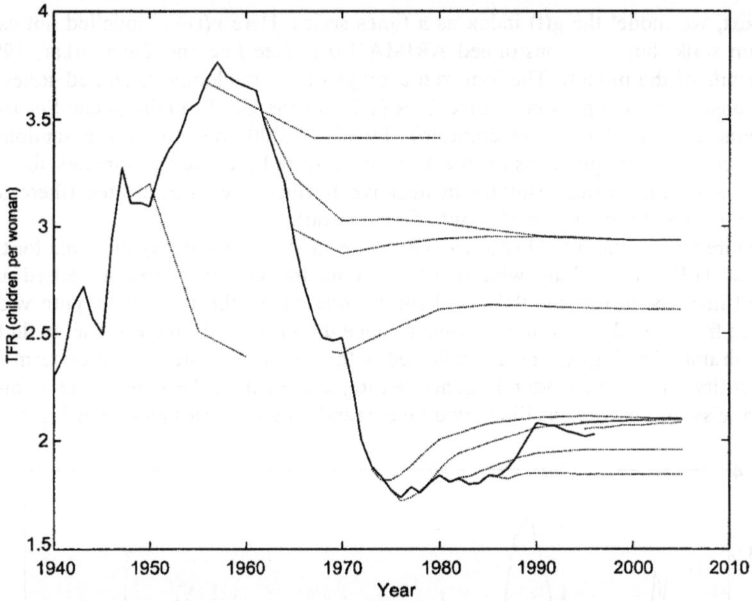


Note: Medium forecasts are the average of high and low forecasts where none existed.
Dotted lines denote forecasts and continous lines actual fertility rates.

*Figure 5. TFR in the US, with Census Bureau's Medium Forecasts*

Nonetheless, today's forecasters remain undaunted. The Social Security Administration's most recent forecasts of the TFR use a High-Low range of 1.7 to 2.2 over the next 75 years. Experts now argue that the widespread availability of effective contraception and tubal ligations has made a return to higher fertility rates unlikely (in which case the SSA may be seriously overestimating the low boundary on fertility in its Low estimate). On the other hand, there is nothing to prevent similar technological advances from restoring the possibility of higher fertility (e.g., fertility-enhancing drugs or a lengthening of the child-bearing years). Most importantly, it is nearly impossible to predict what is perhaps the most important variable – individuals' future predilection for children. For these reasons, we approach fertility forecasting with a greatly increased respect for the unexpected.

Our model of fertility is similar to the model for mortality, except that we model the actual age-specific fertility rates at time t, f(x,t):

$$f(x,t) = a(x) + b(x)g(t) + error(t)$$

where a(x) and b(x) are age-specific constants, and g(t) is an index of fertility over time (i.e. the TFR). For the US, this model is fitted to age-specific fertility rates starting in 1917.

Next, we model the g(t) index as a times series. Here g(t) is modelled not as a random walk, but as a constrained ARIMA(1,0,1) (see Lee and Tuljapurkar, 1994 for details of the model). The long-run average of the randomly generated series is then constrained to a pre-determined TFR (1.95 for the US, from the Social Security Administration's Medium assumption). Finally, 1,000 trajectories are randomly generated on a computer, using the historically-fitted parameter estimates for the model. Any trajectories resulting in negative fertility rates are rejected (there are typically several such trajectories out of a thousand).

Figure 6 plots the fitted historical TFR series and the probability intervals for the forecast TFR series, along with several random trajectories plotted as dotted and dashed lines. Note that the 95% probability interval for the forecast is quite wide, ranging from 1 to 3 children per woman. Since the historically fitted model includes rather dramatic swings which are reflected in the variance of the innovation term for the fertility model, the randomly generated trajectories from the same model exhibit dramatic swings as well, as illustrated by the random trajectories plotted in Figure 6.

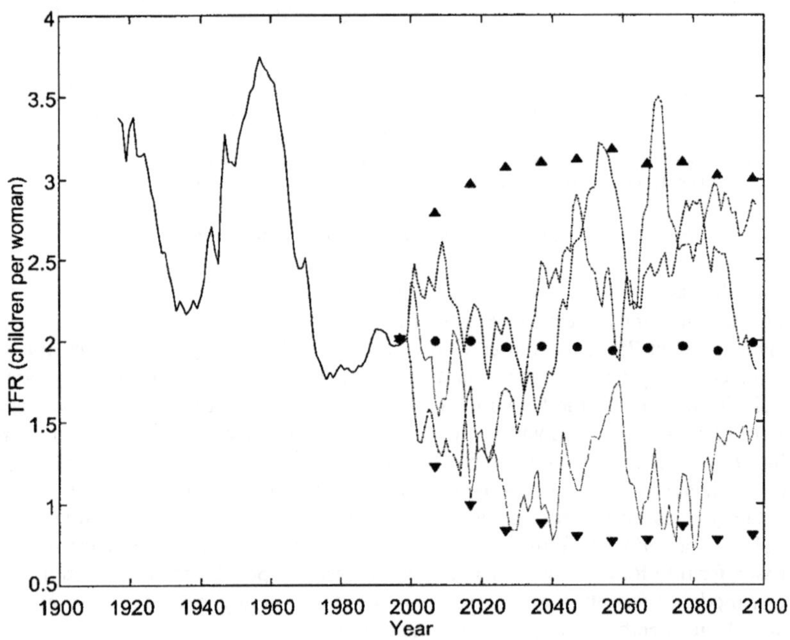


*Figure 6. Total Fertility Rate, fitted (1917-1999) and forecast (2000-2098)*

Tuljapurkar and Boe (1999) have conducted validation experiments using the historical US fertility data, which suggest that the model performs quite well in characterising the uncertainty of the US fertility experience. In particular, they analyse the additional prediction uncertainty that arises from incorporating the constraint that the long-run average converge to some predefined asymptote.

### *2.1.3. Immigration*

For statistical modelling, immigration is the most problematic of the three demographic components. In the US, for example, the magnitude of legal immigration is a matter of policy, and so *a priori* stochastic modelling seems inappropriate. Historical immigration in the US fluctuates more dramatically than do historical fertility rates. In the early part of the century immigration skyrocketed, only to drop drastically by the depression years and reverse direction yet again after World War II, rising steadily throughout the remainder of the century. Most of these changes are driven by policy. Illegal immigration is hard to estimate accurately.

As a result, it is difficult to define a meaningful measure of uncertainty based on history. We simply model immigration deterministically. For our G7 forecasts, we have used official immigration projections.

### *2.1.4. Population dynamics and their implications*

Together with an initial population pyramid, forecasts of mortality, fertility and immigration by age and sex can be used to construct population forecasts. Since our fertility and mortality forecasts are stochastic, so are the population forecasts. We generate 1,000 fertility and mortality trajectories independently and combine them one by one to construct 1,000 population trajectories (by age and sex) over time.

The result is that we have 1,000 forecasts of population by age and sex, typically for a horizon of 50 to 100 years. We can then estimate the distribution of any demographic measure we like, including the proportion of the population at any age group.

The old-age dependency ratio (OADR) is the ratio of the size of the population over age 65 to the size of the population 20 to 65. Thus, the higher the OADR for any given population, the more retired (dependent) persons there are relative to the number of persons in the working years. For any fiscal system that pays benefits primarily to persons in the elderly years while relying on tax payments from young to middle aged workers, this ratio has great relevance.

Figure 7 plots forecasts of the old age dependency ratio for the G7 countries for 2050 (2040 for Canada). The circles show the median of the stochastic forecasts, the triangles represent the 67% probability intervals, and the diamonds show the official medium forecast. With the exception of Canada, the median of our stochastic forecasts exceeds the official medium forecast for all countries. For France, Germany, Italy and Japan, the official medium forecasts are well outside the 67% probability intervals from the stochastic forecasts.

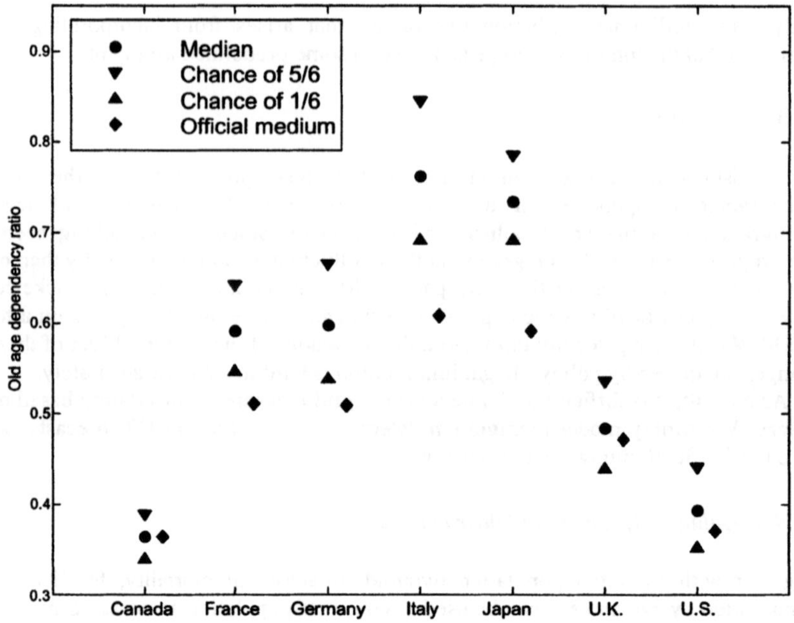


*Figure 7. Forecasts of the old-age dependency ratio in 2050 (2040 for Canada)*

For fiscal planners in Japan and Italy (and to a lesser extent Germany and France), the forecasts have rather pessimistic implications. In the most dire scenarios, age at retirement would have to be increased by as much as ten years to avoid drastic tax increases or benefit cuts.

## 3. PENSION SYSTEMS AND POLICY ANALYSIS

### *3.1. The general structure of pension system forecasts*

The structure of a pension system is often described as either "fully funded" or "pay-as-you-go". In a fully funded system, contributions to the pension system are held and invested for a participant until the money is returned in the retirement years. In a pay-as-you-go pension system, today's contributions are used to pay for the benefits of today's retirees.

The latter type of system can only function with long-term financial stability provided that the benefit payments exacted do not exceed the income collected. Since such systems are typically intended to operate with a margin of security, pay-as-you-go systems are usually modified to include a reserve fund. In the United States' OASDI Trust Fund, the holdings of the system are federal securities, and the "fund" consists of federally-held debt.

A fund balance earns interest, is subject to withdrawals in the form of benefit payments, and receives deposits in the form of worker contributions (usually in the form of tax payments). We model these changes by a straightforward accounting method. Starting with a launch year (initial year) balance, we forecast contributions and benefit payments for each subsequent year, as well as interest earned. This procedure yields a trajectory of fund balance over time.

Future contributions depend both on how many workers contribute how much to the system. Future benefit payments depend on how many beneficiaries receive how much in the future. Our population forecasts do not directly yield a breakdown in terms of workers and retirees. Therefore, we estimate and forecast per-capita averages by age and sex, for both contributions and benefits. We combine these age- and sex-specific "profiles" with age- and sex-specific population forecasts to obtain total inflows and outflows for each forecast year.

Contribution profiles evolve over time according to two factors. First, increases in contributions depend in turn on increases in the real wage. We forecast real wage increases stochastically (as described below), and contributions increase in proportion to wages. Second, changes in the labour force participation rates also affect contributions; we forecast labour force participation rates deterministically.

Benefit profiles evolve over time in response to several factors. In our model of the US Social Security system, we disaggregate benefits into disability benefits and retirement benefits. Retirement benefit levels reflect past changes in real wages because they depend on a worker's lifetime wages. Also, legislated or proposed changes in the Normal Retirement Age (the age at which beneficiaries become eligible to collect 100% of their benefits) will reduce benefits at the old NRA.

### *3.2. Age at retirement, the dependency ratio and pension policy*

As mentioned above, the old-age dependency ratio for a population is the ratio of the number of persons aged 65 and over (the retirement years) to the number of persons aged 20 to 64 (the working ages). Thus, the higher the ratio, the more retirees-per-worker there are in the population, which implies greater stress on a pay-as-you-go pension system which relies on today's workers to pay the benefits of today's retirees.

An interesting insight into the demographic impact of ageing on the dependency ratio can be created by asking the following question. If the age 65 cut-off could be changed arbitrarily, how high would we have to raise this cut-off in order to keep the dependency ratio constant? Figure 8 shows a plot of this cut-off, calculated from our stochastic population forecasts. The step functions show the median cut-off value, with a 95% prediction interval on either side of the median. The smooth line shows the average value. There is a 50% chance, then, that the cut-off would have to be raised to 74 by 2060 in order to keep the dependency ratio constant. There is a 5% chance that the required cut-off would have to be raised above 78 or below 69.

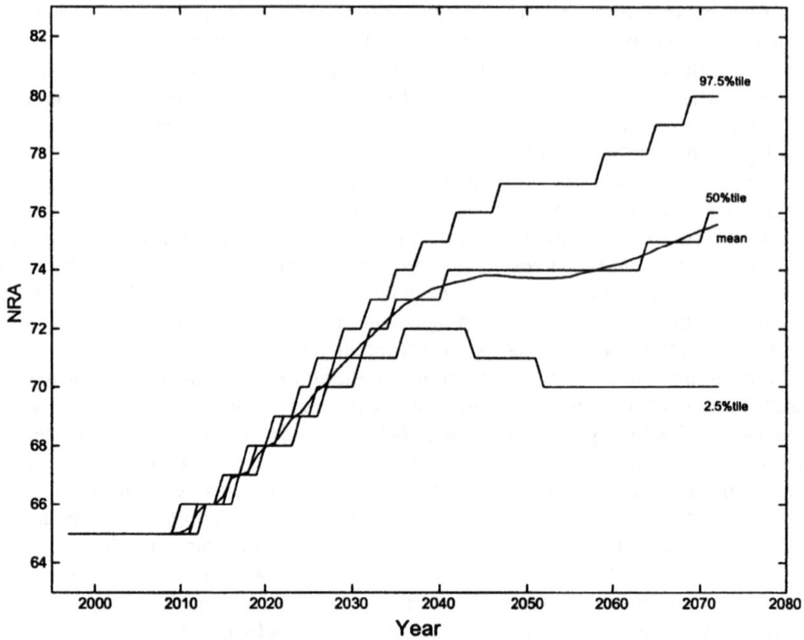


*Figure 8. Normal retirement age required to maintain the old-age dependency ratio, 1997-2072*

### *3.3. Economic uncertainty*

Demographic variables are obviously not the only source of uncertainty facing fiscal planners; there are sizeable economic uncertainties as well. Taxes and future benefits usually depend in some way on wage increases (economic productivity) and funds can accumulate interest or investment returns on tax surpluses.

In our model of the OASDI Trust Fund for the US, we combine inflationary uncertainty with uncertainty in productivity and investment returns by converting productivity to real 1999 dollars, subtracting out increases in the CPI. We then model productivity rates and investment returns stochastically.

Historical and forecast real wage increases (adjusted for inflation and changes in the labour force composition) are shown in Figure 9. This series, w(t), is modelled as a constrained AR(1), with the constraint being that the long-run average of the series is equal to the Social Security Administration's medium forecast (1% annual growth). Figure 9 shows the probability intervals for the forecast series, as well as a random trajectory. It appears that the random trajectory (dotted line) fairly matches historical fluctuations in magnitude and character.

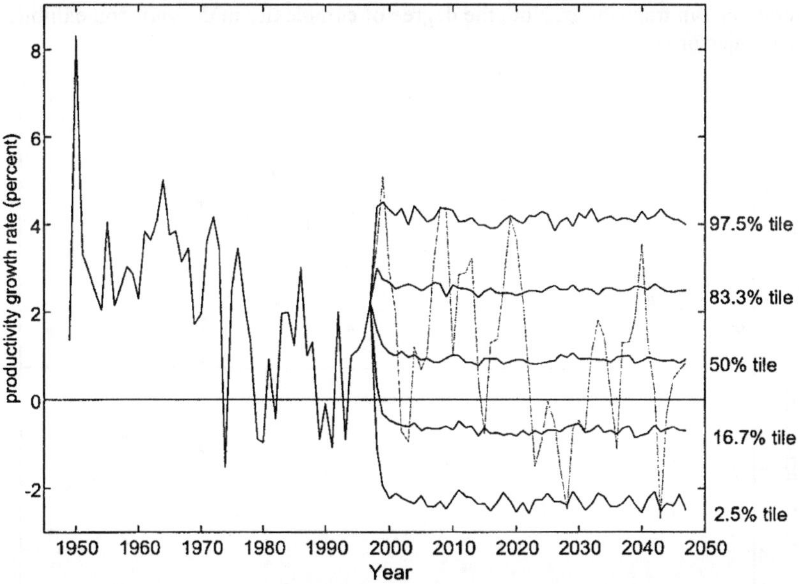


*Figure 9. Real increase in wages, historical (1949-1997) and simulated (1998-2047)*

There is substantial correlation between interest rates on government bonds and returns to equities, so it is important to model these two variables jointly. For our historical interest rate series we use the actual, effective real interest rate earned by the OASDI trust fund, and for historical stock market returns we use the real returns on the S&P500 as a proxy.

These two series are modelled jointly as a vector auto-regressive process.

### *3.4. Example from OASDI*

At the end of calendar year 1999, the combined OASDI fund held a total of $896 billion in 1999 dollars, in the form of government securities. Expenditures for 1999 totalled $393 billion, but income totalled $527 billion, so the fund balance increased by $134 billion from the end of 1998.

Using the modelling procedure described above, we proceed by simulating a trajectory of future changes in real wages, interest rate and other variables, and obtain a time trajectory of the fund balance. Repeating this procedure many times gives us a large sample of "futures" from which we may estimate probabilities and other statistical measures of the system's dynamics.

Figure 10 shows a forecast of the future fund balance in real 1999 dollars. The outer triangles show the 67% probability interval, and the dotted/dashed lines show several random trajectories. Note the degree of complexity in the variation exhibited by the trajectories.

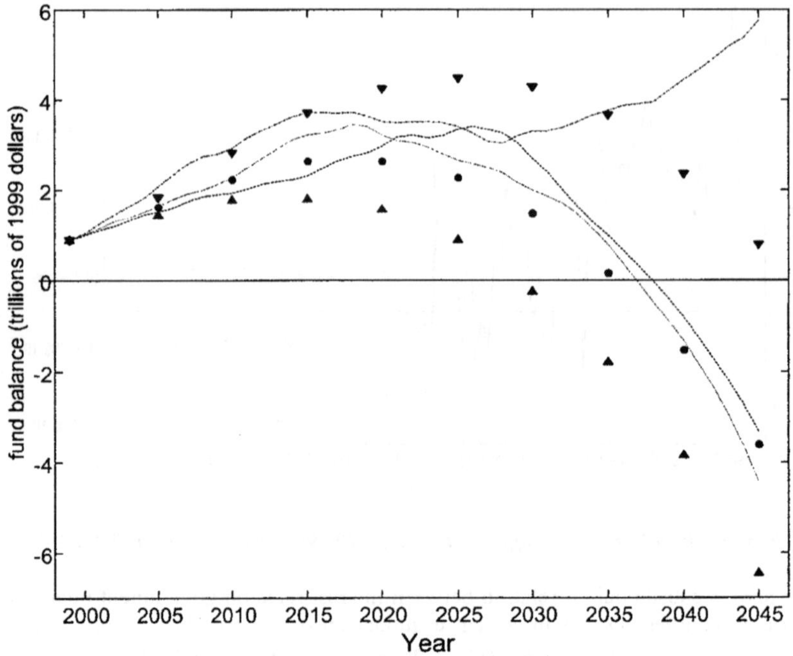


*Figure 10. Forecast fund balance, 1999-2045*

### *3.5. Using stochastic analyses*

The preceding simulation method may be used to explore the probability that particular policy outcomes are achieved: for example that the "fund" stays above a zero balance for a specified period of years, or that the level of borrowing by the fund should not exceed some specified threshold.

As an illustration we show the impact of two proposed types of policy change on the probability of solvency for the US Social Security system: 1) an increase in the Normal Retirement Age; 2) an increase in the payroll tax rate.

Presently, the NRA is scheduled to increase by two months of age per year for six years, starting in 2000 (raising it to 66 by 2005), and again starting in 2017 (raising it to 67 by 2022). We modelled five different NRA schedules, each using six years of time for each year of NRA adjustment. The first is the legislated schedule (resulting in a final NRA of 67 by 2022), the second is an accelerated shift to age 67 by 2012, and the three remaining shifts each add one additional year of NRA increase in an additional six-year period of time. The tax increases are modelled in

0.5% steps, from the presently-legislated 12.4% up to 14.9%. Finally, we modelled all thirty possible combinations of these tax rates and NRA schedules.

Figure 11 shows the probability that the trust fund will remain solvent through 2047, for any given combination of tax increase and NRA change (this result is from a forecast starting in 1997). The lowest point on the surface is for the presently-legislated rules. Tax increases alone can raise the likelihood of solvency to nearly 90% for the next fifty years, but even these fairly aggressive NRA shifts fail to raise the probability of solvency above 25% if taxes are not changed. A moderate combination of both shifts, such as an NRA of 68 by 2020 and a 1% tax increase, results in a fairly substantial improvement. This raises the chance of solvency to 58% and extends the median year of insolvency out to 2050.

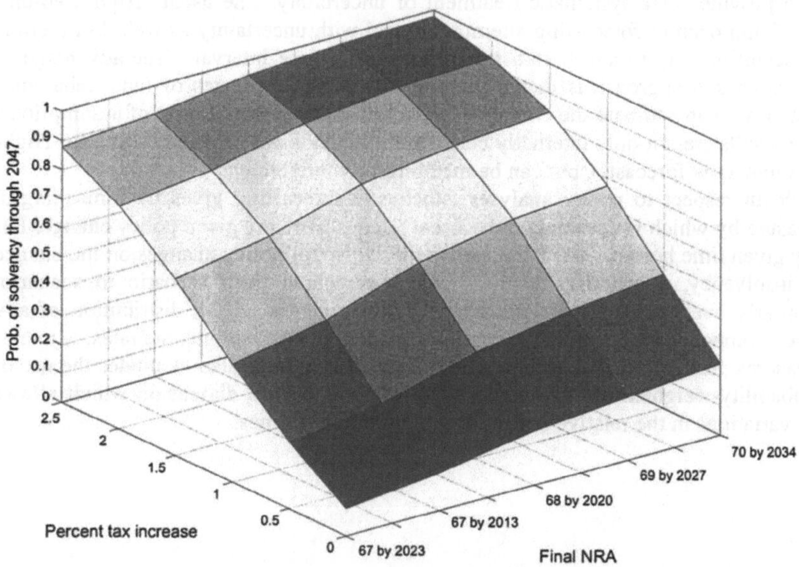


*Figure 11. Chance of solvency until 2047, by tax increase and NRA change*

Interestingly, the combinations of tax increase and NRA change reveal an important synergy between policy changes. In particular, when two policy tools are used in combination, the total impact is more than the sum of the effects from each change by itself. This is mostly because the extra money saved also earns interest over time; hence the sum impact of reforms can grow exponentially, provided they are enacted soon enough to allow for the substantial accumulation of extra interest.

## 4. CONCLUSION

Forecasting pension systems stochastically involves gauging uncertainty from many different sources. We treat demographic and economic uncertainty by stochastically modelling mortality, fertility, increases in real wages, and the interest rate. Where stochastic modelling is inadequate or unfeasible (e.g. immigration levels, changes in labour force participation), we incorporate some expert opinion about the future behaviour of these variables.

Our general concern, however, is not so much with the exact form of these stochastic models; indeed, the approach lends itself to many statistical models, and the reader is encouraged to experiment in this respect. Rather, our central motivation is to provide *some* systematic treatment of uncertainty. The usual "High-Medium-Low" approach to forecasting attempts to deal with uncertainty as well, but there is no scientific way to attach statistical meaning to these intervals. The advantage of the stochastic approach is that it yields probabilistic estimates of fund behaviour; that is, we can estimate the *chance* of solvency under any given set of assumptions. The results are not only internally consistent (which is not necessarily true for High-Medium-Low forecasts), but can be meaningfully interpreted.

With respect to policy analyses, stochastic forecasting gives us a meaningful measure by which we can gauge the fiscal adequacy of any given policy change. For any given time horizon, we can estimate the impact of policy changes on the chance of insolvency, a quantity which is easily compared from scenario to scenario. Similarly, we can gauge the impact of policy changes on the distribution of any given component of the system (e.g. interest earned, cost and income rates, actuarial measures, and so on). The estimation of these distributions also facilitates the use of probability-weighted utility functions, an important extra dimension which allows for variations in the relative desirability of certain outcomes.

## REFERENCES

ANDERSON M., TULJAPURKAR S. and LEE R. (1999), "Chances are: Stochastic forecasts of the social security trust fund and attempts to save it", paper presented at the Conference on Retirement Research, Center for Retirement Research, Boston College.

LEE R. (1999), "Population forecasts, public policy, and risk", *Bulletin of the International Statistical Institute, Proceedings of the 52nd Annual Meeting*, ISI, Helsinki, August.

LEE R. and TULJAPURKAR S. (1997), "Death and Taxes: How Longer Life Will Affect Social Security", *Demography*, 34: 67-81.

LEE R. and TULJAPURKAR S. (1998), "Uncertain demographic futures and Social Security finances", *American Economic Review*, 88(2):237-241.

LEE R. and TULJAPURKAR S. (2000), "Population forecasting for fiscal planning: Issues and innovations" in Auerbach A. and Lee R. (eds.) *Demography and Fiscal Policy*, Cambridge University Press (in print).

TULJAPURKAR S. (1997), "Taking the Measure of Uncertainty", *Nature*, 387:760-761.

TULJAPURKAR S. and BOE C. (1999), "Validation, information and probabilistic priors in stochastic forecasts", *International Journal of Forecasting*, 15:259-271.

TULJAPURKAR S. and LEE R. (1998), "Stochastic forecasts for Social Security" in Wise, D. (ed.) *Frontiers in the Economics of Aging*, University of Chicago Press, Chicago.

TULJAPURKAR S. and LEE R. (2000), "Demographic uncertainty and the United States OASDI fund" in Mason A. and Tapinos G. (eds.) *Intergenerational Economic Relations and Demographic Change*, Oxford University Press (in print).

TULJAPURKAR S., ANDERSON M. and LEE R. (1998), "Effects of Changing the Social Security Retirement Age on the Dynamics of the OASDI Program", paper presented at the meeting of the Social Security Advisory Board, Capitol Hill, Washington DC, October.

TITO BOERI, AGAR BRUGIAVINI AND CAROLE MAIGNAN

# EARLY RETIREMENT: REASONS AND CONSEQUENCES

## INTRODUCTION

One of the most dramatic demographic trends in the post-war period has been the withdrawal from the labour force of older male workers. In the early 1960s, the participation rate for people aged 60 and over was above 70% in each country and above 80% in several of them. By the mid-1990s, the rate had fallen to below 20% in Belgium, Italy, France and the Netherlands, to about 35% in Germany and up to 40% in Spain. But are the reasons for this decline in participation rates attributable to worker's preference for leisure, to legislation, to employer's choice or to social security generosity? This paper looks at the extent to which early retirement plays a role in explaining this trend and focuses on the monetary incentives built into social security systems (or private pensions schemes) which encourage early exits. One important message, if not the main message of our analysis, is that even the basic stylised facts are hard to describe and quantify because of lack of data. In fact, in this framework, it is relevant to consider how different workers take retirement decisions, given the institutional setting and given all other individual characteristics (age, schooling experience, family composition, etc.). The ideal data set would be a micro-level survey which should contain all these characteristics and could be used for policy experiments. Even more valuable would be the possibility of having full comparability of this "ideal sample" across different countries, hence learning about retirement choices from differences in the institutional environment.

In section 2 we outline the problems encountered in the analysis of early retirement: this rests on the definition of early retirement on the one hand, and on data informational content on the other. In section 3 we provide a descriptive analysis of the labour force in selected OECD countries. We describe the historical trends in the labour force participation, cross-sectional evidence, and we explore the "hazard rate" which provides a dynamic measure of the labour force retiring from work. In section 4 we give a brief summary of the different economic theories explaining early retirement. This provides a basic guide through the empirical work in this area. Section 5 presents a review of statistical results concerning early retirement. Many authors make use of simulations to explain early retirement behaviour, while extensive econometric studies have been developed in the Anglo-Saxon context and are essentially lacking for other OECD countries. The last section outlines the main policy issues.[1]



*T.Boeri, A.Börsch-Supan, A.Brugiavini, R.Disney, A.Kapteyn and F.Peracchi (eds.), Pensions: More Information, Less Ideology*, 29—53.

## 1. DEFINING AND MEASURING EARLY RETIREMENT

Before addressing the issue of early retirement it is useful to start by distinguishing a "first pillar" pension provision, which is normally financed on pay-as-you-go (PAYG) basis and in some countries corresponds to social security, while in others it is simply a public pension system, and a "second pillar" provision, which is normally funded and corresponds to group pension-contracts known as occupational pensions or firm plans. The majority of the OECD countries have implemented some combination of these two forms of old age insurance, the mix between first and second pillar and the actual provision within each system varies considerably across countries.

Early retirement corresponds to the period of retirement starting before the "normal retirement age" (NRA).[2] The normal retirement age in the US is 65. In Western Europe, the NRA has varied considerably over time, though age 65 now seems the norm in most countries, at least for men (see Table 1 and Table 2). There is also variability within a country depending on whether the worker is a private- or public-sector employee or whether he or she is self-employed. Furthermore, changes in NRA have occurred in most countries in recent years due to reforms aimed at curtailing pension expenditures within the first pillar provision.

In this paper we refer to *early retirement* (ER) in a broad sense, as the main problem in defining early retirement is that in some countries individuals can stop working before they reach NRA even though they are not officially retired, and a variety of situations could apply. In Denmark, for example, old-age pensions are payable to everyone over the age of 67 and anticipatory pensions may be granted to persons between 18 and 67 according to health conditions and needs of the claimant. In particular, they are payable to people whose working capacity has been permanently reduced by at least one half due to a physical or mental disability, or to people over the age of 50, where social and health circumstances so warrant. In many countries, special pre-retirement programmes were introduced in the mid-1970s with the purpose of easing the industrial restructuring process or accommodating the downsizing of the public sector, i.e. a general policy of labour shedding.

There is a whole spectrum of opportunities offered to workers to leave the labour market prematurely, with different financial conditions attached to them. Such options include early retirement *strictu sensu* (in the US this is retirement before NRA at reduced benefits), entitlement to unemployment benefit in the absence of an obligation to be available for work, and provisions for occupational disability and work incapacity pensions, plus the pre-retirement programmes described above.

It is useful to describe the cross-country variability in normal retirement ages (Table 1) and to compare the legal retirement ages (normal and early, when applicable) with the average age of retirement (Table 2).[3] In countries where pre-pension plans exist, and where social security provides incentives to leave the labour force early, the average retirement rate for men is even lower than the early retirement age (for example, in Belgium, Germany, Italy).

*Table 1. Normal retirement age in selected countries (legislation prevailing in the year 2000*

| | public flat-rate pension | public earnings-related pension | (early) retirement or age policy | occupational pensions |
|---|---|---|---|---|
| AUSTRALIA | 65.5 years for men and 61 years for women (65 for all in 2013) | none | none | 55 years (increasing to 60 by 2025) |
| AUSTRIA | 65 men, 60 women | 65 men, 60 women | 60 men (57 if reduced working capacity), 55 women | |
| CANADA | 65 both | 65 both | basic pension: 65, not allowing early or deferred benefits.<br>income-related pension: payable on actuarial basis as early as age 60 and as late as age 70 | voluntary |
| DENMARK | Basic old age pension: 67 (65 for persons who are 60 years old after July 1 1999) | 67 (65 for persons 60 years old after July 1 1999) for both | over 60 if certain requirements are met; over 50 for social or health reasons | |
| FINLAND | 65 both | 65 both (is an occupational compulsory p., thus as public related) | 60- 64 (or as early as 55 if certain contribution and age-cohort requirements met. | |
| FRANCE | 65 both | 60 both | 57 (in special cases 56) | |
| GERMANY | none | 65 for males and 63 (65 in 2004) for females | 65 for all groups as of 2001 | |
| GREAT BRITAIN | 65 men, 60 (65 from 2020) women | | 50 and over may retire | |
| ITALY | social pension and top-up pension at age 65 | 64 for men and 59 for women (to be increased by one year to 65 for men, 60 for women). For those entering labour market after 1995, flexible retirement age between 57 and 65 will apply | 35 years of contributions, increasing to 40 years | voluntary |
| JAPAN | 65 | 60 both (65 for all in 2018). | 60 | |
| NETHERLANDS | 65 | none | 59 or even 55 depending on collective | |
| SPAIN | 6 | 5 both | 60 | |
| SWITZERLAND | 65 for men and 62 (64 in 2005) for women | 65 for men and 62 (64 in 2005) for women | framework legislation sets a corridor of 5 years under or over legal retirement age | partly compulsory |
| SWEDEN | 65 both | 65 both | guaranteed pension 65, earnings-related pension flexible from 61 | |
| USA | SSI: 65 | OASDI: 65 (67 from 2027) for both | SSI: from 65. OASDI: "early retirement" p. from 62 | voluntary |

*Source: USA – Social Security Administration, Social security programmes throughout the world and individual countries' social security offices. Further details can be obtained from the Fondazione FRDB at www.frdb.org.*

*Table 2: Legal versus effective retirement age (legislation in 1996)*

| men | Normal Retirement age | Early Retirement age | Effective Retirement age |
|---|---|---|---|
| COUNTRIES | | | Average for 1995 |
| **BELGIUM** | 65 | 60 | 57.6 |
| **CANADA** | 65 | 60-64 | 62.3 |
| **DENMARK** | 67 | 60 | 62.7 |
| **FINLAND** | 65 | 60-64 | 59.0 |
| **FRANCE** | 60 | 57 | 59.2 |
| **GERMANY** | 65 | 63 | 60.5 |
| **ICELAND** | 67 | 65 | 69.5 |
| **ITALY** | 62 | 35 years of contributions | 60.6 |
| **JAPAN** | 65 | 60-64 | 66.5 |
| **NERTHELANDS** | 65 | 58-63 | 58.8 |
| **NORWAY** | 67 | 60-66 | 63.8 |
| **SPAIN** | 65 | 60-64 | 61.4 |
| **SWEDEN** | 65 | 60-64 | 63.3 |
| **UK** | 65 | | 62,7 |
| **US** | 65 | 62-64 | 63.6 |

*Source: Blondal & Scarpetta (1999)*

### *1.1 Retirement Paths*

During the 1980s early exit from work soon became a widespread phenomenon embracing nearly the entire workforce in Western countries; now, however, there are marked differences in early retirement across OECD countries. Very early exit, before age 60, was relatively common in France and the Netherlands, and also in Germany and Italy. On the other hand, the level of Japanese participation hardly changed. The second pre-retirement age group (60-64) shows that Japan, Scandinavia and Anglo-Saxon countries experienced some long-term decline in participation rates but remained above the OECD average, while continental European countries experienced a dramatic decline.

These differences can be explained by the different opportunities to "bridge" the transition period between early withdrawal from work and NRA. Pathways to early retirement often combine different income programmes. For example, unemployment benefits were originally extended to older workers as a social policy for the hard-to-reemploy, though with rising mass unemployment these rights became the first step on a popular pathway leading to early exit. There are a multitude of possible pathways: lowering the normal pension age, partial or gradual pensions, special pre-retirement programmes, long-term unemployment, disability insurance, employer policy.

In Sweden, there are several permanent ways to leave the labour market. Palme and Svensson (2000) provide a definition of "retirement path" based on income receipts. They use 10 possible sources of income and compute the percentage share of workers who receive their main income from one of these income sources (see Figure 1). Main income is defined as the income representing more than 50% of total income and two groups emerge: (1) old age pension programmes, i.e. state old-age pension, occupational pensions, pensions provided by the employer or severance payments, private pensions, partial retirement benefits; (2) insurance programmes against income loss from bad health or unemployment (disability insurance, income support for disabled persons within the family, sickness insurance and unemployment insurance). A final group is constituted by survivor's pension. Figure 1 provides indirect evidence of the existence of many different modes of retirement. On top of this, future retirees may switch from one mode to another over their life cycle, thus creating a pathway to retirement, which in turns explains the complexity of defining early retirement.

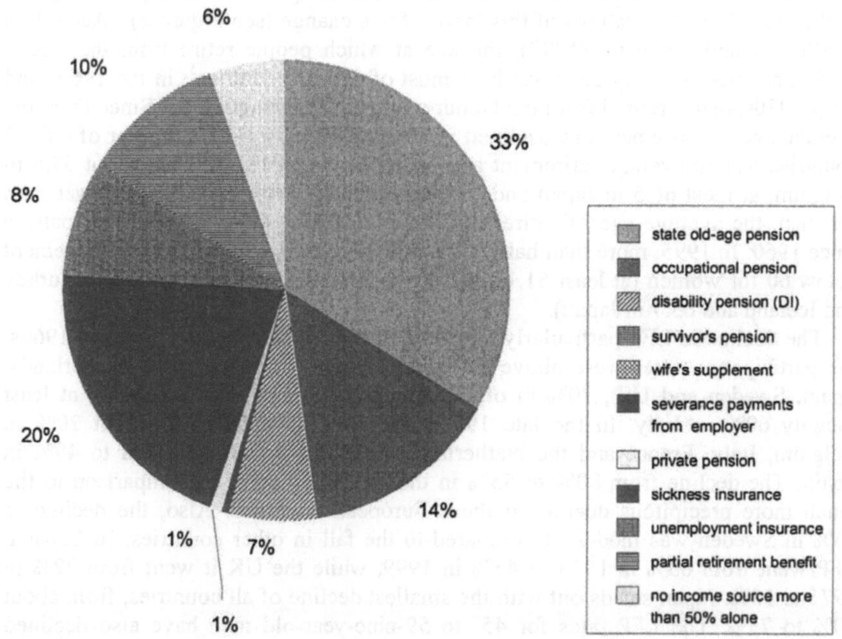


*Figure 1: Pathways to retirement in Sweden, men*

*Source: Palme and Svensson (2000). Calculations based on the panel data set LINDA (Longitudinal Individual Data). The sample used by the authors has been restricted to those born between 1927 and 1932, as these birth cohorts reached "normal" retirement age of 65 in 1997 (last year of data available).*

## 2. SOME FACTS ON EARLY EXITS

In this section, we present the evidence on the labour market for older men and women by selecting as examples two industrialised countries. We give a description of the historical evolution of labour force participation from 1960 until 1999, pointing out the decline for the group aged 60 to 64, then we look at cross sectional analysis based on current labour force participation rates by age, and finally we present hazard rates by age. From this analysis, it is possible to see the important role that social security can play in the participation decisions of older persons. It is also possible to identify the most pressing data requirements. Better information is indispensable for a better understanding of the actual determinants of retirement decisions.

### 2.1 *Historical trends in the labour force participation of older men and women*

The labour market position of the older workforce has changed over the past several decades. The decline in the labour force participation[4] (LFP) of older persons is one of the most dramatic features of this labour force change (see Figure 2). According to Blondal and Scarpetta (1999), the age at which people retire from the labour market has been drifting downwards in most of OECD countries[5]: in the 1960s and early 1970s, males retired from the labour market after the age of 65. Since then, the average age of retirement has declined in all countries: by 1995 a quarter of OECD countries had an average retirement age below 60 for males (at least about 57.6 in Belgium, at most 66.5 in Japan and 69.5 in Iceland). While historically lower than for men, the average age of retirement for women has followed a similar pattern since 1960. In 1995, more than half of the OECD countries had an age of retirement below 60 for women (at least 51.1 for Belgian women, at most about 66 in Turkey and Iceland and 63.7 in Japan).

The decline in LFP particularly concerns men aged 60 to 64: in the early 1960s, the participation rates were above 80% in several countries (Japan, Netherlands, Spain, Sweden and US), 70% in others (Belgium, France and Germany), at least roughly 60% in Italy. In the late 1990s, the rates have fallen to about 20% in Belgium, Italy, France and the Netherlands, to 30% in Germany, and to 40% in Spain. The decline from 80% to 55% in the US was modest in comparison to the much more precipitous decline in these European countries. Also, the decline to 55% in Sweden was modest if compared to the fall in other countries. In Canada, LFP went from 65% in 1976 to 45% in 1999, while the UK it went from 72% in 1971 to 50%. Japan stands out with the smallest decline of all countries, from about 80% to 75%. The LFP rates for 45- to 59-nine-year-old men have also declined substantially.

The LFP trends for older women are just as dramatic. The growth in the aggregate LFP rate often observed for women is due to the existence of cohort effects (younger more educated cohorts enter the labour force in higher percentages than older cohorts did).

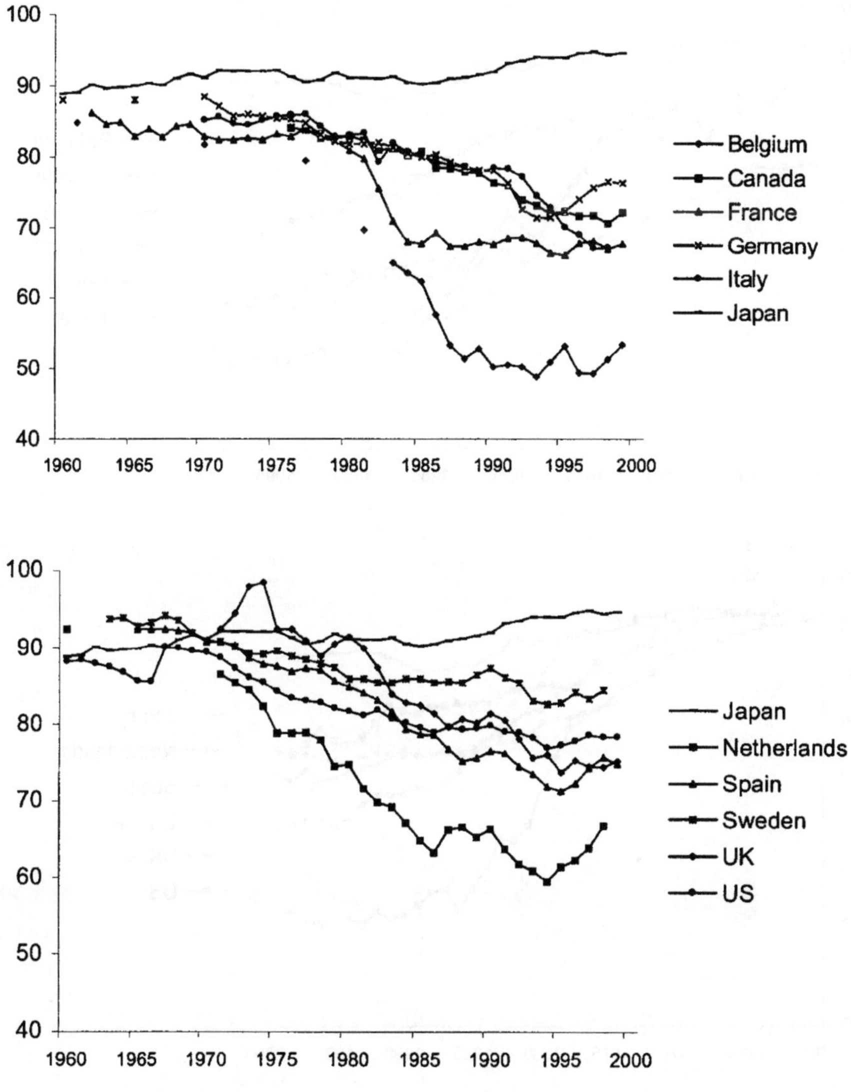


*Figure 2: Labour Force Participation trends for men aged 55 to 59*

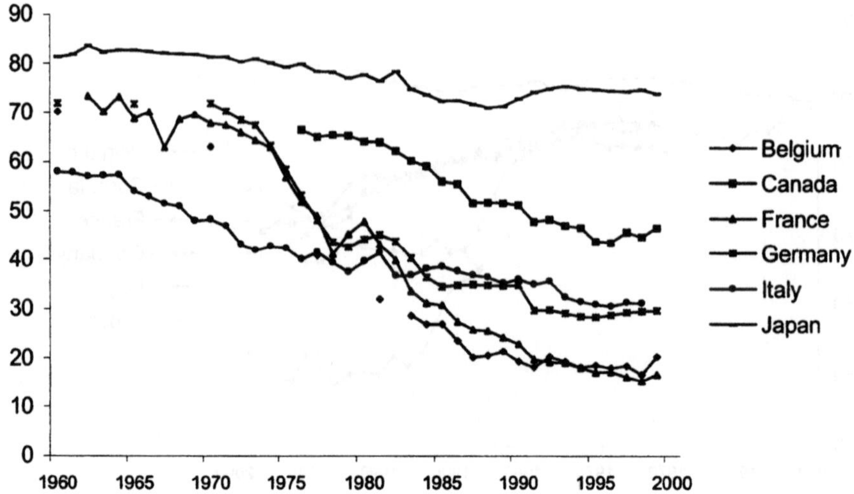


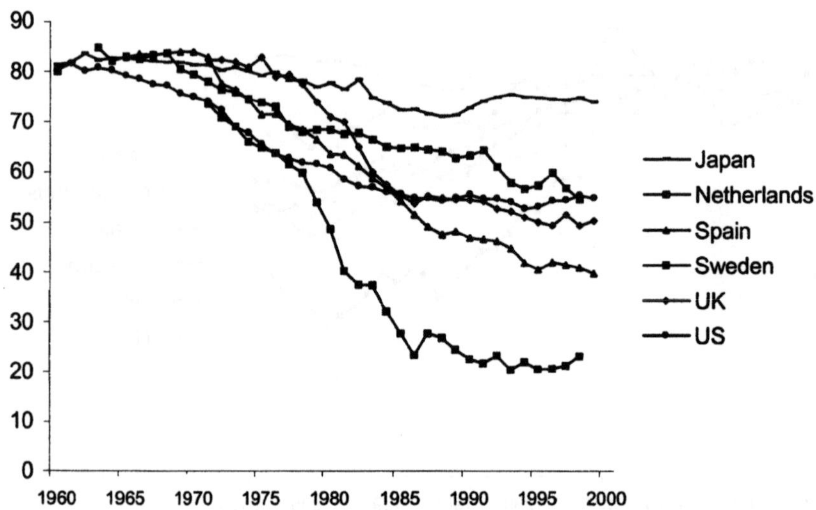


*Figure 2 (continues): Labour Force Participation trends for men aged 60 to 64*

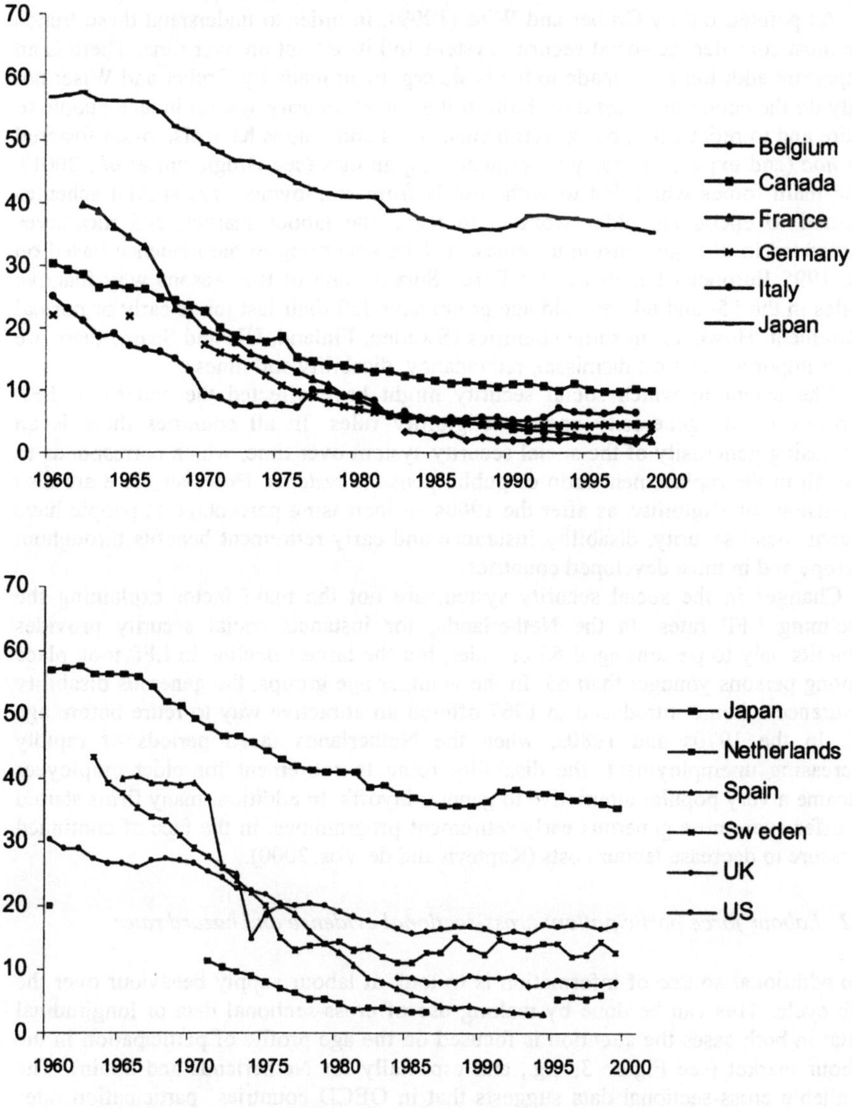


***Figure 2 (continues): Labour Force Participation for men aged 65 and over***

***Source: European Union Labour Force Survey, over several years***

As pointed out by Gruber and Wise (1999), in order to understand these trends we must consider the social security system and its evolution over time. There is an important addition to be made to the basic argument made by Gruber and Wise: not only do the economic incentives built in the social security system induce people to retire and to retire early, but governments, firms and unions have also often fostered *ad hoc* (and expensive) early retirement programmes (see Brugiavini *et al.*, 2001). The main forces which led to withdrawals from employment are special schemes created to encourage older workers to leave the labour market, and incentives embedded in old-age pension schemes. In fact, according to the evidence based on the 1995 European Union Labour Force Survey, one of the reasons why inactive males in the 55- and 64-year-old age group have left their last job is early or normal retirement. However, in some countries (Sweden, Finland, UK and Spain) there are other important causes: dismissal, redundancy, disability and illness.

The extent to which social security might have affected the pattern of LFP depends on its generosity and on eligibility rules. In all countries there is an increasing generosity of the social security system over time, which corresponds to growth in the replacement ratio of public pension systems. However there are also extensions of eligibility, as after the 1960s an increasing percentage of people have drawn social security, disability insurance and early retirement benefits throughout Europe and in most developed countries.

Changes in the social security system are not the main factor explaining the declining LFP rates. In the Netherlands, for instance, social security provides benefits only to persons aged 65 or older, but the largest decline in LFP took place among persons younger than 65. In the younger age groups, the generous disability insurance scheme introduced in 1967 offered an attractive way to retire before age 65. In the 1970s and 1980s, when the Netherlands faced periods of rapidly increasing unemployment, the disability route to retirement for older employees became a very popular alternative to general layoffs. In addition, many firms started to offer even more generous early retirement programmes, in the face of continued pressure to decrease labour costs (Kapteyn and de Vos, 2000).

### 2.2 *Labour force participation: cross-sectional evidence and hazard rates*

An additional source of information is to look at labour supply behaviour over the life cycle. This can be done by making use of cross-sectional data or longitudinal data: in both cases the attention is focused on the age profile of participation in the labour market (see Figure 3, e.g., and especially for Netherlands and Spain). The available cross-sectional data suggests that in OECD countries participation rates decrease with age both for men and for older women.[6] However the shape of the age profile is different for men and women: in all countries LFP rates are higher for men than for women and in some countries this difference is significant. At age 45 LFP rates for men range between 90% and 100%, while LFP rates for women are about 44% in Italy and Spain and about 88% in Sweden. After that age, LFP rates start to decline gradually, and a marked drop is normally observed between the ages

55 and 65. An explanation for this precipitous drop for men seems to be early or partial retirement.

An alternative way of analysing LFP over the life cycle is through the age-profile of the *hazard rates* that provide, at each age, the percentage increase of the labour force retiring from work, conditional on the existing stock of workers. The empirical hazard rate is obtained as the flow of individuals leaving the labour force at each given age over the stock of people in labour force at that age.

Figure 4 displays hazard rates for Netherlands and Spain, which provide two extreme examples social security system arrangements.[7] In both cases hazard rates present a number of spikes. For each country the spikes occur after 50 but not always at the same ages and not to the same extent. It seems that the most important spikes can be explained by eligibility rules, even though the amount of variability around these important spikes is also impressive.

For example, in the Netherlands, hazard rates for men leaving the labour force are greater than 20% around age 57 and peaks at age 60, which is consistent with the proliferation of early retirement programmes. For women, exits from the labour force occur more frequently at earlier ages but a spike is also observed around age 60. For Spanish men, hazard rates increase smoothly with age and show clear spikes at ages 60 and 65, corresponding to early and normal retirement ages in Spain. Among women, the behaviour of the hazard rates is very erratic at almost all ages: there is action in the data between ages 52 and 61, followed by a pronounced spike at 65. The spike at 54 can be explained by the interaction between eligibility requirements and minimum pension provisions (Boldrin, Jimenez-Martin and Peracchi, 1999).

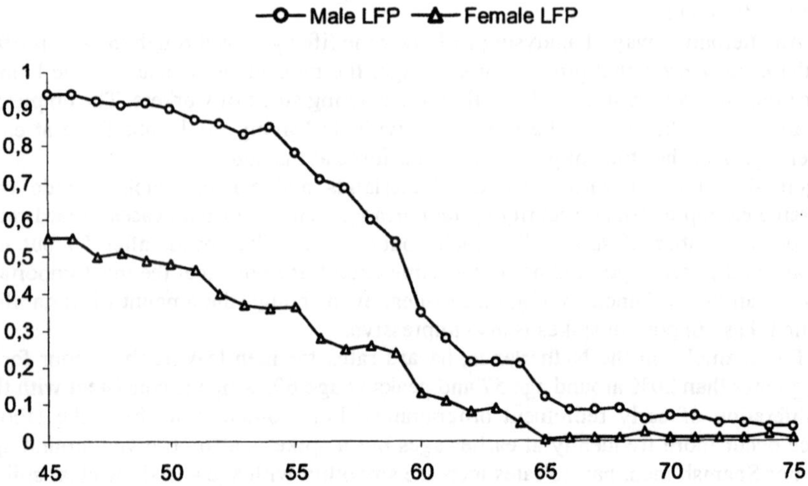


*Figure 3: Age profile of LFP – The Netherlands*

*Source: Kapteyn and de Vos (1999)*

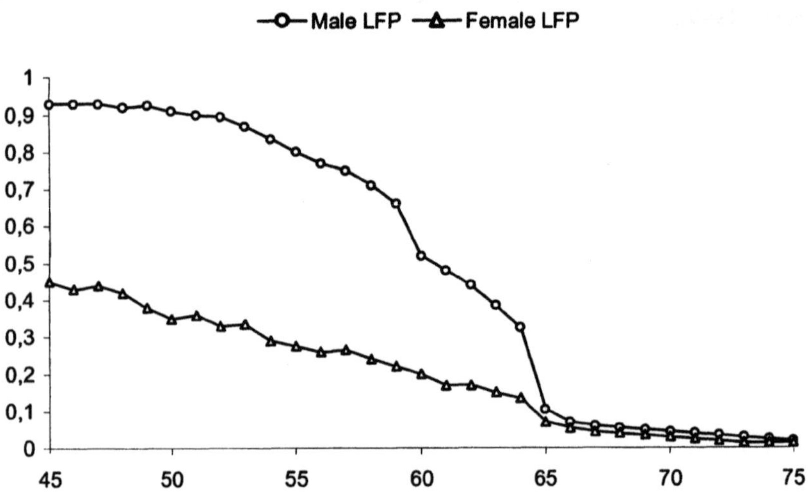


*Figure 3 (continues): Age profile of LFP – Spain*

*Source: Boldrin et al. (1999a)*

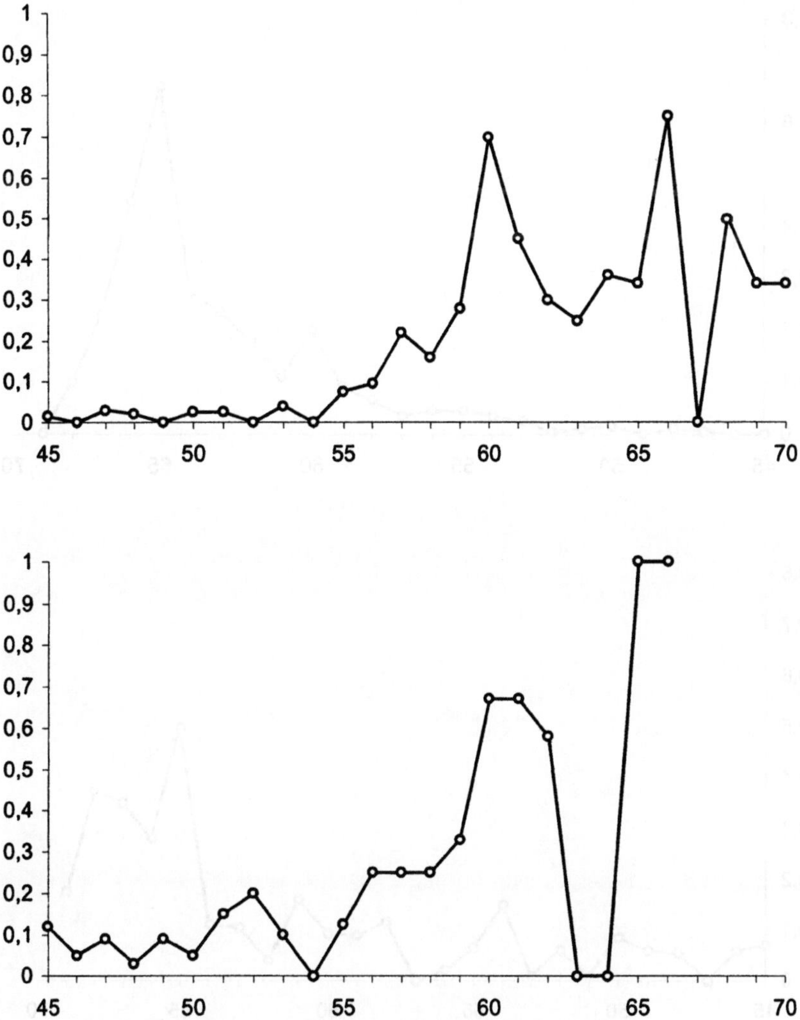


*Figure 4: Hazard rates for men and women, The Netherlands*

*Source: Kapteyn and de Vos (1999)*

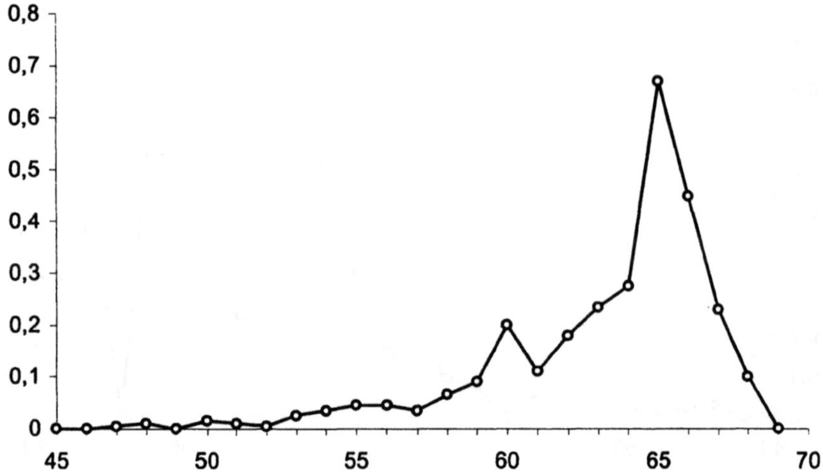


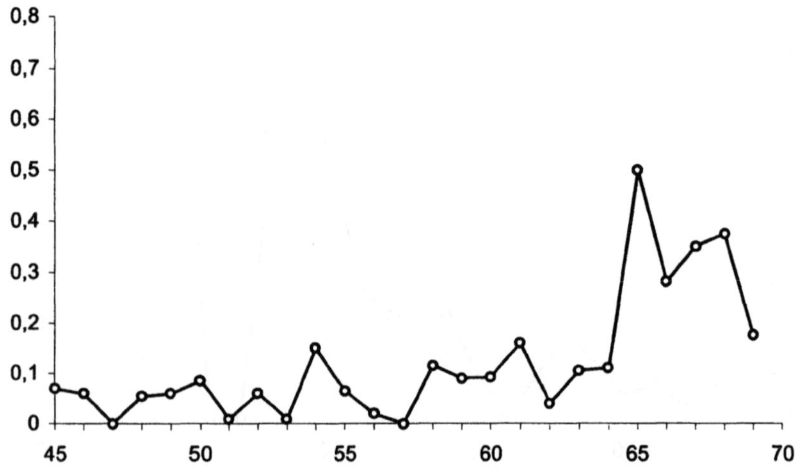


*Figure 4 (continues): Hazard rates for men and women, Spain*

*Source: Boldrin et al. (1999a)*

## 3. WHY DO PEOPLE RETIRE? A REVIEW OF THEORY AND METHODOLOGY

The determinants of the retirement decision can be summarised in the following keywords: retirement rules (eligibility, earnings rules etc.), health-related factors, existence of non-pension alternatives for old age (more general availability of different sources of income in old age), actuarial (un-)fairness of pension schemes, social norms, labour demand factors (for older workers) and firms' productivity considerations. Within households, decision-making could also play a role (Blau, 1998 and Coile, 2000), as well as care responsibilities. A number of models have been used to analyse the retirement decision: these have emphasised one or more of the above aspects. We present a brief summary by focusing on those models which best suit the purpose of explaining early retirement. Furthermore, we focus on empirical evidence, and this is often limited to objects that we can actually measure. The tension in the literature is between comprehensive and general models, which are often complex to deal with, and models which are a partial view of the story but are tractable. In all cases however it is clear that the major hurdle is implementation, as almost invariably these approaches require high-quality longitudinal data. Hence the scarce empirical evidence obtained so far is often based on poor substitutes of the "ideal data set", i.e. samples drawn from cross-sectional data or from pooled cross-sections.

### *3.1 Preference theory*

#### *3.1.1 "Stochastic optimisation" method*

The most general models are dynamic stochastic optimisation models, such as those in Rust (1989). These models attempt to provide a complete description of the choice set available to consumers in terms of labour supply and saving decisions, including situations of missing or incomplete markets (whereby consumers are constrained to make sub-optimal choices). The problem with this approach is that it requires a fully developed backward induction solution under uncertainty. As this is hardly tractable, many authors have resorted to numerical solutions and simulations to analyse the properties of the resulting economic outcomes. The approach is also extremely demanding when it comes to actual applications in terms of data, as it requires a very rich panel data sample of households. A simpler form of these models is the "option value" approach.

#### *3.1.2 "Option value" theory*

Stock and Wise (1990) use an "option value" model to analyse the effects of firm pension plan provisions on the retirement decisions of older employees in the US. The "option value" of continued work is the central feature of the analysis. This is based on two key ideas: firstly, the individual will continue to work at any age if the expected present value in utility units of continuing work is greater than the expected present value of immediate retirement. Secondly, the individual re-evaluates his or her retirement decision as more information about future earnings becomes available with age. Simulations of the effects of alternative pension plans show that plan provisions may have important effects on retirement rates.

### 3.2 *Incentives models*

Along the same lines, "incentives models" use a detailed computation of plan retirement incentives where, rather than using utility units, a money metric is implemented. Gruber and Wise (1999) suggest the use of the present discounted value of expected future benefits at a certain age (social security wealth – SSW) and look at the dynamics of this variable under continued work. The question is: "what is the change in social security wealth for a worker of age X if he or she retires at age (X+1) instead of retiring at age X?" The difference between social security wealth at age (X+1) and social security wealth at age (X) is called social security wealth accrual. They compare this SSW accrual to potential earnings over the extra year of work. If the accrual is negative (positive) the ratio of SSW accrual to net wage earnings is an *implicit tax* (subsidy) on earnings, which discourages (encourages) work. The Gruber and Wise study is probably the most recent and complete attempt at providing consistent cross-country evidence based on micro data, and yet data limitations have obviously hampered the potential of the analysis as results could be obtained only for a specific cohort of individuals. Some selected results from their study are presented in section 5.

## 4. EMPIRICAL EVIDENCE ON RETIREMENT DECISIONS

### 4.1 *Some empirical measures*

As we argued in section 4, above, a useful concept in analysing retirement choices is *social security wealth* (*SSW*), which is the present discounted actuarial value of future expected benefits under a given legislation. It is an "actuarial" value because discounting is done allowing both for time preference and mortality adjustments. We have also defined the concept of *accrual*[8]: the *accrual rate* is the percentage change in SSW from one year to the next. A more traditional measure used in describing a social security system is the forward *replacement rate*, i.e. the rate at which social security replaces the earnings of the worker should he or she continue working in that year.

To provide an example we follow Gruber and Wise (1999) and analyse the case of a "typical worker" born in 1930 who began work at age 20 and is married with a wife who is 3 years younger and does not work; he has no dependent children and he is receiving standard fiscal deductions. Table 3 shows a comparison of the different incentive calculations computed for this "typical worker". Each row of this table represents the age of the worker in the last year that he worked; that is, the first row represents the effect of working during the 54th year and retiring on the 55th birthday.

*Table 3: A comparison of incentive calculations*

| Country | Age | Replacement Rate | Tax/Subsidy |
|---|---|---|---|
| Belgium | 59 | 0.749 | -0.157 |
| | 65 | 0.874 | 0.529 |
| Canada | 59 | 0.176 | 0.038 |
| | 65 | 0.6124 | 0.367 |
| Sweden | 59 | 0.459 | 0.146 |
| | 65 | 0.785 | 0.039 |
| UK | 65 | 0.464 | 0.01 |
| US | 61 | 0.403 | 0.064 |
| | 65 | 0.749 | 0.188 |
| Japan | 59 | 0.552 | -0.138 |
| | 65 | 0.549 | 0 |
| Spain | 59 | 0.59 | 0.279 |
| | 65 | 0.998 | 0.729 |
| France | 59 | 0.92 | 0.05 |
| | 65 | 0.93 | 0.52 |
| Italy | 55 | 0.726 | 0.245 |
| | 59 | 0.798 | 0.401 |
| | 65 | 0.809 | 0.756 |

*Source: Gruber and Wise (1999). For Italy we consider the situation under the pre-1992 legislation. For Canada we distinguish the case in which the family has no outside income from that in which the income is equal to $4,818, because a critical parameter is the level of asset income available, since the GIS and SPA benefits are means tested. We focus on social security only and exclude private pensions. For Belgium and France we also consider the case in which the worker is entitled to unemployment benefits. In the UK there is no provision for early receipt of SERPS and of the basic pension.*

For all but two countries (Japan and Belgium at age 59), the implicit tax is positive, which implies that the social security system brings about a disincentive to additional work. The disincentive measured by the implicit tax rate is higher for Southern European countries such as France, Italy and to a certain extent Spain, whereas it is lower in Anglo-Saxon countries.

The replacement rate is very high in France, Belgium and Italy, and below average in Japan, Canada, UK and US.

In a parallel study, Blondal and Scarpetta (1999) have looked at the implicit tax on work for a number of OECD countries. Figure 5 illustrates the correlation between the implicit tax and labour supply for 1995: countries where the implicit average tax on work (for people aged between 55 and 64) was the lowest also had the lowest average retirement age. Further evidence can be obtained by looking at replacement rates, though this is less clear-cut: eyeball econometrics suggests a negative relationship between the replacement rate and average rate of retirement (Figure 6). This is another area where lack of suitable data is most felt, as defining replacement rates requires a detailed knowledge of the different income sources before and after retirement and a good knowledge of eligibility rules for each individual (or groups of individuals).

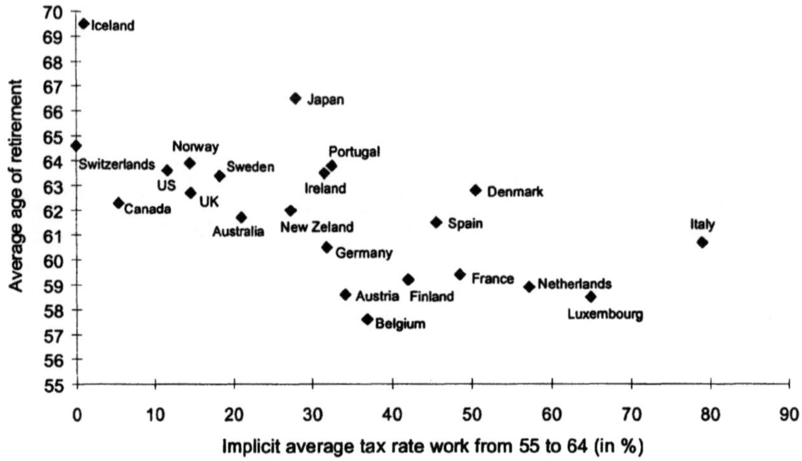


*Figure 5: Implicit tax rates on continued work and average age of retirement, men, 1995*

*Source: Blondal and Scarpetta (1999)*

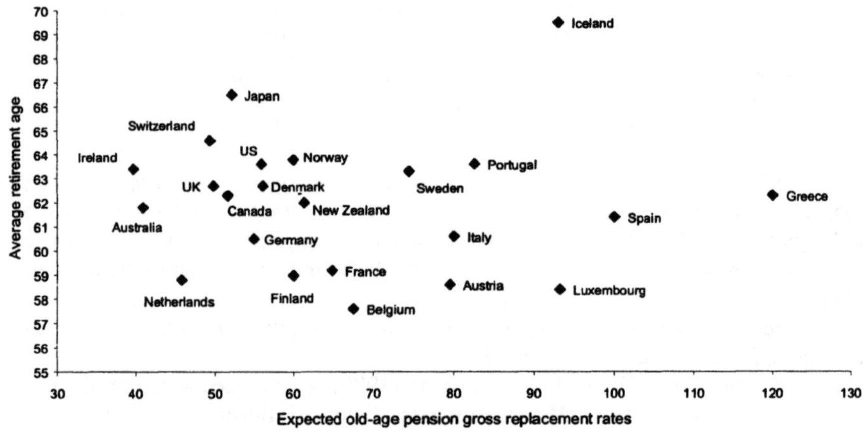


*Figure 6: Expected old-age pension gross replacement rates and average age of retirement, 1995*

*Source: Blondal and Scarpetta (1999)*

## 5. POLICY IMPLICATIONS

The studies discussed so far show a strong link between early retirement/normal retirement age and departure from the labour force. Furthermore, social security provisions place a heavy tax burden on work past the age of early retirement eligibility (in most countries). The implicit tax on work is clearly an important component of the incentives existing in different countries to leave the labour force. However, unemployment and disability programmes also serve as early retirement programmes and private pension schemes have been offering early exits in countries where occupational pensions are important.

In this section we will focus on three policy issues linked with early retirement. First, we will look at estimates of the costs of early retirement, then we will briefly discuss the role of pension plans, and occupational pensions on early retirement. Finally we illustrate one link between labour market performance and early retirement.

### *5.1 The cost of early retirement*

It is clearly very hard to provide precise numbers for the cost of early retirement for the economy. In a recent paper Herbertsson and Orszag (2001) attempt to provide this measure by building on the idea of "unused capacity" also developed in Gruber and Wise (1999). This is the complement to 100 of the labour force participation and it provides a rough measure of the percentage of people, in each age group, who could potentially participate in the labour force, but have left the labour market. It is *prima facie* evidence of the resources available for production which are not used up, without taking account of behavioural responses. Herbertsson and Orszag estimate the cost of early retirement as the share of potential GDP which is effectively lost, again simulating the basic trends without attempting a fully developed behavioural model. This cost peaks for all OECD countries during the 1980s and it gradually declines in the 1990s (but no definite reversal is observed). There is also a marked cross-country variation as the cost, in 1998, is as high as 13% in Luxembourg and Austria and 0.5% in Iceland. The OECD average is 6.3% and EU countries tend to be above average.

This exercise is very useful in helping us understand the overall macroeconomic implications of early retirement, but a lack of detailed information on responses in labour supply to, say, pension reforms, prevents any further developments.

### *5.2 Early retirement options and macroeconomic performance*

In several countries, governments, facing politically sensitive unemployment problems in declining sectors, have implemented and subsidised various soft landing plans (early retirement, disability, long-term unemployment benefits) to reduce labour supply. These are restricted to a number of industries or firms within an industry that are restructuring. In these cases the eligibility requirements for retirement are less stringent than the general rules: a worker becomes eligible even if he or she is younger than the normal retirement age and has a lower number of payroll tax payments (in years) than normally required. Workers have a strong incentive to accept the deal, as this is usually quite generous. We call this situation a "pre-retirement option".

Pre-retirement options offer older workers a soft landing at a cost to the active population and tax payers. Bridging pensions, paid at rates equivalent to the standard retirement pension, with no penalty, have been used extensively in Austria, Finland, Italy, Sweden, West Germany and the Netherlands (see OECD, 1992). They are often accompanied by disability pensions. Firms and unions find them appealing because part of the cost falls on the taxpayer (see also Brugiavini *et al.*, 2001).

The macro-economic consequences of early retirement and pre-retirement options have been studied theoretically by Saint-Paul (1995). Such programmes may create strategic complementarities between economic allocations and political processes. In one possible equilibrium, such programmes will promote the emergence of even more declining sectors, due to the macroeconomic distortions they generate, enhancing the political demand for such early retirement plans. This will create a "low" equilibrium with a large number of declining sectors, high political demand for soft landing plans, overuse of those plans and stagnant growth. On the other hand, such programs could make firms and workers more willing to accept change and mobility. This will produce a "high" equilibrium with a small number of declining sectors, a moderate political demand for soft landing plans, a moderate implementation of such plans and a high macroeconomic growth rate. This kind of explanation may therefore help to explain the variety of experiences observed by western welfare states on these issues.

These "soft landing" plans were popular during the 1980s in countries where unemployment was reaching unaffordable levels. The political reasons given for encouraging early exits both in state-provided pensions and firm-organised plans can be summarised in two typical views: "early exits allow ageing high-wage workers to be replaced by young low-wage unemployed", or "placing an older worker in retirement would free the same job for a younger possibly unemployed worker". As we have argued, these ideas suit both governments and firms, normally at the expenses of tax-payers, because it would provide cheap rent-seeking and vote-buying activities.

Even if a "high" equilibrium of the type advocated by Saint-Paul (1995) existed in theory, there is no clear empirical evidence that this is the direction being taken. Boldrin, Dolado, Jimeno and Peracchi (1999) have tested this hypothesis on labour market data for European countries over the period 1986-1996. They look for empirical support to the idea that negative variations in labour force participation rates among the elderly (55+) should be associated to reduced unemployment in younger cohorts (aged 21-30). Figures 7 and 8 plot the relationship between the exit rate from the labour force and the variation in the unemployment rate. There is no evidence of a negative correlation: early retirement of older workers does not seem to cause a reduction of unemployment among younger individuals.

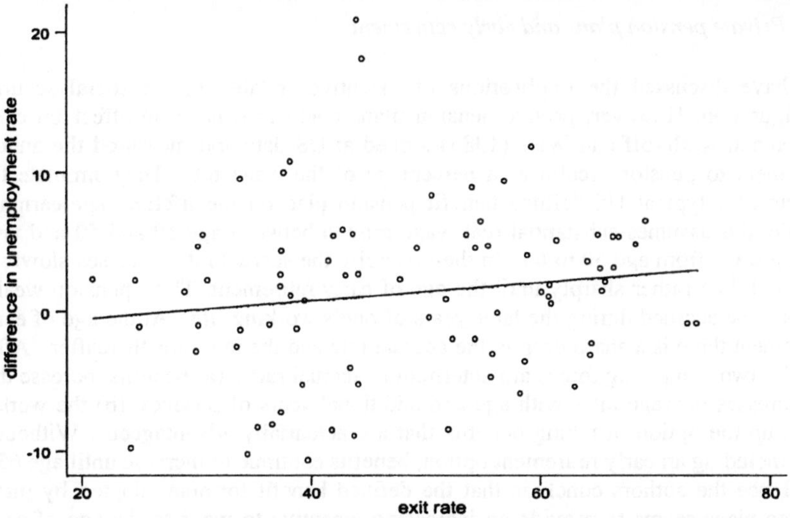


***Figure 7: Early retirement and changes in youth unemployment (aged 21-30), men***

***Source: Boldrin et al. (1999b), using three European Labour Force Surveys for the years 1986, 1991, 1996***

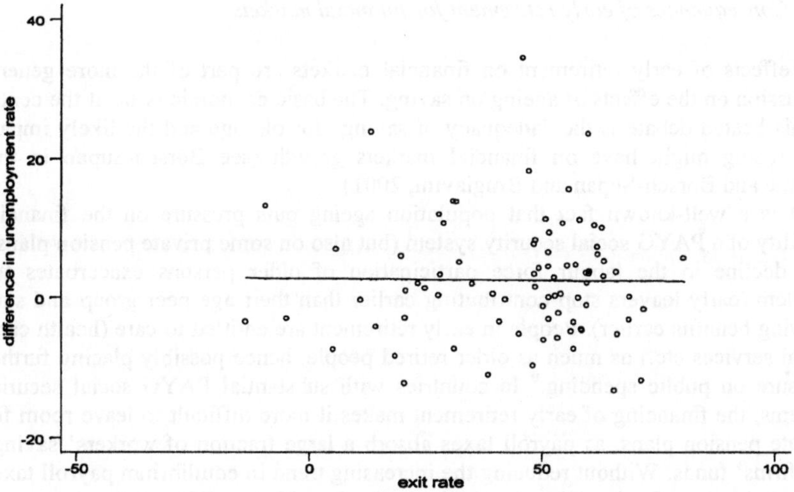


***Figure 8: Early retirement and changes in youth unemployment (aged 21-30), women***

***Source: Boldrin et al. (1999b), using three European Labour Force Surveys for the years 1986, 1991, 1996***

### *5.3 Private pension plans and early retirement*

We have discussed the implications of incentives related to the social security configuration. However, private pension plans could also have an effect on early retirement. Kotlikoff and Wise (1985) looked at US data and measured the annual increment to pension wealth as a percentage of the wage rate. They simulate the effects of a typical US-defined benefit pension plan on the lifetime age-earnings profile, this assumes substantial real wage growth between age 30 and 50 and very little growth from age 50 to 65. In their exercise the accrual rate increases slowly at first and then rather sharply until the age of early retirement. Thus, pension wealth tends to be accrued during the later years of one's working life. At the age of early retirement there is a sharp drop in the accrual rate and the rate falls thereafter. After age 55, two competing forces are determining accrual rates: (a) benefits increase due to increases in wage rates with age and additional years of services; (b) the worker gives up the option of taking benefits that are actuarially advantageous. Without a plan including an early retirement option, benefits continue to increase until age 65.

Hence the authors conclude that the defined benefit formula adopted by many private plans seems to provide an increasing incentive to work to the age of early retirement and a strong disincentive to work after the age of normal retirement. Indeed workers in these plans are observed to leave the work force within the window of early retirement age and normal retirement age.

### *5.4 Consequences of early retirement for financial markets*

The effects of early retirement on financial markets are part of the more general discussion on the effects of ageing on saving. The basic economic issue at the centre of this heated debate is the "adequacy of saving" for old age and the likely impact that ageing might have on financial markets growth (see Börsch-Supan in this volume and Börsch-Supan and Brugiavini, 2001).

It is a well-known fact that population ageing puts pressure on the financial viability of a PAYG social security system (but also on some private pension plans). The decline in the labour force participation of older persons exacerbates the problem (early leavers stop contributing earlier than their age peer group and start drawing benefits earlier). People in early retirement are entitled to care (health care, social services etc.) as much as older retired people, hence possibly placing further pressure on public spending.[9] In countries with substantial PAYG social security systems, the financing of early retirement makes it more difficult to leave room for private pension plans, as payroll taxes absorb a large fraction of workers' savings and firms' funds. Without reducing the increasing trend in equilibrium payroll taxes (those clearing the social security budget), it will be difficult to encourage individuals to switch resources from a public, unfunded, basis to a private, prefunded, or funded basis. Hence, early retirement could make some pension reforms harder to implement and, at the same time, could create impediments to the development of a funded component.

There is also a large body of literature discussing the "beneficial" effects that ageing could have on stock markets and financial markets precisely because there should be an increased desire for saving in pension products. Early retirement could in turn make this argument more compelling. One could also expect direct positive effects on the structure of financial markets if preferences of households change as a result of ageing. If the time horizon of the working life is longer, there will be more incentives to invest in riskier assets in exchange for the expectation of higher returns coupled with a different attitude to risk taking (Gollier and Zeckhauser, 1997).

## 6. CONCLUSIONS

Governments seem to ignore the relevance and magnitude of early retirement. However, costs of early retirement, in terms of foregone output, are already large (they can add to anything up to 10-15% of GDP) and originate much of the problems of fiscal sustainability of public pension systems. The way in which the transition to a mixed system is phased in and the pace of growth of private pension plans also greatly depends on the future developments on the "early retirement front". Hence early retirement will have important implications for financial markets as well.

Governments and employers can do much to discourage early retirement. Labour market institutions and old-age provisions play a very important role in stimulating early retirement. This holds true for both the design of social security provisions and that of private, second pillar, occupational pension plans.

It is usually argued that the features of pension systems encouraging early retirement can hardly be removed as there is a powerful coalition – composed mainly of employers and insiders in the labour market – in favour of it. However, it may be possible to reduce disincentives to early retirement simply by marginally adjusting the pension formulas and the relevant eligibility criteria. The literature reviewed in this chapter points to a strong responsiveness of early retirement decisions to the implicit tax on work imposed by the presence of many early exit to retirement and "soft landing schemes" in OECD countries.

In a nutshell, not only is early retirement important, but Governments can also do much about it. Economists can offer guidance to policy-makers by highlighting the features of pension systems that should be adjusted in order to reduce incentives to early retirement. Better data, such as those advocated in other parts of this volume, would also be very important in this respect as information on health, family wealth and labour market histories is essential in making precise inferences as to the likely impact of these reforms.

---

## NOTES

1. This paper is a brief survey of the literature. More details both on the legislation and on the statistical evidence can be found in an Appendix available at www.frdb.org.
2. In the US this is the age at which a person may first become entitled to unreduced retirement benefits. For persons reaching age 62 before 2000, the normal retirement age was 65. It increases gradually to

67 for persons reaching that age in 2027 or later, beginning with an increase to 65 years and 2 months for persons reaching age 65 in 2003.

3. The only study we know where a comparison between normal retirement age and effective retirement age is made on a consistent basis is Blondal and Scarpetta (1999). Unfortunately the evidence in their study is based on 1995-1996 data.
4. Labour force participation rate is defined as the proportion in each age group counting as economically active, in employment or self-employment or unemployed and actively seeking work.
5. Retirement is defined as complete withdrawal from work, with no possibility of returning to the labour force.
6. There are some exceptions, e.g. in Sweden for young women and for men aged about 65.
7. These examples are drawn from the Gruber and Wise (1999) volume. Other examples can be found in that volume.
8. The difference between social security wealth if retirement is at age $a$ and social security wealth if retirement is at age $a+1$, $SSWa+1 - SSWa$, is called social security wealth accrual.
9. See the contribution by Nazroo and Marmot in this volume.

## REFERENCES


BLAU D. (1998), "Labour force dynamics of older married couples", *Journal of Labour Economics*, vol. 16, n°3.

BLONDAL S. and SCARPETTA S. (1999), "The retirement in OECD countries", OECD, Economics Department Working Papers, N°202.

BOLDRIN M., JIMENEZ-MARTIN S. and PERACCHI F. (1999a), "Social security and retirement in Spain", in Gruber J. and Wise D. (eds.), *Social security and retirement around the world*, NBER, University of Chicago Press.

BOLDRIN M, DOLADO J. J., JIMENO J. F. and PERACCHI F. (1999b), "The future of pensions in Europe", *Economic Policy*, 29:289-320.

BÖRSCH-SUPAN A. and BRUGIAVINI A. (2001), "Savings: the policy debate in Europe", *Oxford Review of Economic Policy*, 17(1):116-143.

BRUGIAVINI A. *et al.* (2001), "What do unions do to the welfare states?", in Boeri T., Brugiavini A. and Calmfors L. (eds.), *The Role of the Unions in the Twenty-First* Century, Oxford, Oxford University Press.

COILE C. (2000), "How do couples decide to retire?", prepared for presentation at the second Annual Joint Conference for the Retirement Research Consortium, "The Outlook for Retirement Income", Washington, DC.

EUROPEAN UNION LABOUR FORCE SURVEY, over several years.

GOLLIER C. and ZECKHAUSER R. (1997), "Horizon length and Portfolio risk", NBER Working Paper 216.

GRUBER J. and WISE D. (1999), *Social security and retirement around the world*, NBER, University of Chicago Press.

HERBERTSSON T, ORSZAG M. (2001), "The cost of early retirement in the OECD", University of Iceland, Institute of Economic Studies Working Paper 1:02.

KAPTEYN A. and DE VOS K. (1999), "Social security and retirement in the Netherlands", in Gruber J. and Wise D. (eds.), *Social security and retirement around the world*, NBER, University of Chicago Press.

KAPTEYN A. and DE VOS K. (2000), "Micro-modelling of retirement in the Netherlands", mimeo, Tilburg University.

KOTLIKOFF L. and WISE D. (1985), "Labor compensation and the structure of private pension plans: evidence for contractual versus spot labor markets", in Wise D. (ed.), *Pension, Labor and Individual Choice,* NBER, The University of Chicago Press.

OECD, (1992), Employment Outlook, Paris.

PALME M, SVENSSON I. (2000), "Micro-modeling of retirement in Sweden", mimeo.

RUST J. (1989), "A dynamic programming model of retirement behaviour", Wise, D. A. (ed.), *The Economics of Aging*, National Bureau of Economic Research Project Report series, Chicago and London, University of Chicago Press, pp. 359-98.

SAINT-PAUL G. (1995), "Some political aspects of unemployment", *European Economic Review*, 39.
STOCK J. and WISE D. (1990), "Pensions, the option value of work and retirement", *Econometrica*, 58(5):1151-1180.
THE MINISTRY OF SOCIAL AFFAIRS, SOCIAL POLICY IN DENMARK, "Social Pensions and Semiretirement Pension", Feb. 1995.
U.S.A. SOCIAL SECURITY ADMINISTRATION (SSA), Social security programs throughout the world, www.ssa.gov.

HOWARD OXLEY [1]

# OECD EXPERIENCE WITH PROJECTING AGE-RELATED EXPENDITURE

## INTRODUCTION

This note briefly reviews the experience of the OECD in making long-term projections of age-related expenditure and draws some lessons and caveats from this experience. Some of the issues regarding age-related spending were discussed in the early 1970s (OECD, 1975, 1976 and 1977). However, the longer-term issues of ageing only began to receive active attention around the middle of the 1980s. By that time, it had become apparent that the trend decline in fertility among most OECD countries could not be easily reversed and that the associated impact on population growth and structure would have implications for future patterns and levels of spending.[2] This, combined with the widespread increase in general government expenditure during the latter half of the 1980s and the large government deficits and debt as many OECD economies moved into recession in the 1990s, led to a growing concern about the implication of population ageing for longer-term fiscal sustainability.

Four different studies have been carried out at the OECD in the period from the mid-1980s to the mid-1990s. The first was prepared for the OECD Social Policy Committee (OECD 1988*a* and 1988*b*), and took a broad approach to ageing, examining all spending components likely to be affected by the change in the population levels and structure (pensions, health, unemployment, family benefits and education). (Referred to hereafter as OECD). This study covered most OECD countries but certain estimates were limited to only 12. The remaining three studies were examined by the Working Party No 1 on Macroeconomic and Structural Policy Analysis of the Economic Policy Committee. Hagemann and Nicoletti (1989) (referred to hereafter as HN) looked at the United States, Japan, Germany and Sweden and examined pension spending alone; Van den Noord and Herd (1993 and 1994) (referred to as NH) also looked at pension spending but covered the major seven countries. Liebfritz, Roseveare, Fore and Wurzel (1995) for seven countries and Roseveare, Liebfritz, Fore and Wurzel (1996) for 20 countries also examined education and health expenditure as well as pensions (these two studies are hereafter referred to as LR).

This study compares the methodology and results of these four exercises. The first section looks at differences in population projections in the four studies. It then



*T.Boeri, A.Börsch-Supan, A.Brugiavini, R.Disney, A.Kapteyn and F.Peracchi (eds.), Pensions: More Information, Less Ideology, 55—74.*

turns to the spending projections themselves starting with OECD (1998*a*). Because it is now possible to compare the first part of the projections with outcomes, this study is considered independently and in somewhat greater length. The discussion then examines the other three papers, focusing on pension spending. In many cases, comparisons are made difficult because the data are for different years and the information needed for a fuller analysis was often not complete. The costs of other age-related spending are then reviewed. A concluding section describes the most recent exercise currently underway at the OECD and the EU and raises some policy issues and areas for further work.

## 1. POPULATION PROJECTIONS

Since the key issue underlying ageing is demographic, a comparison of different population projections is a good place to start. Population projections were the same for OECD (1988*a*) and for HN (1989) and were based on data collected at the OECD from national sources. NH (1993) and LR use estimates prepared by the World Bank. These two sets of projections are compared with more recent population projections collected by the Secretariat in a projection exercise that is currently underway.

The data indicate the well-known patterns of a sharp fall in the growth rates of the total and the working-age population. This decline in growth is particularly marked in Europe where, by the end of the period, both the total and working-age population will be below levels in 1995. At the same time, there is a sharp increase in the share of the elderly in the population. As regards youth, an initial fall in the youth dependency ratios reverses itself within the projection period, reflecting the assumed rise in the fertility rate embedded in the projection. This leads to a subsequent increase in the number of children and, by the end of the period, the youth dependency ratio is not far off its level in 1995 in most countries.

A comparison of the projections indicates that this story is broadly the same for all three sources (Table 1 first three columns). (Data in Table 1 are shown in index form with 1995=100). However, a comparison of the countries shows quite different results in terms of dependency across the three projections.[3] In particular the World Bank/UN projections used in the HN and LR studies are more pessimistic for the age dependency ratios of the three. Most recent projections from Eurostat and national statistical agencies and the UN are often closer to the earlier projections. But a comparison with the most recent UN updates (last two columns) indicates that there can be quite different values even in projections produced around the same time. A message from this is that significant changes can occur over a relatively short period of time in the outlook for ageing over a period as long as 50 years. Further, there is not always a consensus on the underlying parameters to be used and this can lead to quite different outcomes. A hard look at the population projections and the underlying assumptions are therefore needed when assessing the relevance of long-term projections.

*Table 1: Comparison of population projections in 2040 (index 1995=100)*

| | Total population | | | | Working-age population [2] | | | | Old-age dependency ratio [2] | | | | Youth dependency ratio | | |
|---|---|---|---|---|---|---|---|---|---|---|---|---|---|---|---|
| | OECD | World Bank/UN | Eurostat/ National projections[3] | UN 1998 Revision | OECD | World Bank/UN | Eurostat/ National projections[3] | UN 1998 Revision | OECD | World Bank/UN | Eurostat/ National projections[3] | UN 1998 Revision | OECD | World Bank/UN | Eurostat/ National projections[3] |
| | mid 1980s | early 1990s | late 1990s | late 1990s | mid 1980s | early 1990s | late 1990s | late 1990s | mid 1980s | early 1990s | late 1990s | late 1990s | mid 1980s | early 1990s | late 1990s |
| Australia | 139.6 | 126.5 | 138.5 | 138.5 | 128.2 | 112.4 | 128.2 | 126.9 | 188.5 | 226.8 | 197.1 | 199.0 | 94.56 | 92.61 | 96.36 |
| Belgium | 92.0 | 94.9 | 102.4 | 93.0 | 83.6 | 82.1 | 89.9 | 80.8 | 163.0 | 186.6 | 193.5 | 199.3 | 103.82 | 110.39 | 96.36 |
| Canada | 126.7 | 123.3 | 126.0 | 137.7 | 111.1 | 106.7 | 117.1 | 121.1 | 211.2 | 238.1 | 221.7 | 224.4 | 102.78 | 96.90 | 74.56 |
| Denmark [1] | 79.0 | 98.5 | 110.6 | 95.5 | 67.5 | 85.2 | 100.7 | 82.9 | 191.5 | 184.6 | 167.3 | 189.5 | 118.08 | 117.81 | 99.17 |
| France | 99.5 | 107.1 | 109.4 | 105.1 | 89.7 | 94.8 | 97.9 | 93.5 | 173.2 | 191.0 | 196.8 | 189.2 | 100.13 | 98.74 | 89.33 |
| Germany | 75.1 | 86.1 | 97.7 | 93.7 | 62.8 | 68.8 | 82.2 | 79.7 | 202.4 | 246.4 | 233.8 | 218.8 | 119.03 | 117.21 | 96.36 |
| Italy | 85.1 | 87.5 | 90.0 | 79.6 | 73.6 | 69.1 | 74.1 | 62.3 | 191.9 | 239.6 | 241.5 | 262.8 | 112.61 | 125.55 | 91.79 |
| Japan | 95.8 | 94.5 | 89.0 | 89.0 | 83.5 | 76.7 | 80.7 | 71.4 | 194.9 | 242.2 | 272.4 | 259.3 | 111.49 | 119.32 | 96.36 |
| Netherlands | 92.4 | 100.1 | 115.7 | 96.9 | 79.2 | 82.0 | 98.1 | 79.7 | 220.3 | 245.1 | 227.6 | 265.3 | 104.39 | 113.38 | 105.01 |
| Sweden | 95.1 | 107.0 | 103.2 | 100.5 | 87.2 | 98.1 | 97.0 | 90.5 | 142.8 | 146.7 | 154.9 | 171.9 | 110.34 | 104.84 | 87.11 |
| UK | 101.5 | 103.1 | 108.2 | 100.0 | 95.8 | 92.5 | 99.0 | 91.0 | 146.3 | 172.8 | 173.4 | 172.6 | 95.66 | 100.05 | 91.40 |
| United States | 120.4 | 126.3 | 133.5 | 128.3 | 111.3 | 113.8 | 125.1 | 120.4 | 175.9 | 200.6 | 172.9 | 182.8 | 95.27 | 92.26 | 90.96 |

1. Base year in 2000 for population projections in the late 1990s
2. Data for the working-age population refer to 15-64, except for the column Eurostat/National projections where data refer to 20-64.
3. As furnished by national sources, except for Australia, Germany and Japan, where based on latest Eurostat or national data available from OECD Demographics Database.

*Source: OECD; Bos, E. et al. (1994) World Population Projections, 1994-5; IBRD, Washington; Eurostat revised projections 2000; UN Population Division (1998), World Population Prospects: the 1998 Revisions, New York.*

## 2. SOCIAL SPENDING PROJECTIONS IN THE MID-1980S – OECD (1988)

Social spending projections prepared in the mid-1980s (OECD, 1988*a*) considered the impact of population developments alone on five areas of social expenditure: education and family/child allowances, unemployment benefits, and pensions and health-care expenditure, both of which tend to be higher among the elderly. The approach used to calculate spending projections was analytically straightforward. A profile of spending by age for each of these components was first established for 1980. This was then multiplied by the number of individuals in three age groups (0 to 15, 16 to 64 and 65+) to obtain estimates of the level of spending. These levels were then extended to 2040, using the strong assumption that real benefits *per capita* in each age group would remain constant over time. Spending was not compared directly with an estimated path of real GDP nor was the impact of the slower growth of population on GDP and GDP *per capita* assessed.

The key results are highlighted in Table 2. These projections show, in fact, relatively modest population-related increases in spending over the period to the year 2040, averaging only 30 per cent. Much higher increases were expected for Australia, Canada, Japan and the United States, while declines were expected for Belgium and Germany. A simple decomposition can help to understand these projections better. Since *per capita* spending by age group for each spending component is held constant over time, spending increases depend on three factors: the overall increase in population; the change in population structure and the implicit spending weights for each spending component attached to each age group.[4] Dividing spending by population growth and the total dependency ratio provides an estimate of the impact of the residual item.[5] The results in Table 2 – which are expressed in the form of indices with 1980 equal to 100 – suggest that:

- Seen over a 60 year period, the population-related increase in spending is not that large for many countries and, in two countries, spending might even decline;
- While overall population growth probably explains, on average, only one fifth of the expected increase in spending, it is the factor that contributes the bulk of the difference in projected spending across countries;
- The changing structure of the population explains more than half of the total increase in spending but cross country differences are much narrower;
- Finally, the residual effect is almost always positive because the share of the elderly increases rapidly and they are more costly in terms of social spending, on average, than the young.

The study then went on to calculate what would be the necessary rate of GDP growth to keep the ratio of social spending to GDP constant over time. It was found that the rate was below 1 per cent *per annum* for all but two countries.[6] As a result it was concluded that "the social expenditure effects of demographic change appear unlikely to give rise to financial strain in any of the countries examined". It was recognised, however, that to achieve this result, there would need to be a major shift from the spending on the young (as their number fell) to the old (as their number increased) which would require considerable skill to manage. It was also stressed that there were many other reasons why social spending could increase.

*Table 2: Comparisons of social spending projections and outcomes 1980 to 2040 (index 1980=100)*

| | Projected increase in total spending (1) | Part due to increase in population | Part due to increase in dependency | Residual |
|---|---|---|---|---|
| Australia | 207.2 | 168.4 | 111.0 | 110.9 |
| Belgium | 102.2 | 91.6 | 113.7 | 98.1 |
| Canada | 187.4 | 146.3 | 124.9 | 102.5 |
| Denmark | 87.8 | 77.0 | 116.3 | 98.1 |
| France | 128.2 | 104.4 | 111.9 | 109.7 |
| Germany | 97.0 | 73.6 | 127.0 | 103.8 |
| Italy | 107.5 | 84.7 | 116.0 | 109.4 |
| Japan | 140.2 | 102.4 | 122.8 | 111.5 |
| Netherlands | 121.1 | 97.9 | 121.1 | 102.1 |
| Sweden | 109.3 | 95.2 | 111.4 | 103.1 |
| United Kingdom | 110.4 | 102.9 | 106.4 | 100.8 |
| United States | 165.2 | 135.9 | 114.4 | 106.3 |
| *average* | 130.3 | 106.7 | 116.4 | 104.7 |

*Source : OECD.*

How do these projections and the policy conclusions stand up to hindsight? Table 3 shows the expenditure projections over the period 1980-95 compared with most recent data. This comparison needs to be treated with some caution as the study aimed to isolate only the population-related component. Further, it is difficult to know whether like is being compared with like. Data for 1980 used by OECD (1988a) were drawn in large part from national sources while the source of the actual outcomes for 1980 to 1995 come from the OECD Social Expenditure Data File, which is based on common definitions across countries. Thus, the levels at the beginning of the period do not always coincide although the errors are, most often, not large. Ignoring these possible problems, the results show that there were large differences between projections and outcomes. They averaged around 50 per cent with estimates for old-age pensions and health slightly less.

What reasons can be attributed to the differences between the projections and the outcomes and what can this tell us about the way to interpret these exercises?

- First the differences in expenditure appear little related to errors in the population projections. Aside from Italy, Japan and the UK and for Sweden (youth dependency ratio) the projection errors in the dependency ratios appear small.
- Thus, the key differences appear to have been in the estimate of the average benefits *per capita* which has risen much more rapidly than projected. This may reflect the following factors:

- First, the projections make no allowance for the maturing of pension systems or for the reduction in the participation rates of older workers on a variety of programmes (long-term unemployment benefits and early retirement and disability arrangements). Both of these factors have led to an increase in the number of recipients of pensions and in overall income transfer spending;
- Second, the assumption of constant real benefits takes no account of the rules governing, for example, pension systems, or economic and political pressures to increase spending. Thus, salaries of civil servants have tended to rise in line with private sector wages so as to be able to attract staff (for example, in education and in health); and transfer payments have tended to rise in line with the general standard of living. Thus, it is probably unwise to use constant real spending per recipient as the base case when making projections;
- Third, there is no allowance for the impact of the steady increase in the size of cohorts entering retirement. Since these groups would have higher pension than those in retirement in many pension systems, the average benefit – when measured over the entire retired population – will rise;
- Fourth, it has proved politically difficult to offset increases in spending to the elderly by declines elsewhere. Even though the number of children may fall, pressures remain to maintain (or even increase) education spending: the number of children staying on in school has increased in most countries, as has participation in higher education. Since upper secondary and tertiary education is more expensive than lower education levels, this limited any major economies in spending for this component. There are also strong pressures to increase family benefits so as to improve horizontal equity and reduce child poverty;
- Finally, there have been growing demands for new types of social spending. For example, increases in female participation rates have led to a rising demand for childcare. With families less able to care for the elderly, the need for public services for the frail elderly has risen as well.

Several lessons can be drawn from these results. First, over the past twenty years, population has explained only a limited portion of the total change in spending. Second, and associated with this, there are likely to be strong autonomous factors pushing for increases in spending over any time period. Third, projection exercises need to take into account, where possible, rules governing pension schemes and allow for other pressures on spending arising, in large part, from the feed-back effects from rising living standards. The following section asks how well the following three studies resolved these problems.

*Table 3a: Comparisons of social spending projections and outcomes 1980 to 1995 (index 1980=100)*

| | Projected increase in total spending [1] | Actual increase in total spending [2] | Projected old age dependency ratio | Actual old age dependency ratio | Projected youth dependency ratio | Actual youth dependency ratio |
|---|---|---|---|---|---|---|
| Australia | 123.2 | 204.9 | 115.7 | 123.1 | 84.3 | 83.6 |
| Belgium | 96.5 | 133.5 | 100.2 | 109.4 | 89.8 | 87.2 |
| Canada | 117.5 | 174.1 | 127.0 | 128.2 | 87.2 | 89.1 |
| Denmark | 93.7 | 137.3 | 98.4 | 102.2 | 73.9 | 78.9 |
| France | 107.9 | 163.7 | 101.1 | 104.6 | 86.1 | 85.3 |
| Germany [3] | 98.5 | 117.7 | 101.9 | 95.8 | 81.4 | 84.8 |
| Italy | 103.4 | 172.7 | 102.5 | 120.4 | 75.2 | 62.7 |
| Japan | 118.3 | 181.8 | 143.7 | 156.2 | 74.5 | 65.7 |
| Netherlands | 108.1 | 121.5 | 109.4 | 111.3 | 78.1 | 79.7 |
| Sweden | 99.2 | 141.7 | 103.6 | 108.4 | 86.1 | 95.8 |
| UK | 96.6 | 159.2 | 97.4 | 104.0 | 91.7 | 91.1 |
| United States | 109.7 | 168.2 | 107.6 | 113.7 | 94.9 | 99.8 |

1. OECD, 1988, Ageing populations: the social policy implications.
2. OECD Social Expenditure Database, OECD Education Database.
3. Germany refers to western Germany for spending and population projections. Spending data compares the period 1980 to 1995. Population data compares the period 1980-95 with actual data based on western and eastern Germany combined.

*Source : OECD*

*Table 3b: Comparisons of spending projections and outcomes 1980 to 1995 (index 1980=100)*

| | Pensions | | Health | |
|---|---|---|---|---|
| | Projected increase [1] | Actual increase [2] | Projected increase [1] | Actual increase [2] |
| Australia | 136.1 | 221.7 | 132.4 | 198.2 |
| Belgium | 102.6 | 129.0 | 101.3 | 178.6 |
| Canada | 142.1 | 217.4 | 128.9 | 176.1 |
| Denmark | 99.5 | 162.4 | 101.4 | 112.3 |
| France | 119.7 | 159.4 | 107.3 | 170.5 |
| Germany [3] | 107.4 | 113.4 | 102.9 | 119.7 |
| Italy | 113.5 | 212.1 | 107.1 | 126.3 |
| Japan | 159.5 | 242.4 | 126.6 | 192.8 |
| Netherlands | 120.9 | 130.4 | 111.8 | 156.2 |
| Sweden | 100.6 | 153.8 | 107.7 | 104.2 |
| United Kingdom | 100.1 | 181.2 | 102.9 | 164.7 |
| United States | 116.4 | 160.6 | 117.4 | 257.2 |

1. OECD, 1988, Ageing populations: the social policy implications.
2. OECD Social Expenditure Database, OECD Education Database.
3. Germany refers to western Germany for spending and population projections. Spending data compares the period 1980 to 1995.

*Source: OECD*

## 3. STUDIES IN THE LATE 1980S AND THE 1990S

In the course of the 1980s, the OECD economies moved from a position of large fiscal imbalance and restrictive expenditure policies in the downswing to rapid increases in revenues and declining deficits in the second half of the decade. At the same time, the restrictive expenditure policies were relaxed and, while fiscal positions appeared to improve, there was little change on a cyclically adjusted basis. With little improvement in the underlying fiscal position, the downswing in the 1990s was accompanied by a sharp widening in general government deficits.

Against this background, the issue of ageing and spending took on new urgency, particularly as there was growing evidence from national sources that the impact of accelerated ageing on pensions could be much stronger than the earlier studies, including those at the OECD, would have suggested.[7] Reforms were already being implemented in the United States and considered in a few other countries.

While the three studies took quite different approaches to the estimation of expected pension outcomes, they found in general, that ageing would have an important fiscal impact. This required policies to adapt, particularly in the area of old-age pensions. Table 4 presents the key results of these studies. For a number of reasons these projections are difficult to compare:

- The dates of the beginning and end years do not always correspond. In these comparisons, HN and NH have 1990 as the start date. The LR study begins in 1995, such that the increases compared to the two others over the period to 2040 is underestimated. In addition, the coverage of expenditure for some countries (e.g. Germany) appears to be different.
- The HN study presents results in terms of projected increases in the contribution rates (which is applied to some part of wages), while spending in the other two studies is shown as a share of projected GDP. Since the contribution base used in HN is smaller than GDP, the same rise in pension spending will lead to a larger increase in contribution rates than in the share in GDP. Furthermore, HN contribution rates do not include government subsidies (transfers) to the public old-age pension system. These were estimated to represent 20% of pension spending in Japan, 15% in Sweden and 18% in Germany. Including these amounts would increase both the effective contribution rate as well as the increase in this effective rate over time.[8]
- The assumed growth rate of GDP differs between the NH and LR studies.[9] Both estimated GDP growth by multiplying the growth rate of the working-age population by productivity growth. However, NH assumed 2% productivity growth through the period (except for the US where it was 1%). LR applied a rate of 1.5% to all countries.

*Table 4: A comparison of pension projections in the late 1980s and early 1990s (Contribution rates and % of GDP)*

| | Hagemann and Nicoletti | | Van den Noord and Herd | | Leibfritz *et al.* and Roseveare *et al.* | |
|---|---|---|---|---|---|---|
| **Original data** | | | | | | |
| | Level in 1990 | Maximum change to 2040 | Level in 1990 or near year | Maximum change to 2040 | Level in 1995 | Maximum change to 2040 |
| | (contribution rate) | | (shares in GDP) | | (shares in GDP) | |
| United States | 12.1 | 4.7 | 5.1 | 4.4 | 4.1 | 3.0 |
| Japan | 4.5 | 18.5 | 5.7 | 6.8 | 6.6 | 9.9 |
| Germany | 13.5 | 15.7 | 6.9 | 6.2 | 11.1 | 7.3 |
| France | .. | .. | 9.2 | 5.5 | 10.6 | 3.8 |
| Italy | .. | .. | 11.0 | 11.9 | 13.3 | 8.1 |
| United Kingdom | .. | .. | 6.3 | 4.8 | 4.5 | 1.0 |
| Canada | .. | .. | 3.9 | 6.3 | 5.2 | 3.9 |
| Sweden | 15.8 | 5.2 | 0.0 | 0.0 | 11.8 | 3.1 |

| **Adjusted data** | Hagemann and Nicoletti | | Van den Noord and Herd (No adjustments) | | Leibfritz *et al.* and Roseveare *et al.* | | | |
|---|---|---|---|---|---|---|---|---|
| | Level in 1990 (adjusted using wage share and impact of subsidies)[1] | Maximum change to 2040 (adjusted using wage share and impact of subsidies)[1] | Level in 1990 or near year | Maximum change to 2040 | Estimated level in 1995 (allowing for growth in spending 1990-5)[2] | Maximum change to 2040 with adjustment for period 1990-95[2] | Maximum change to 2040 with adjustment for different GDP growth[3] | Maximum change with adjustment for 1990-5 and GDP growth[3] |
| | (shares in GDP) | | (shares in GDP) | | (shares in GDP) | | | |
| United States | 5.7 | 2.2 | 5.1 | 4.4 | 3.6 | 3.5 | 1.6 | 2.1 |
| Japan | 2.5 | 10.5 | 5.7 | 6.8 | 5.3 | 11.2 | 5.9 | 7.2 |
| Germany | 7.3 | 7.6 | 6.9 | 6.2 | 9.9 | 8.5 | 3.6 | 4.8 |
| France | .. | .. | 9.2 | 5.5 | 9.5 | 4.9 | 0.3 | 1.5 |
| Italy | .. | .. | 11.0 | 11.9 | 11.6 | 9.8 | 3.8 | 5.5 |
| United Kingdom | .. | .. | 6.3 | 4.8 | 2.9 | 2.6 | 0.1 | 1.7 |
| Canada | .. | .. | 3.9 | 6.3 | 4.7 | 4.4 | 1.4 | 1.9 |
| Sweden | 7.8 | 2.6 | 0.0 | 0.0 | 11.1 | 3.8 | -0.8 | -0.1 |

1. *Adjustments aimed at making the HN and the LR study results closer to those in the NH study. For the HN study, the data on contribution rates were very roughly transformed into ratios of spending relative to GDP by a) grossing up the contribution rates using the share of wages in GDP, and b) adding in government transfers to public pension funds as a share of GDP.*
2. *For the LR study, two different and separate adjustments were made. First data from the Social Expenditure Data File were used to estimate the level of spending in 1995 using growth rates from between the starting year around 1990 and 1995. The change is equal to the change in the LR study plus the estimated difference in level between 1990 and 1995. Maximum change refers to the highest level reached over the period rather than the end of the period itself.*
3. *In the second adjustment, the ratios including the change from 1990 to 1995 were recalculated using growth rates for GDP corrected for the differences in productivity growth. The two adjustments are combined in the last column.*

*Source: Hagemann and Nicoletti (1989), van den Noord and Herd (1991), Roseveare et al. (1996), author's estimates drawing on the OECD Social Expenditure Data File.*

The second panel presents the data after a number of adjustments have been made to the HN and LR studies to bring them closer in line with the NH study: in the first two columns, adjustments aim at translating the contribution rates in HN into expenditure shares by multiplying the contribution rates by the wage share in GDP with an allowance for the amount of government transfers to public pension systems. In the last four columns two separate adjustments have been made to the LR study. In the first two of these, the outcomes in LR were adjusted by the actual change in pension spending between 1990 and 1995 to make them more comparable with the NH results. In the third column, shares of spending in GDP in the LR study were changed by revising GDP growth to allow for the difference in the productivity growth between the LR and the NH studies and the two modifications were combined in the fourth column. These adjustments are approximate and need to be treated with considerable caution for the following reasons. The contribution base used in the HN study may be less than the total wage bill in some countries.[10] Furthermore, the adjustment to GDP growth for productivity (made to the results of the LR studies) does not take into account the feedback effects of higher productivity on pension spending. Since the associated increase in spending is not taken into account, the adjustment to productivity growth probably overstates the impact on the *share* of spending in GDP. Finally, these adjustments take no account of reforms undertaken in some countries between the first and the last of these studies.

Even after these adjustments, an examination of the data in Table 4 indicates how very difficult it is to compare either the starting point or the maximum projected changes over time. This is particularly the case for Germany, where the coverage does not seem to be the same between the NH and the LR studies. Significant differences also appear for the United Kingdom and Canada. The changes over time show considerable variation in results for each country which are hard to explain *a priori* without fuller information of the projection methods:

- The HN baseline results (for four countries) show quite large increases in contribution rates for Germany and Japan and more modest but still significant increases for the United States and Sweden, the latter two countries being less affected by the demographic shock (see Table 1).
- Compared with this, the NH study finds a much lower increase for Japan and to a lesser extent Germany but a higher increase for the United States. This is the case despite a projection of more rapid ageing in the NH study (Table 1).
- A comparison of the NH and LR studies indicates, depending on the adjustment made, lower increases in pension spending for LR with the possible exception of Japan and Germany.

Some part of the differences appears to be embedded in the projection models used, and a few salient differences in the approach used are worth highlighting. As noted, the HN study approaches the problem of the fiscal implications of ageing by calculating pension contribution rates. Their model is based on a social security budget constraint in which the revenues of the fund plus returns on assets of the state schemes (where these funds exist) must be equal to pension expenditure (taking account of government transfers to the fund) plus the change in the pension fund assets over the period.[11] After defining revenues, expenditures and pension fund assets on a *per capita* basis and assuming that these grow in line with nominal wages, an identity is derived in which the tax (contribution) rate is largely affected by the replacement ratio and the dependency ratio.[12]

This simplification of the pension system leaves less place for the modelling of the underlying pension systems. In calculating the time paths the authors took into account reforms in the United States and Japan in the 1980s (essentially affecting the dependency ratios) and allowed for a progressive run-down in pension fund assets over time for all countries except for the US where it first increases and then falls.[13] Although replacement ratios were adjusted to allow for the impact of maturing pension systems in Japan and Sweden, a key implicit assumption is constant average replacement ratios over the period – i.e. that all pensions rise in line with wages, for new entrants and existing retirees alike. This was fully the case (at that time) in Germany.[14] However, for Japan and the United States and Sweden (the basic pension only), pensions are, in fact, indexed to prices after retirement such that the average benefits/replacement rates could be affected by the changing size of cohorts and lengthening lifetimes.[15,16]

The subsequent two papers paid progressively greater attention to cohort effects and to the impact of the rules governing pension benefits in each country. Cohort analysis allowed the authors to assess the importance of unfunded (implicit) pension debt of government and the degree to which current systems will lead to transfers between generations. In the NH paper, pension benefits for each cohort were established as the basis of a standardised model in which individuals were estimated to have worked 40 years and to retire at 60 on a pension which is a fixed percentage of the lifetime earnings.[17] Each period receives pensions up until he or she dies and the last cohort with existing pension rights is assumed to pass away in 2050. The pensions received by individuals in each cohort in retirement was then summed to establish total pension spending in any given year. The pension benefits were set on the basis of the contribution history at the time of retirement and were then indexed only to prices. The pension benefits of current children and future generations are estimated in a similar manner, assuming that a constant share of those aged 60+ receive benefits over time. The entry level of pension benefits was calibrated on levels around the end of the 1980s.

The LR studies built on this framework by adding in a better representation of pension systems in each individual country. In each case, allowance was made for the different kinds of benefits, retirement ages and the rules governing the calculation of benefits. In addition, more recent reforms were taken into account, although they may not have done full justice to the impact of the reforms – e.g. Italy.[18] For several countries (e.g. Germany and Japan), pensions were indexed on wages net of tax and social security increases. These factors could explain the larger increases in spending in the LR study for these two countries. On the other hand, the smaller increase for the United Kingdom probably reflects the modifications to the retirement age to 65 for both men and women. Differences in the assumed retirement age may also explain the differences for Canada, along with the assumption that the flat rate benefit would fall relative to wages.

One conclusion that can be drawn from these studies is that small changes in assumptions can give significantly different results. Thus, careful attention needs to be paid to appropriate modelling of pension system rules within a context which, at the very least, isolates individual cohorts as they enter and leave the system. This is being attempted in the forthcoming round of projections at the OECD and the EU where greater reliance is being placed on more detailed country models of pension expenditure (see below).

## 4. EDUCATION AND HEALTH-CARE SPENDING

The fiscal impact of ageing will also have important effects through health care and education, although in different directions. The latter, it has sometimes been argued, will provide an offset to the increase in spending among the elderly. The LR paper projected education spending to 2030. The projections were based on estimated unit costs from primary to tertiary education. Costs in this sector were assumed to rise in line with aggregate productivity. The results suggested that this area of spending was unlikely to provide much offset to the effects of rising age-dependency ratios: among the Major Seven countries, spending would decline only marginally. These projections, if carried out today, would be likely to show more significant declines as the most recent population projections project a much smaller rise in fertility. However, this does not take into account the effects of progressively longer stays in education, a factor which continues to place pressure on education systems in many countries and the more general difficulty in the area of budget policy of transferring resources from areas where needs (as measured by the population) are declining.[19]

Projecting health-care spending is a much more difficult exercise than for pensions, where existing rules provide a basis for calculating future pension liabilities. No such framework exists for public health care. Levels of spending vary considerably across countries, even those at the same level of *per capita* income, reflecting the share of total health spending paid for by general government, patient expectations as regard to health care and conditions of supply, which, in turn, is conditioned by government budgetary policies, regulation and payment systems and technology. These various factors are mixed in different ways across countries and within any country over time.

Focusing on the demand component alone, the development of health-care costs depends on mortality, morbidity, disability and whether these increase or decrease as lifetimes lengthen. Since there is little information in this area to guide the policymaker, projections are open to considerably wider margins of error than for pension expenditure.

Most projections of public health-care expenditure have used the profile of health-care spending by age group as a starting point. These are generally U shaped with higher spending *per capita* for the very young, lower spending for those of prime working age and, then, a progressive increase with age. A key question, however, is whether spending patterns by age group are related to mortality. Since mortality is strongly correlated with age, the large share of total health-care costs that is consumed by the elderly may, in fact, reflect the high cost of treatment just before death rather than a steady increase in "ordinary" health services among all of the elderly. If a large share of individual lifetime health-care spending occurs in the period just before death, lengthening lifetimes may delay these health-care costs, leading to a slower rise in aggregate health spending as the population ages. In this context, the LR study provided two extreme estimates for ageing-related health-care costs to 2030: in the first, public spending is entirely related to the age structure of the population; in the second it is totally related to mortality/longevity by age group (Table 5).[20] These results suggest that while health-care costs as a share of GDP are likely to increase over the period to 2030, lengthening lifetimes could significantly limit the size of the increases if the bulk of costs are associated with the "cost of dying". However, the outcome may also depend on the profile of ageing over time. For example, the projection for health-care spending is higher in Japan in the LR results when it is assumed that costs are fully driven by mortality, possibly because ageing has begun earlier than in other OECD countries (Table 5).[21]

*Table 5: Projections of health care cost to 2030*

| Country | Public health care costs in 1995 | Projected health care costs in 2030 assuming cost depends on: | |
|---|---|---|---|
| | | Number of elderly | Number of deaths |
| United States | 6.4 | 8.2 | 6.9 |
| Japan | 4.9 | 6.3 | 7.2 |
| Germany | 6.2 | 7.8 | 7.4 |
| France | 7 | 8.9 | 8.3 |
| Italy | 6.4 | 8.1 | 7.7 |
| United Kingdom | 6 | 7 | 6.2 |
| Canada | 7.4 | 10.3 | 9.3 |
| Sweden | 6.2 | 7.9 | 6.7 |

*Source* : OECD

A final health-cost issue concerns the type of care. Earlier studies have often not distinguished between acute care in hospitals and ambulatory care from long-term care or home help for the elderly. In this context, one of the features of the expected population developments is the sharp increase in the very old – i.e. those over 80 years old. For the eight countries examined here, the number of the very old are expected to increase rapidly. At the same time, there is likely to be increased demand for support for the elderly outside the family unit as older-worker and women's labour market participation increases. In certain Nordic countries, where participation rates are already high, spending on the frail elderly already represents a substantial share of GDP.[22]

## 5. DEFICITS, DEBT AND DEBT INTEREST PAYMENTS: CLOSING THE MODELS

A final issue in assessing the impact of ageing is that these projections need to be embedded in a wider fiscal approach which takes into account the impact of higher spending on deficits and debt dynamics. While this approach is highly sensitive to the starting point and the interest rate assumptions, it provides some measure of the overall cost of the system if there is no change in policies to compensate. Under the assumption that there is no increase in taxes or in other spending as a share of GDP (the latter a strong assumption in itself) the LR studies show that increase in primary deficits or the fall in surpluses leads to increased debt of substantial portions for all but a few countries.

## 6. MOST RECENT PROJECTIONS AND MAIN CONCLUSIONS

The issues of ageing are likely to remain in the forefront of the policy debate for some time to come. Many countries have high levels of implicit government debt in the form of future pension rights that have been or will be built up by generations currently alive. If reforms are not undertaken, there will need to be increases in tax/contribution rates of substantial proportion over the next few decades. Alternatively, widening defects will lead to a sharp rise in government debt and pressure on government budgets through rising debt interest payments. With tax pressure already high in a number of European countries, such increases can lead to non-linear increases in efficiency losses. In some cases, when combined with high levels of debt, they have already led to financial market pressures.

This suggests that projections which provide measures of the potential impact of ageing on the sustainability of public finances will be essential for assessing current policy, and the need for (and the impact of) further reform. But if past work in this area is a guide, there remains considerable uncertainty concerning population developments and the results are very sensitive to the projection methodology and system parameters employed. For projections to be useful they need to be credible and based on well-developed projection models which describe accurately future trends in pension benefits. Most countries have already undertaken this task even though there is not always the necessary degree of transparency because projection models are sometimes not made available for public inspection.

At the same time, the resulting projections are often weakly comparable with those of other countries as they are based on macro assumptions which differ. The current work on age-related spending projections at the OECD (in conjunction with a similar exercise in the EU) aims at using national models within a framework of common assumptions for the macro environment. These have been constructed as follows:

- Eurostat (EU countries) and national population projections (other OECD countries) provide estimates of the dependent and working age population up to 2050.

- Employment is then established on the basis of assumptions concerning participation rates and unemployment. Participation rates for women are allowed to converge towards those of men and to approach levels in countries where participation rates are highest. Little further change in prime-aged male workers (aged 20 to 54) or male older workers (55-64) was assumed. Unemployment rates were set to fall to their structural component by 2005 and remain constant thereafter except for countries where recent labour market reforms could lead to lower structural unemployment. In the latter case, unemployment rates could be reduced by a third from their current structural levels.
- Labour-augmenting productivity growth was assumed to rise by 1.75% with countries allowed a transition period.
- Wages were assumed to rise in line with productivity and price inflation and real interest rates were arbitrarily set at, respectively, 2 and 4% annually.
- Government revenues and non-age-related expenditure rise in line with GDP.

This scenario, which may be a fairly optimistic picture of future GDP growth trends, assumes no further decline in the participation rates of older workers, no change in the share of part-time working, and productivity rates which are somewhat above historical trend rates in a number of countries. Using this framework as a starting point, 21 OECD countries have provided projections up to 2050 using their own models (OECD, 2001 and Dang *et al.*, 2001).

The results of this work (Table 6) provide greater transparency for international policy assessment and analysis. They show an increase in spending on public old-age pensions of between 3 and 4 percentage points of GDP but the increases are above 4 percentage points in 10 countries and 5 or above in 7. The number of countries providing health-care spending projections is not as wide. But for those countries providing estimates, the increase averages around 3 to 4 percentage points of GDP. Based on a yet smaller sample of countries, increases in these first two components might be offset by declines in child-related spending (education and family benefits) but the impact on overall spending is small – in the range of 1 percentage point. Thus, spending projections point to substantial fiscal pressures from ageing in general, with a significantly larger impact for a substantial number. If these problems are not addressed, this will lead to a significant deterioration in the primary balance, significantly offsetting the improvements in underlying fiscal positions achieved over the last 5 to 10 years.

*Table 6: Age-related spending: recent projections (% of GDP, changes in percentage points)*

| | Total age-related spending[1] | | Old-age pension | | Health care and long-term care | |
|---|---|---|---|---|---|---|
| | Panel A | | Panel B | | Panel C | |
| | level 2000 | change 2000-50 | Level 2000 | change 2000-50 | level 2000 | change 2000-50 |
| Australia | 16.7 | 5.6 | 3.0 | 1.6 | 6.8 | 6.2 |
| Austria | 10.4 | 2.3 | 9.5 | 2.2 | .. | .. |
| Belgium | 22.1 | 5.2 | 8.8 | 3.3 | 6.2 | 3.0 |
| Canada | 17.9 | 8.7 | 5.1 | 5.8 | 6.3 | 4.2 |
| Czech Republic | 23.1 | 6.9 | 7.8 | 6.8 | 7.5 | 2.0 |
| Denmark | 29.3 | 5.7 | 6.1 | 2.7 | 6.6 | 2.7 |
| Finland | 19.4 | 8.5 | 8.1 | 4.8 | 8.1 | 3.8 |
| France[2] | .. | .. | 12.1 | 3.9 | .. | .. |
| Germany | .. | .. | 11.8 | 5.0 | .. | .. |
| Hungary | 7.1 | 1.6 | 6.0 | 1.2 | .. | .. |
| Italy | .. | .. | 14.2 | -0.3 | .. | .. |
| Japan | 13.7 | 3.0 | 7.9 | 0.6 | 5.8 | 2.4 |
| Korea | 3.1 | 8.5 | 2.1 | 8.0 | 0.7 | 0.5 |
| Netherlands | 19.1 | 9.9 | 5.2 | 4.8 | 7.2 | 4.8 |
| New Zealand | 18.7 | 8.4 | 4.8 | 5.7 | 6.7 | 4.0 |
| Norway | 17.9 | 13.4 | 4.9 | 8.0 | 5.2 | 3.2 |
| Poland | 12.2 | -2.6 | 10.8 | -2.5 | .. | .. |
| Spain | .. | .. | 9.4 | 8.0 | .. | .. |
| Sweden | 29.0 | 3.2 | 9.2 | 1.6 | 8.1 | 3.2 |
| United Kingdom | 15.6 | 0.2 | 4.3 | -0.7 | 5.6 | 1.7 |
| United States | 11.2 | 5.5 | 4.4 | 1.8 | 2.6 | 4.4 |
| **OECD average[3]** | **16.9** | **5.5** | **7.4** | **3.4** | **6.0** | **3.3** |

1. Does not include countries only providing old-age pension spending (shown in panel B)
2. For France, the latest available year is 2040
3. OECD averages exclude countries where information is not available. The total change in Panel A is the sum of the average changes of each one of the age-related spending components (each of which is a different sub-sample of countries). Thus the average could be interpreted as a "typical" country with spending per component equal to the sub-sample averages. The total includes, in addition to old-age pensions and health care, other programmes permitting early withdrawal from the labour force (e.g. disability), family benefits and education.

*Source*: OECD.

Nonetheless it is important to recognise factors which have not been taken into account and which will affect outcomes over such a long time horizon.

- Projections of this kind need to be placed in an international general-equilibrium context to assess the impact of ageing on savings and investment and how this might affect overall growth, the foreign balance, exchange rates and rates of return. Recent work at the OECD (Turner *et al.*, 1998) finds, for example, that growth will slow because of the effect of lower savings and the possible build-up of debt.
- As pointed out by Blondal and Scarpetta (1998) there are strong incentives in most systems to retire early and many countries have allowed a variety of arrangements (long-term unemployment benefits, disability etc.) to absorb older workers before the official retirement age is reached. These incentives appear to strongly affect the timing of retirement and explain a significant portion of the decline in the effective age of retirement in many OECD countries. While recent reforms have reduced incentives to retire early, not all countries have made the necessary changes and, unless further progress is made, there may be further declines in the participation rates of older workers.
- The projections are to some degree policy inconsistent. Much higher rates of female participation are assumed but no allowance is made for increased costs of childcare, which may well need to be supplied or subsidised by the public sector if women's labour force participation is to increase to the degree assumed. No allowance is made for the need for retraining of older workers.
- Government spending from other sources is assumed to rise in line with GDP. As illustrated by the discussion of the projections in OECD (1988*a*), policy makers are confronted with continuing demands for extensions of existing programmes and additional spending as new needs arise. The difficulty in making cuts to existing programmes remains a continuing feature of budget policy.
- Finally, the reforms in some countries may not be sustainable over the longer haul. In practice, many changes to pension systems have aimed at a progressive reduction in average benefits. In the absence of additional measures to encourage individuals to supplement incomes through continued labour-market activity or higher savings, levels of income replacement among the elderly will fall and poverty could increase. This raises the importance of broader strategies for retirement incomes (see OECD, 1998) – if pressures to raise benefits are to be avoided.

In all of these areas, more research in necessary. This is particularly the case for Europe: the impact of ageing is likely to be stronger there than elsewhere and the fiscal impact higher, reflecting the more important role of the state in income replacement for the elderly. Projections are highly uncertain, in part because they make strong assumptions about future labour market trends, particularly as regards women's labour market behaviour and the retirement decision. More and better data, which provide policy makers with a better fix on likely developments, is desirable. In this context, constructing improved panel data – which trace the behaviour of individuals through time – is particularly desirable.

## NOTES

1. The views expressed in this note are personal and do not necessarily reflect those of the OECD. Thanks go to Debbie Bloch, Thai-Thanh Dang, Sarah Kennedy and Muriel Duluc for technical assistance. The author is grateful for comments from Pablo Antolin, Giuseppe Nicoletti, Paul van den Noord, Deborah Roseveare and Jonathon Coppel. The usual disclaimer applies.
2. See, for example, Steinmann G. (ed.) (1984) and Davis K. *et al.* (eds.) (1996).
3. In particular, the fertility rate does not return to a level necessary to stabilise the population or at least does so only over the very long run in the most recent projections.
4. $$\frac{EXP_t}{} = POP_t * \frac{POPD_t}{POP_t} * RES_t$$
   Where EXP is expenditure, POP is total population, POPD is the dependent population (age groups 0 to 14 plus 65+). RES is the residual equal to expenditure divided by the dependent population.
5. Note that the cross product terms are entirely attributed to the residual in this case, which should lead to an overestimate of the impact of the structural effect.
6. Canada and Australia. However, this was partly offset by the fact that total population and, more importantly, the working-age population was expected to grow more rapidly than for the average of the countries considered.
7. Hagemann and Nicoletti (1989) provide an exhaustive bibliography of the literature during this period.
8. Although, in the case of Germany, it was assumed that this share would decline from 18 to 11.4% over the projection period.
9. This problem is "avoided" in HN by making estimates for contribution rates.
10. For example where there are ceilings on contributions or on income over which contributions are calculated.
11. REV(t) + I(t) F(t-1) = EXP(t)(1-S(t)) + F(t) - F(t-1). Where REV and EXP are revenue and expenditure, I is the interest rate on F, the fund assets, and S is the share of spending financed by the budget.
12. The full model is affected by other factors. The tax rate is defined
    $$\tau(t) \equiv \phi(t-1) + \frac{g(t)+n(t)-i(t)}{1+g(t)+n(t)}\phi(t-1) + \beta(t)[1-S(t)]DEP(t)$$
    where $\phi$ is the pension fixed *per capita*; "g" and "n" are the growth rates of taxable wages and the number of contributors, "i" is the real rate of return on pension fund assets. $\beta$ is the replacement rate, S is the share of pension benefits financed by the government and DEP is the "economic" dependency ratio – i.e. the actual ratio of beneficiaries to contributors. Thus, the tax rate is directly related to *a)* the growth in (de-cumulation of) pension fund assets, *b)* an average replacement rate, and *c)* the dependency ratio (ratio of beneficiaries to contributors). The tax rate is negatively related to difference between the average real rate of return on the fund assets and the rate of growth of real taxable income and the fraction of expenditure paid for by the government budget.
13. This is in line with the intention of the 1983 Social Security reform.
14. Pensions indexing was changed to wages net of taxes and social security contributions in 1991.
15. Consider a situation where the number of pension beneficiaries is constant and the number of entrants just equal to the number of exits and benefits are set in terms of past wages. The increase in the number of entrants as the baby boom moves into retirement leads, in this case, initially to an increase in the average benefit (measured over all pensioners). But as these cohorts age, and the number of new entrants grows more slowly, the average benefit should fall as their pensions fall relative to the

average wage over time. This would be accentuated by lengthening lifetimes, as the difference between the average wage and the pension benefit will continue to widen in real terms.

16. However, as the authors note, the estimate of benefit rates at the end of the period for the United States are almost identical with estimates of the Social Security Administration.
17. Except for the United Kingdom and Canada where allowance is made for the introduction of an earnings-related scheme.
18. The LR estimates appear to significantly underestimate the impact of the series of reforms undertaken in the course of the 1990s. See OECD (2000).
19. The increases for education between 2000 and 2030 were the following:

| Country | 2000 | 2030 |
|---|---|---|
| United States | 5.4 | 5.1 |
| Japan | 2.8 | 2.7 |
| Germany | 3.1 | 3.0 |
| France | 5.0 | 5.0 |
| Italy | 4.3 | 4.6 |
| United Kingdom | 4.9 | 4.6 |
| Canada | 6.2 | 6.1 |

20. Projections were based on a cost per person below 65 and 65 and over. Thus this does not take into account the increase in the very old and the possible increase in needs for long-term and nursing care.
21. Note that mixed models have been used which fix a value for the "average costs of death". This value, multiplied by mortality by age group is then subtracted from total health-care costs by age group to estimate "current" health-care costs. Projections are then based on ordinary health-care costs multiplied by the number of individuals in each age group and the costs of death multiplied by mortality in each age group. See Van Ewijk *et al.*(2000).
22. In the early 1990s Sweden and Norway spend around 2¾% of GDP.

## REFERENCES

BLONDAL S. and SCARPETTA S. (1998), "The retirement decision in OECD countries", OECD Economics Department Working Papers, No.202, Paris.

DANG T-T, ANTOLIN P. and OXLEY H. (2001), "The fiscal implications of ageing: projections of age-related spending", OECD Economics Department Working Papers, forthcoming, Paris.

DAVIS K. *et al.* (eds.) (1996), *Below –Replacement Fertility in Industrialised Countries: Causes, Consequences, Policies*, Cambridge University Press, Cambridge Mass..

HAGEMANN R and NICOLETTI G. (1989), "Population ageing: economic effects and some policy implications for financing public pensions" OECD Economic Studies, No.12, Spring.

LIEBFRITZ W., ROSEVEARE D., FORE D. and WURZEL E. (1995), "Ageing population, pension systems, and government budgets: how do they affect savings", OECD Economics Department Working Papers, No.156, Paris.

OECD (1975), *Public Expenditure on Education*, Studies in Resource Allocation No.2, Paris.

OECD (1976), *Public Expenditure on Income Maintenance Programmes*, Studies in Resource Allocation No.3, Paris.

OECD (1977), *Public Expenditure on Health*, Studies in Resource Allocation, No.4, Paris.

OECD (1988a), *Ageing Populations, the Social Policy Implications*, Paris.

OECD (1988b), *The Future of Social Protection*, Paris.

OECD ([1998]), *Maintaining Prosperity in an Ageing Society*, Paris.

OECD (2000), *Economic Survey of Italy*, Paris.

OECD (2001), Economic Outlook No.69, Paris.

ROSEVEARE D., LIEBFRITZ W., FORE D. and WURZEL E. (1996), "Ageing population, pension systems, and government budgets, simulations for 20 countries", OECD Economics Department Working Papers, No.168, Paris.

STEINMANN G. (ed.) (1984), *Economic Consequences of Population Change in Industrialised Countries*, Springer-Verlag, Berlin.

TURNER D., GIORNO C., DE SERRES A., VOURC'H A. and RICHARDSON P. (1998), "The macroeconomic implications of ageing in a global context", OECD Economics Department Working Papers No.193, Paris.

VAN EWIJK C., KUIPERS B., TER RELE H., VAN DE VEN M. and WESTERHOUT E. (2000), *Ageing in the Netherlands*, Netherlands Bureau for Policy Analysis, The Hague.

VAN DEN NOORD P. and HERD R. (1993), "Pension liabilities in the seven major countries", OECD Economics Department Working Papers, No.142, Paris.

VAN DEN NOORD P. and HERD R. (1994), "Estimating pension liabilities: a methodological framework", OECD Economic Studies, No.23, Winter.

MARCO BUTI AND DECLAN COSTELLO [1]

# POPULATION AGEING AND THE SUSTAINABILITY OF PUBLIC FINANCES IN EMU

## 1. INCREASED ATTENTION TO AGEING POPULATION AT EU LEVEL IN LIGHT OF EMU

Over the coming decades, the size and age-profile of the population of European Union Member States will undergo substantial changes due to a fall in fertility rates to levels well below what is needed for a natural replacement of the population and significant increases in life expectancy. These changes will pose economic, budgetary and social challenges for policy makers, especially managing the increased pressure for spending on public pensions and health care. Several studies have shown that the impact on public finances in EU countries could be particularly severe given that public pensions systems are for the most part financed on a pay-as-you-go (PAYG) basis and high levels of public debt.[2]

Concern over the long-term sustainability of public finances in light of ageing populations acquired significance with the launch of the Euro in 1999. In Economic and Monetary Union, increased age-related spending cannot be financed by running up large structural deficits and public debt. A return to large structural deficits would undermine fiscal consolidation achieved in the run-up to EMU and would be contrary to the Stability and Growth Pact (SGP). Unsustainable public finance positions would complicate the implementation of the single monetary policy by the European Central Bank and undermine confidence in the EMU process, possibly resulting in interest rates being higher than they otherwise would be.[3] Increased EU surveillance of the long-term sustainability of public finances in light of ageing population can therefore be justified with a view to internalising such negative cross-border spillover effects.

EU involvement is not, however, limited to ensuring sound public finances. As pointed out in McMorrow and Roeger (1999), ageing populations will potentially have important consequences for labour supply, private savings behaviour and economic growth. The policy responses of Member States to population must also address these effects. For example, raising contribution rates to public pension systems (which are already very high in many Member States) would widen the wedge between labour costs and net wages, and create disincentives to hire workers and participate in the labour market. Similarly increasing the overall tax burden could exacerbate disincentives towards employment and investment. Alternatively,



*T.Boeri, A.Börsch-Supan, A.Brugiavini, R.Disney, A.Kapteyn and F.Peracchi (eds.), Pensions: More Information, Less Ideology, 75—94.*

cutting back on other essential public spending items such as infrastructure, education and training could be counter-productive as such expenditures can contribute to raising the potential output of the EU.

This paper outlines the growing involvement of the EU in the debate on ageing populations, in particular the steps being taken to ensure the long term sustainability of public finances in EMU. The next section briefly summarises the latest Eurostat population projections up to 2050. Section 3 considers how the long-term sustainability of public finances is dealt with in the existing EU framework for budgetary surveillance, and comments on budgetary developments in the first two years of EMU. Section 4 reviews recent attempts at EU level to develop more comparable projections for the impact of ageing on public finances. Section 5 closes with a description of the emerging policy stance at EU level.

## 2. RECENT DEMOGRAPHIC PROJECTIONS

Updated Eurostat population projections for the period 2000 to 2050 show that the EU working-age population (aged between 15 and 64) will stay broadly stable at some 250 million until 2015. Thereafter, it will decline to 244 million by 2025 and 211 million by 2050, a drop of over 40 million or some 16%. As well as declining in size, the labour force will be "greying", with workers over the aged between 55 and 64 accounting for a larger share of the total workforce. At the same time, the numbers of elderly persons aged 65 and above will rise from 61 million in 2000 to 103 million by 2050. The largest increase will take place amongst the very old (aged 80+), whose numbers will almost triple from 14 million in 2000 to 38 million in 2050.

The old-age dependency ratio (defined as persons aged over 65 as a percentage of working age population 15-64) will more than double from some 24% in 2000 to 49% in 2050 for the EU. In other words, the EU will move from having 4 to only 2 persons of working age for every elderly person by 2050, thus placing an increased burden on the economically active population in supporting the inactive.

These figures for the EU as a whole mask considerable variations in both the timing and size of demographic changes across individual Member States. Whereas large falls in the size of the total population between 2000 and 2050 are projected in Germany, Italy and Spain, it is expected to grow in France, Ireland, the Netherlands, Portugal and the UK. Striking differences across Member States are evident on graph 1 displaying old-age dependency ratios. In terms of starting position, Ireland has the lowest old-age dependency ratio at 17% compared with ratios of 25% in Belgium, Greece, Italy and Spain. The timing of the demographic changes also differs. Steep increases in the old-age dependency ratio start to occur after 2005 in Germany, Greece, Italy, the Netherlands and Austria, and somewhat later, around 2010, in Belgium, Spain, France, Finland and Sweden. In most Member States, the old-age dependency ratio will reach a new plateau around 2040, with the highest ratios of some 60% in 2050 forecast for Spain and Italy (an increase of 35 percentage points over the projection period!).

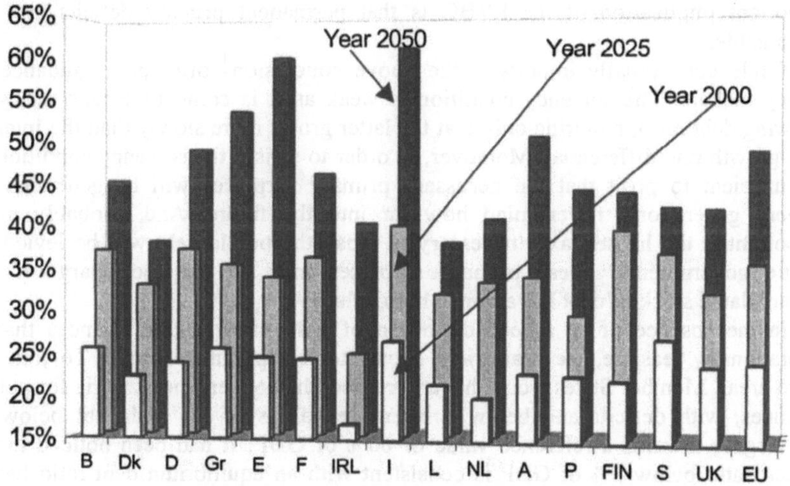


*Figure 1. Old-age dependency ratios 2000-2050 (baseline scenario)*
*Source: Eurostat*

Although caution must be exercised when using long-term population projections, they do provide broadly reliable evidence of substantial demographic changes in the coming decades. This is because the old-age dependency ratio largely depends upon the life expectancy of generations currently alive (which tend to change in a stable fashion) and on past fertility rates. Increased migration could mitigate the projected increase in the old-age dependency ratio, but would have to reach levels vastly above those experienced in the past to have a significant impact.

## 3. SUSTAINABILITY IN THE BUDGETARY FRAMEWORK OF EMU

### *3.1. How sustainability is addressed in the Maastricht Treaty*

The Euro area has a unique macroeconomic framework for a monetary union, in that monetary policy is centralised under the ECB whereas fiscal policy remains under national authority. The Treaty recognises that a decentralised approach to fiscal policy, and ultimately the viability of the EMU project, hinges upon sustained budgetary discipline on the part of participating Member States.

Intuitively, fiscal sustainability is ultimately about avoiding government bankruptcy. Although the intuition is straightforward, the analytical and operational definition of sustainability has proven elusive. The so-called Present Value Budget Constraint (PVBC) translates formally the principle that sooner or later the public debt has to be repaid. Barring Ponzi games, this implies that today's government debt has to be matched by the present value of cumulated primary surpluses. An important implication of the PVBC is that permanent primary deficits are not sustainable.

While conceptually important, the above conclusions offer poor guidance to policy makers. The solvency condition is weak as it is compatible with an ever-growing debt ratio, requiring only that the latter grows more slowly than the interest rate-growth rate differential. Moreover, in order to satisfy the solvency condition, it is sufficient to posit that the necessary primary surpluses will be generated by unborn generations, never mind how far into the future. And, probably more importantly, the higher taxes necessary to repay the public debt will be levied by future governments. These primary surpluses may be extremely large if the accumulated stock of debt has attained high values.

In the absence of an agreed definition of sustainable public finances that is operationally feasible, the Maastricht Treaty took a pragmatic route. To join the Euro area,[4] Member States would have to respect the convergence criteria for public finances, with deficits and below a reference values of 3% and debt below or converging towards a reference value of 60% of GDP. It had been noticed that a deficit ratio below 3% of GDP is consistent with an equilibrium debt ratio below 60% of GDP if the yearly nominal growth of GDP is 5%.

These provisions were substantially reinforced in EMU via the SGP which commits Member States to achieve medium-term budgetary positions "*of close to balance or in surplus*": it also provides for a detailed surveillance procedure involving the submission of annual stability and convergence programmes.[5] Although the SGP only imposes commitments on Member States for budgetary positions in the medium-term (3 to 5 years), and does not require explicit long-term commitments, sustainability is *de facto* ensured[6] as the SGP must be respected at all times in EMU. If countries do so, this will lead to the virtual disappearance of public debt in the long run.

This pragmatic approach, with sustainability implicitly defined as non-violation of pre-determined levels of deficits and debt, stemmed from earlier efforts to operationalise the theory of sustainability. To do so, economists introduced *ad hoc* requirements such as the debt ratio eventually converging back to its initial level (Blanchard *et al.*, 1990) or the ratio of net public sector worth to output remaining constant at its current level (Buiter, 1985).

To shed light on the political dimension of public debt sustainability, a useful concept is Blanchard's "maximum sustainable level of public debt" (Blanchard, 1984). This value of debt – let us call it $b_{MAX}$ - is defined by the ratio of the maximum politically-feasible primary surplus $s_{MAX}$ and the long-run interest rate – growth rate differential $r$-$y$. Let $s_{MAX}$ be seen the level of primary surplus that cannot be exceeded persistently without triggering political or social resistance.

For given $r$-$y$, if the actual stock of debt exceeds $b_{MAX}$, there is no way to bring it back under control because this would require a primary surplus higher than $s_{MAX}$ which is, by definition, impossible. If the reference value of 60% of GDP is interpreted as $b_{MAX}$, and we assume that $r$-$y$ is 2%, then $s_{MAX}$ is 1.2% of GDP. If $r$-$y$ is 1%, $s_{MAX}$ is 0.6% of GDP. These are relatively small values by recent historical standards: in 2000, the structural primary surplus of the Euro area was above 3% of

GDP. Hence, $b_{MAX}$ = 60% would signal a scepticism by Treaty founders on the feasibility of high and persistent primary surpluses.

### *3.2. Budgetary consolidation in the run-up to EMU and beyond*

The previous section shows that public finances will be sustainable, provided that Member States respect the rules based approach of the SGP. The question arises whether they will do so. Only time will tell, but some insights can be gleaned by examining efforts towards meeting the convergence criteria in the run-up to EMU and by assessing progress towards meeting the first two years of EMU.

As shown on table 1, public finance positions in the EU have improved dramatically as a result of a budgetary consolidation that was partly driven by the Maastricht convergence process. From a deficit for the EU of 4.2% of GDP in 1995, to a deficit of 0.6% in 1999 and budget balance in 2000 (net of UMTS receipts[7]). Public debt has also been placed on a steady downwards path, falling from 70% for the EU as a whole in 1995 to below the 60% reference value in 2000. At Member State level, some spectacular turnarounds have been achieved from what were clearly unsustainable trajectories. A good deal of the improvement can be attributed to more favourable economic conditions in recent years and a lower interest burden. Nonetheless, public finances are in a much stronger position to meet the budgetary consequences of ageing populations compared with 5 or 6 years ago.

*Table 1 : Public finance developments, 1995-2004 (% of GDP)*

| | Deficit/surplus | | | Debt | | |
|---|---|---|---|---|---|---|
| | 1995 | 2000 | 2004* | 1995 | 2000 | 2004* |
| B | -4,3 | -0.1 | 0.6 | 134 | 101 | 93 |
| DK | -2,3 | 2.7 | 2.7 | 69 | 48.3 | 37 |
| D | -3,5 | -1,0 | 0,0 | 57 | 60 | 55 |
| EL | -10,2 | -0.8 | 2.0 | 109 | 104 | 84 |
| E | -6,6 | -0.3 | 0.3 | 64 | 61 | 50 |
| F | -5,5 | -1.4 | 0,2 | 54 | 58 | 52 |
| IRL | -2,2 | 4.7 | 4.6 | 84 | 39 | 24 |
| I | -7,6 | -1.3 | 0.0 | 123 | 112 | 95 |
| L | 2,3 | 3.0 | 2.5 | 6 | 6 | 5 |
| NL | -4,2 | 1.0 | 1.9 | 77 | 57 | 42 |
| A | -5,1 | -1.4 | 0.0 | 69 | 63 | 55 |
| P | -4,6 | -1.5 | 0.0 | 64 | 56 | 48 |
| FIN | -3,7 | 4.5 | 4,9 | 57 | 42 | 32 |
| S | -7,9 | 3.4 | 2.0 | 77 | 59 | 48 |
| UK | -5,8 | 1.1 | -1,0 | 52 | 40 | 36 |

*Source: Figures for 1995 from AMECO database. Figures for 2000 and 2004 from updated stability and convergence programmes. Debt is Maastricht definition of gross general government consolidated debt. Deficit figures for 2000 are net of UMTS license receipts.*
** = Figures for IRL, L and S are for 2003.*

Table 1 also presents the medium-term budgetary targets which Member States have set themselves in the most recent stability and convergence programmes.[8]. The updated programmes provide for a gradual improvement in the actual budgetary position as well as in cyclically-adjusted terms, although several larger Euro area Member States clearly still have some progress to make towards meeting the SGP goal of cyclically adjusted positions of "close to balance of surplus". By 2004, all countries are expected to have reached the medium-term target of the SGP.

### *3.3. The composition of budgetary adjustment*

Although the framework for fiscal policy in stage 3 of EMU has still to be severely tested in a major economic downturn, Member States appear to be on track towards the SGP medium-term target. The question is whether the EU's pre-emptive co-ordination can be sustained to ensure the long-run sustainability of public finances.

Some critics have pointed to a slackening in the pace of budgetary consolidation since 2000 as an indication of fiscal fatigue and that the commitment to budgetary discipline is waning. However, a slower pace of deficit reduction is the result of new budgetary priorities coming to the fore as compliance with the SGP target is approached. In particular, many Member States are taking steps to lower the tax burden. On the basis of the recent stability programmes, the tax burden in the twelve Euro area countries is projected to decline by over 2 percentage points of GDP (in both nominal and cyclically adjusted terms) between 2000 and 2004. While a lower tax burden could make a positive contribution towards meeting the challenge of ageing population by promoting employment and growth, it is vital that the tax cuts are sustainable and do not have to be reversed if the economic situation deteriorates.

A key factor emerging from the literature in determining the success and durability of budgetary consolidation is the composition of budgetary adjustment.[9]. Table 2 presents the adjustment for the Euro area as a whole and the sources of the retrenchment (whether it comes from the revenue side or from various spending categories). The consolidation period has been selected by looking at the years of virtually uninterrupted improvement in the cyclically-adjusted primary balance. It is possible to discern two distinct sub-periods during the run-up to the launch of EMU.

*Table 2: Composition of budgetary consolidation in euro-11 countries (p.p. of GDP)*

| | | | | Of which | | |
|---|---|---|---|---|---|---|
| **Period** | **Change in structural balance** | **Change in structural revenue** | **Change in structural primary spending** | **Capital spending** | **Primary current spending** | **Change in interest payments** |
| **1992-93** | 0.7 | 3.1 | 1.8 | -0.2 | 2.0 | 0.6 |
| **1994-97** | 3.1 | 0.7 | -2.0 | -.04 | -1.6 | -0.4 |

*Source: Commission services*

To begin with, in 1992 and 1993 the consolidation was essentially revenue-based. Strong increases in structural revenue more than offset continued rises in structural primary expenditures to achieve a reduction of 0.7% of GDP in the overall structural balance. This tightening of the fiscal stance brought a halt to the increase in actual deficits, and may have yielded positive expectation effects by sending a strong signal that serious steps at last were being taken to shift budget policies back onto a sustainable path. The period from 1994 to 1997 is less uniform, but overall the budgetary adjustment was more expenditure-based. The structural revenue continued to increase but at a slower pace compared with the first phase of the retrenchment process. As a result, the overall structural balance improved by 3.3% of GDP.

What about the future? To capture in a synthetic manner the composition of the budgetary adjustment in the 2000 stability programmes, figure 2 decomposes the discretionary policy changes into changes in total revenue and in primary expenditure.

The diagonal from north-west to south-east indicates the direction of the budgetary adjustment: the area above it marks a deterioration in the cyclically-adjusted primary balance, while the area indicates a structural consolidation. The diagonal from south-west to north-east marks the composition of the adjustment: in the area above it, revenue change dominates while the opposite holds below it. The triangle in the lower quadrant labelled as "tax cuts *cum* consolidation" shows the area where the reduction of structural revenues goes hand in hand with a larger reduction of primary structural expenditure, allowing for a continued consolidation of public finances while introducing tax reductions.

The figure confirms that, after years of strong tightening up to 1997, the consolidation has *de facto* come to an end. This may have been expected given the elimination of budget deficits in most countries. More importantly, over the time horizon of the programmes, public finances appear to ensure the right combination of tax cuts *and* consolidation, thereby leading to a gradual reduction in the overall size of the public sector. All in all, the "quality" of the budgetary strategies in the programmes appears to be both efficiency- and sustainability-friendly.

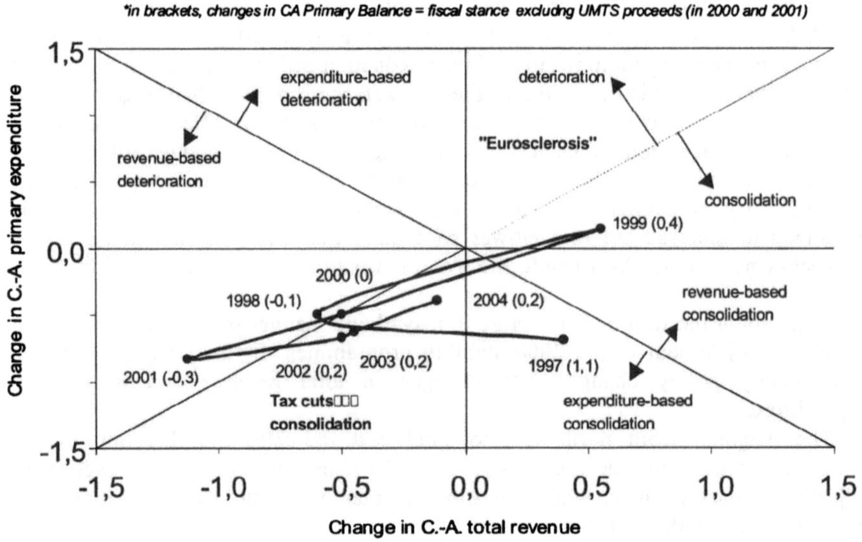


*Figure 2: Composition of the fiscal stance and adjustment, 1997-2004**

*Source: European Commission (2001)*

### *3.4. The challenge of sustaining sound public finances in EMU*

In a joint report to March 2001 European Council in Stockholm, the Commission and Council set down a strategy on how to sustain sound budget positions while at the same time lowering the tax burden and preparing for the budgetary consequences of ageing populations. In the short-run perspective, Member States must avoid pro-cyclical fiscal policies, and to this end more emphasis will be placed on structural budget balances when assessing budget positions at the EU level. In the medium-term perspective, the Commission and Council recognised that tax cuts are not self-financing, and to be sustainable need to be accompanied by a firm control on public expenditure. Moreover, an appropriate balance has to be drawn between cutting taxes and running down public debt, implying that priority should be given to the latter in high debt countries.

The contribution which sound public finances can make towards meeting the additional budgetary costs of ageing populations is illustrated in table 3. This presents illustrative calculations showing that public debt and interest payments will fall substantially over the next three decades if Member States stick to the medium-term targets for 2003/4 set down in their recent stability or convergence programme. This effect is particularly strong for high-debt countries who would bring about a fall in their interest burden of around 3 percentage points of GDP by 2020 and about 5 points by 2030. As we will show in section 4, below, a reduction in the interest burden of this scale would help meet the additional costs of ageing populations.

*Table 3: Projections of the debt level assuming compliance with SGP targets*

| | Debt | | | Change in interest burden | | |
|---|---|---|---|---|---|---|
| | 2010 | 2020 | 2030 | 2010 | 2020 | 2030 |
| B | 69 | 40 | 22 | -2,1 | -3,5 | -4,5 |
| DK | 14 | -13 | -30 | -1,7 | -3,0 | -3,9 |
| D | 42 | 28 | 18 | -0,9 | -1,6 | -2,1 |
| EL | 52 | 17 | -6 | -2,6 | -4,4 | -5,5 |
| E | 36 | 20 | 10 | -1,3 | -2,0 | -2,5 |
| F | 39 | 24 | 14 | -1,0 | -1,7 | -2,2 |
| IRL | -10 | -43 | -64 | -2,5 | -4,1 | -5,2 |
| I | 72 | 44 | 26 | -2,0 | -3,4 | -4,3 |
| NL | 23 | -1 | -16 | -1,7 | -2,9 | -3,6 |
| A | 43 | 28 | 18 | -1,0 | -1,8 | -2,2 |
| P | 36 | 23 | 14 | -1,0 | -1,7 | -2,1 |
| F | -1 | -40 | -66 | -2,2 | -4,1 | -5,4 |
| S | 23 | -1 | -17 | -1,8 | -3,0 | -3,8 |
| UK | 33 | 29 | 27 | -0,4 | -0,5 | -0,6 |

*Source: Authors' calculations. Debt projections assume that Member States continue to stick to the deficit/surplus for 2004 (2003 for IRL, L and S) and are based on an assumption of a growth rate-interest rate differential of between 2 and 2.25%. The change in the interest rate measures the fall in the interest rate burden compared with its level in 2000.*

It must be recognised that maintaining the 2003 budget balances over the long run will be difficult, and possibly not desirable for the countries showing a large budget surplus. Moreover, the above exercise is a partial equilibrium analysis; as shown by McMorrow and Roeger (1999), without structural reforms the demographic impact will have a substantial negative effect on output (which in the above calculations is set exogenously), thereby undermining the sustainability of public finances.

## 4. DEVELOPING MORE COMPARABLE PROJECTIONS OF THE BUDGETARY IMPACT OF AGEING

With the launch of the Euro in 1999, there was a recognition that the long-term sustainability of public finances needed to be assessed in a more comprehensive and systematic manner. Even if one could rely on respect of the SGP to deliver sustainability, additional indicators going beyond the national measures of deficits and debt are needed to help determine the timing and scale of the impact of ageing populations on public expenditures (and revenues) and thereby assist in devising policies that can ensure compliance with the SGP.

A working group on ageing attached to the Economic Policy Committee (EPC), a group of senior advisors to economic and finance Ministers), was established in 1999 with a view to developing more comparable estimates of the impact of ageing on public finances. Long-term budgetary projections need to be interpreted with considerable caution as they require making a number of assumptions on variables such as interest rates, productivity growth and labour market developments. Notwithstanding this caveat, projections should be able to identify serious budgetary imbalances.

A further difficulty is that national projections are usually not comparable as they use different demographic and economic assumptions along with different model specifications and definitions. International organisations have overcome some of these problems by using standard demographic and economic assumptions, but at the cost of less accuracy in the modelling of the institutional detail of national pension and social security systems.

This trade-off between comparability/transparency prompted the EPC Committee to take a new approach in a report on the budgetary implications of ageing populations examined by the ECOFIN Council on November 7 2000.[10] National authorities were invited to run their national models using standard EUROSTAT demographic and economic assumptions. These assumptions provide some flexibility to cope with specific national circumstances.[11] The results presented below are not comparable, but nonetheless represent an important advance in producing more comparable estimates of long-term pension projections.

The starting point was a so-called "current policy scenario", which aimed at projecting pension expenditures on the basis of legislation already enacted. Various sensitivity tests and policy simulations have been conducted, which are set out in full in the EPC report.

*Table 4: Pension expenditure projections 2000-2050 (as % GDP, before tax)*

| | 2000 | 2005 | 2010 | 2020 | 2030 | 2040 | 2050 | Change 2000-peak year |
|---|---|---|---|---|---|---|---|---|
| B | 9.3 | 8.7 | 9.0 | 10.4 | 12.5 | 13.0 | 12.6 | *3.7* |
| DK | 10.2 | 11.3 | 12.7 | 14.0 | 14.7 | 13.9 | 13.2 | *4.5*[12] |
| D | 10.3 | 9.8 | 9.5 | 10.6 | 13.2 | 14.4 | 14.6 | *4.3* |
| EL | 12.6 | 12.4 | 12.6 | 15.4 | 19.6 | 23.8 | 24.8 | *12.2* |
| E | 9.4 | 9.2 | 9.3 | 10.2 | 12.9 | 16.3 | 17.7 | *8.3* |
| F | 12.1 | 12.2 | 13.1 | 15.0 | 16.0 | 15.8 | *N.A.* | *3.9* |
| IRL | 4.6 | 4.5 | 5.0 | 6.7 | 7.6 | 8.3 | 9.0 | *4.4* |
| I | 14.2 | 14.1 | 14.3 | 14.9 | 15.9 | 15.7 | 13.9 | *1.7* |
| L | 7.4 | 7.4 | 7.5 | 8.2 | 9.2 | 9.5 | 9.3 | *2.2* |
| NL | 7.9 | 8.3 | 9.1 | 11.1 | 13.1 | 14.1 | 13.6 | *6.2* |
| A | 14.5 | 14.4 | 14.8 | 15.7 | 17.6 | 17.0 | 15.1 | *3.1* |
| P | 9.8 | 10.8 | 12.0 | 14.4 | 16.0 | 15.8 | 14.2 | *6.2* |
| FIN | 11.3 | 10.9 | 11.6 | 14.0 | 15.7 | 16.0 | 16.0 | *4.7* |
| S | 9.0 | 8.8 | 9.2 | 10.2 | 10.7 | 10.7 | 10.0 | *1.7* |
| UK | 5.1 | 4.9 | 4.7 | 4.4 | 4.7 | 4.4 | 3.9 | *0.0* |

*Source: Report of the EPC working group on ageing populations*

The simulations show that public pension expenditure as a percentage of GDP is predicted to rise substantially in all Member States over the next few decades, except in the UK. However, the size and timing of the increases in expenditure differ across Member States. Only two Member States are projected to have increased spending on public pensions of less that 2% of GDP over the period 2000 to 2050, namely Italy and Sweden.

In the majority of cases the effects of ageing will add between 3% and 5% of GDP to pension expenditure. Somewhat higher upwards pressure on public pension spending are projected for Portugal and the Netherlands, with the highest increase projected for Spain (over 8% of GDP over the forecast period) and Greece (12% of GDP). Although the projected rise in public expenditure is a significant challenge, it remains below the expected increase in dependency ratios. Moreover, the projected increases are substantially below the increases projected in earlier studies, and suggest that the many reforms undertaken in the 1990s have gone some way towards mitigating the impact of ageing populations on public pension schemes.

Other factors should be borne in mind apart from the size of the increase in spending on public pensions. Account needs to be taken of the starting level of spending on public pensions, which in 2000 ranges from some 5% of GDP in Ireland and the UK to over 14% of GDP in Italy and Austria. It is also necessary to take account of taxes levied on pension income, i.e. net public expenditure on pensions. Another relevant factor is that contributions to funded pension schemes, such as in Denmark and the Netherlands, are usually tax deductible i.e. deferred until entitlements are paid out. This means that the increased spending on public pensions will be partly offset by increased tax revenues on income from funded pensions.

Of course pensions are not the only public expenditure item that will be affected by ageing populations. An equally significant impact is expected on health care given that people tend to consume increasing amounts on health care services as they age. The EPC working group on ageing is now trying to produce comparable projections for spending on health care up to 2050, but results are not expected before the end of 2001. Measuring the impact of demographic changes on overall health expenditure is not as straightforward. Recent studies suggest that as life expectancy (as well as the number of elderly people) increases in the future, individuals will enjoy a higher number of years in good health than previous generations. That is to say that although there will be increased numbers of elderly people in the future, this might not lead to a proportional increase in health expenditure. Moreover, a significant proportion of health care services are consumed in the final months of life prior to death, and are therefore not directly age-related.

Over the past three decades, demographic changes have not been a significant driving force in the increase in health expenditure in Member States. The following factors have been more important: increased coverage of public provision of health care or health insurance, increased demand/consumption of health care in line with increased prosperity; and supply-side factors such as the increased use of new and more expensive technology, and medical price inflation higher than overall price inflation. There is little consensus as to whether these factors will continue to be important in the future. Other factors, might also start to play a role in increasing the demand for formal health provision, such as increased household fragmentation as a result of increased female participation in the labour force. On the other hand, an increased awareness of the link between individuals' behaviour and their health status, or more importantly the effect of past reforms in the health sector, might serve to contain pressures for increases in health expenditure.

The existence of many different factors driving health care expenditure considerably complicates the process of projecting future trends in health expenditure and of predicting the particular role of demographic changes. Moreover, cross-country projections for health expenditure are further complicated by the nature of health systems. Health systems by their very nature are extremely complex and their structure can vary considerably between different countries. However, the detailed organisational structure of health systems, and the incentives that they create for different types of agents, can have an extremely important role to play in determining supply and demand pressures for expenditure. As a result, similar trends in medical technology or in medical prices, might lead to very different implications for the evolution of health expenditure in different Member States.

One important issue in the budgetary impact of ageing is the issue of long-term care for the elderly. This type of expenditure will be one of the key sources of increased public expenditure due to ageing. However, in many Member States, long-term care is no longer a formal part of the health sector – this spending is often covered by social budgets. Projections of health care expenditure excluding this type of care are likely to seriously underestimate the impact of ageing populations on overall public expenditure.

Despite these difficulties, there have already been some attempts to project health care expenditures. The OECD (1998) estimate that the direct effects of ageing on public expenditure on health will be an increase of 3% of GDP in the EU and in Japan, and 2% in the US. Several Member States have attempted to quantify future increases in public expenditure on health associated with ageing populations. These point to an increase in public spending of the order of 2 to 3% of GDP. On balance, therefore, there is a consensus that health care expenditure will rise, but there is still some debate as to the scale of the increase.

## 5. AN EMERGING COMMUNITY POLICY

### *5.1. A three-pronged strategy to address the budgetary consequence of ageing*

While caution must be exercised in interpreting the above projections, the combined impact of ageing populations on public pension and health care systems suggests an increase in public spending of between 5 to 8 percentage points of GDP in most Member States. Although this pressure will emerge over several decades, it represents a major challenge to the sustainability of public finances especially in countries having a large stock of outstanding public debt and that rely on PAYG pension systems.

Formal recognition of the need to address the budgetary consequences of ageing populations at EU level came at the Lisbon European Council of March 2000, which called for more emphasis to be placed on the quality and sustainability of public finances. This led to a joint Commission-Council report to the Stockholm European Council of March 2001. This report defined sustainable public finances as not only avoiding structural deficits and rising debt (i.e. with respect to the SGP targets), but also as keeping the tax burden at reasonable levels so that employment and growth are not hindered, and ensuring that essential public expenditures (such as education and investment) are not crowded-out by pressures for increased spending on pensions and health care. It outlined a three-pronged strategy to tackle the budgetary implications of ageing populations, as follows.

First, Member States should *sustain sound public finances reducing public debt levels at a fast pace*, thereby lowering the interest burden. As shown in table 3, sticking to the SGP targets over the long term will lead to substantial future reductions in the interest burden that will offset some, but not all, of the additional spending on pensions and health care. The EU has an important role to play in convincing citizens of the need for sustain budgetary discipline over the long run, and that there is a window of opportunity in the coming decade in advance of the retirement of the post-war baby boom generation.

Just how difficult this will be is demonstrated in table 5 below which presents some illustrative calculations of budget balance and primary balance which would allow to offset the *whole* increase in age-related spending via a fall in interest payments. The basic approach is presented in the annex. The calculations are made under different assumptions concerning the initial level of debt, the impact of ageing and the evolution of nominal interest rates and growth rates. As to the effects of ageing, the variable *a* in the table indicates the expected impact by 2030. The overall effect over the 2000-30 period – variable *a* in the table – is computed by simply assuming a linear increase of spending over the period. All non-age-related budgetary items are assumed to remain constant.

Inspection of the table shows that countries with high debt ratios, which have a lot of potential for interest savings, "can afford" a higher total deficit or a lower surplus to generate the interest savings needed to offset a given rise in age-related spending. For instance, if the expected increase in spending over the next 30 years is 4% points of GDP, a broadly balanced budget would be required if the initial stock of public debt is 100% of GDP, while a surplus of 1.4% of GDP is needed if the debt ratio is 60% of GDP. However, these less ambitious budgetary targets do not imply that high debt countries have an "easier job". Quite the contrary: as shown in the table the required primary surplus is higher in the case of high debt countries. If the primary surplus is taken as a measure of the policy effort, pre-empting ageing requires a tougher adjustment in countries with higher initial debt. The same conclusions is attained if the discretionary policy effort is proxied by the tax gap or other similar indicators.

*Table 5: Pre-empting ageing: medium term total (primary) budgetary targets (% of GDP)*

| b \ a | 2% | 4% | 6% |
|---|---|---|---|
| 60 % | -0.5 (1.8) | 1.4 (3.0) | 3.3 (4.2) |
| 80 % | -1.3 (2.0) | 0.6 (3.2) | 2.5 (4.4) |
| 100 % | -2.1 (2.2) | -0.2 (3.4) | 1.7 (4.6) |

*Source: Buti (2000)*
*a = increase in age-related spending as % of GDP between 2000 and 2030*
*b = level of government debt in 2000*
*Results outside parentheses are actual budget balance required (+=deficit, -=surplus)*
*Results within parentheses are primary surplus required (+=deficit, -=surplus) ;*
*Assumptions*
*Nominal growth rate of GDP = 4%; interest rate= 5%, time horizon=30 year, r-y = 1%*

Second, *comprehensive labour market reform leading to higher employment rates* is needed to offset the negative impact of demographic developments on the ratio of active to inactive persons. While measures are needed to raise employment rates across all age cohorts, particular attention should be paid to raising employment rates amongst older workers and women. Participation rates of men aged over 50 have fallen considerably in the EU in recent decades, and are low (for both men and women) compared with other industrialised countries. These developments cannot only be attributed to an increased demand for leisure as income increases.

There is strong evidence that the tax and benefit system combined with early retirement schemes have led to a bias in favour of early withdrawal from the labour market, i.e. there is a large "implicit tax" on remaining in active employment until the official retirement age. Tax and benefit reforms must address this bias, and return neutrality to the decision as to when to retire. Active measures will also be required to improve access to life-long learning, and facilitate the reconciliation of professional life and family life (e.g. via the provision of affordable child care facilities).

However, it would be inappropriate to presume that higher employment rates alone will resolve the budgetary challenge of ageing populations. Sensitivity tests carried out by the EPC have shown that even meeting the ambitious employment targets agreed in Lisbon do not completely offset the pressure on public finances (which is not surprising as the additional persons employed will acquire pension entitlements higher than they would receive if they remained outside the labour force). Hence, labour market reforms need to be accompanied with reforms that tackle the pressures for increased age-related spending at source.

The EU has an important role to play in helping Member States to raise employment rates. The existing process of issuing annual Employment Guidelines allows Member States to learn from the experiences of other countries and to benchmark their progress in reforming labour markets against their peers. External pressure from Europe has proved to be of considerable help to national policy-makers seeking to introduce painful structural reforms, especially if one can demonstrate that other countries have successfully reformed tax and benefit systems to prepare for ageing populations without jettisoning the commitment to social protection.

Thirdly, *further reforms of pension systems* are urgently required in many Member States to contain pressures on public finances, especially if countries also want to lower the tax burden. There is scope in some Member States to increase the share of public pension schemes that are funded with a view to diversifying the sources of retirement income: this requires a sound legal and fiscal framework to be put in place. Pension reform is also essential to raise employment rates. Indeed, it is difficult to envisage how the Lisbon employment targets can be reached unless effective retirement ages across the EU rise substantially, something which can only be achieved through reform of all kind of early retirement schemes and of the pension and tax systems.

EU involvement in pension reform is sensitive as social policy remains a national responsibility. Nonetheless, as with employment policy described above, there is a growing recognition of the benefits of co-operation and awareness that Member States can learn a great deal from each other. The Stockholm European Council of March 2001 agreed that the so-called "open method of co-ordination" (essentially a peer review process) could be extended to include pensions. It also called for the Barcelona European Council of March 2002 to examine a detailed report on the quality and sustainability of pension systems, with an interim report due by December 2001. A key factor facilitating EU involvement in pensions reform is the recognition that budgetary sustainability must be accompanied with social sustainability, i.e. that social protection systems must continue to provide adequate and fair retirement income to all elderly citizens. In 2000, a Committee on Social Protection, including senior officials of national social security Ministries, was established with a view to upgrading co-operation on the modernisation of social protection systems.[13]

The EU is making a further important contribution to pension reform through its efforts to eliminate tax and administrative distortions affecting cross-border occupational pensions. Such barriers affect the provision of cross-border occupational pensions by financial institutions and can inhibit the free movement of labour throughout the EU. Perhaps an equally relevant contribution of the EU are steps to create an integrated financial market-place in light of the single currency. These measures will help increase the depth and liquidity of financial markets, and facilitate the provision of a wide range of financial instruments for retirement saving.

### *5.2. Factoring sustainability into the EU's budgetary surveillance process.*

One of the most important matters agreed in the Stockholm European Council of March 2001 is that the "Council should regularly review the long-term sustainability of public finances, including the expected strains caused by the demographic changes ahead. This should be done both under the [Broad Economic Policy] guidelines and in the context of stability and convergence programmes". The long-term sustainability of public finances in light of ageing populations will therefore be factored into the assessment of public finance positions of Member States under the SGP.

This does not alter existing commitments or the main purpose of stability and convergence programmes, which is to define a medium-term budgetary strategy. However, addressing the long-term sustainability of public finances in stability and convergence programmes underlines the fact that Member States must respect the SGP over the long term. It also emphasises the need for policy actions anticipating the major demographic changes. Most importantly, it recognises that, although the budgetary impact of ageing populations only becomes evident in the long run, it is determined by short- to medium-term policy decisions taken within the time frame of programmes. Current policy choices, such as the medium-term budgetary target, the pace of debt reduction and the scale and type of tax reforms, will therefore be assessed against the commitment to place public finances on a sustainable footing.

Community institutions are currently considering how to put this agreement into practice (European Commission, 2001). A first attempt was already made to include issues related to ageing population in the 2000 updates to stability and convergence programmes. This served to underline the need for further work in developing comparable data and indicators. The projections for age-related expenditures of the EPC are an important step in this regard. Consideration will have to be given to extending this work beyond pensions and health care to include the impact of ageing on other public expenditure items and on revenues. There may be advantages to producing common projections on a regular basis, say every two years. Further consideration must also given to the merits and feasibility of developing a wider set of indicators of budgetary sustainability at EU level, given the limitations of national accounts data outlined by Disney in this volume.

## 6. CONCLUSION

The EU has a central role to play in helping Member States prepare for the budgetary implications of ageing populations. While EU can support reforms of tax/benefits systems and labour markets as well as promoting integrated financial markets, helping Member States sustain the commitment to fiscal discipline is perhaps the single most important contribution which the Community can make to ensure that the public finances are sustainable. The degree of budgetary ambition in the EU must go beyond avoiding budgetary crises, and hence sustainability should also be viewed in terms of a reasonable tax burden, which avoids the squeezing out of essential non-age-related public expenditures.

The agreement at the 2001 Stockholm European Council is a welcome recognition that incorporating long-term sustainability into the framework of the Stability and Growth Pact is essential for the success of EMU. Regular and systematic assessments of the sustainability of public finances requires the development of comparable data and indicators. The projections of the EPC for spending on public pensions are a step in the right direction, but further work is needed to extend this analysis to other expenditure and revenue items. Moreover, consideration should be given to supplementing these projections with additional indicators of the sustainability of public finances.

Ultimately, the challenge in preparing for ageing populations is a political one, i.e. getting citizens to face up to the realities of major demographic change. The EU can help in getting the central messages across. Budgetary choices today will determine our capacity to meet the additional costs of ageing populations. Having achieved broadly sound public finance positions, we must sustain budgetary discipline over the long-run.

## ANNEX

Pre-empting ageing via a reduction in interest payments

Let us call *B* the cumulated effect of the fall in debt service burden brought about by a fall in the stock of debt, *B*, over the period *0-T*:

$$(1) \qquad B = i\int_0^T (b(0) - b(t))dt$$

where *i* is the nominal interest rate. By substituting in (1) the expression for *b(t)* from the government budget constraint and solving the integral, we obtain:

$$(2) \qquad B = i\left[T - \frac{1}{y+\pi} + \frac{e^{-(y+\pi)T}}{y+\pi}\right]\left\{b(0) - \frac{\bar{d}}{y+\pi}\right\}$$

where, $d$ is the budget deficit, and $y+\pi$ is rate of growth of nominal GDP. In the simulations, the nominal interest rate and the GDP growth rate are assumed to be given.

Denote by *A* the estimated exogenous effect on the budget of the ageing of the population over the period *0-T*. Setting $A = -B$, we can solve for the budget balance which allows the overall budgetary effect of ageing to be offset by a reduction in the interest burden:

$$(3) \qquad d = \frac{A(y+\pi)}{i\left[T - \frac{1-e^{-(y+\pi)T}}{y+\pi}\right]} - b(0)(y+\pi)$$

While *d* in equation (3) is a negative function of *b(0)*, it is easy to show that a country with a higher (lower) stock of debt requires a higher (lower) primary surplus to offset the budgetary impact of ageing. This is shown in equation (4) which gives the primary surplus required to offset a rise in age-related spending (an increase of A) over the 0-T period:

$$(4) \qquad s = (r-y)\left\{b(0) - \frac{A}{i\left[T + \frac{1-e^{(r-y)T}}{r-y}\right]}\right\}$$

## NOTES

1. Officials in the Directorate General for Economic and Financial Affairs of the European Commission. The views expressed herein are personal and should not be attributed to the European Commission or its services. We would like to thank our colleague, Gabriele Giudice, for comments and suggestions.
2. Roseveare *et al.* (1996), Chand and Jaeger (1996)
3. ECB (2000).
4. The Treaty provides additional safeguards via the independence of the ECB and the no-bail out clause. Coupled with a better integrated capital market in the Euro area, these may result in financial markets becoming more sensitive to the build-up of government debt and lead to higher risk premia being attached to the debt of individual Member States. Irrespective of Treaty rules and the enhanced discipline imposed by financial markets, it has been argued that a Member State with an unsustainable public finance position may seek an accommodating monetary policy. As all Member States could lose from the default of an individual Member State, and given the potential systemic risk of default for the financial system of the Euro area, financial markets may perceive monetary discipline to be vulnerable with consequent pressure on Euro interest and exchange rates.
5. For a description and one in-depth analysis of the SGP, see Brunila, Buti and Franco (2001).
6. Balassone and Franco (2000).
7. All Member States have benefited from the sale of third-generation (or UMTS) mobile phone licenses. In accordance with a decision of Eurostat, these are recorded in ESA95 national accounts as the sale of real assets by the government sector which causes a jump in the actual budget balance and government expenditure series for 2000 and 2001. The positive impact on the budget balance for the EU as a whole is estimated as 1.3% of GDP for 2000 and 0.1% of GDP for 2001. See European Commission (2001).
8. An overview assessment of these programmes is contained in European Commission (2001).
9. Von Hagen, Hughes Hallet and Strauch (2001).
10. *Report of the impact of ageing populations on public pension systems, EPC/ECFIN/581/00-EN.* The work of the EPC is proceeding in parallel with an exercise under way in the OECD (Working Party 1). The demographic and economic assumptions were drawn up in collaboration with the OECD Secretariat to ensure consistency between the two exercises.
11. For example, participation rates were based on ILO projections, but adjustments to 2010 were allowed to reflect cross-country differences in labour markets policy reforms and legislated reforms to social institutions. Unemployment is assumed to fall to its structural level by 2005 as defined by the OECD and held at that rate to 2050. However, this rate could be adjusted to reflect reforms to the labour market already enacted, provided the adjustment does not exceed one third of the estimated structural rate of unemployment in 2005. Labour productivity should converge towards 1.75% annually between 2020 and 2030.
12. For Denmark, net of the supplementary, semi-funded scheme, ATP, the increase from 2000 to the peak year is only 3.1 % of GDP.
13. The Committee on Social Protection submitted a report on *The future evolution of social protection – pensions* to the European Council of Nice in December 2000 (Council Document 2949/00 of 06.11.00). This progress report was prepared on the basis of a Commission Communication on *The Future Evolution of Social Protection from a Long-Term Point of View: Safe and Sustainable Pensions* (COM (2000) 622 final).

## REFERENCES

BALASSONE F. and FRANCO D. (2000), "Assessing Fiscal Sustainability: a Review of Methods with a View to EMU" in Banca d'Italia (2000).

BANCA D'ITALIA (2000), *Fiscal Sustainability*, Public Finance Workshop, Research Department.

BLANCHARD O. (1984), "Current and Anticipated Deficits, Interest Rates and Economic Activity", *European Economic Review*, 25(1): 7-28.

BLANCHARD O. (1990), "Suggestions for a New Set of Fiscal Indicators", OECD Working Paper No. 79.

BLONDAL S. and SCARPETTA S. (1998), "The Retirement Decision in OECD Countries", OECD Economics Department Working Papers No 202, Paris.

BRUNILA A., BUTI M. and FRANCO D. (eds.) (2001), *The Stability and Growth Pact – the Fiscal Architecture of EMU*, Palgrave, forthcoming.

BUTI, M. (2000), "Comment", in Banca d'Italia (2000).

CHAND S. and JAEGER A. (1996), "Ageing Populations and Public Pension Schemes", IMF Occasional Paper N°147, Washington.

EUROPEAN CENTRAL BANK (2000), "Population Ageing and Fiscal Policy in EMU", ECB Monthly Bulletin, July 2000.

EUROPEAN COMMISSION (1999), "Towards a Europe for All Ages: promoting prosperity and intergenerational solidarity", Communication of the European Commission, COM(1999) 221 final.

EUROPEAN COMMISSION (2000a), "Public Finances in EMU – 2000", *European Economy - Reports and Studies*, No 3.

EUROPEAN COMMISSION (2000b), "The Contribution of Public Finances to Growth and Employment: Quality and Sustainability", COM(2000)846.

EUROPEAN COMMISSION (2001), *Public Finances in EMU – 2001*, European Economy-Reports and Studies.

VON HAGEN J., HUGHES HALLET A., STRAUCH R. (2001), "Budgetary Consolidation in EMU", Economic Papers N° 148, Directorate General for Economic and Financial Affairs, European Commission.

MCMORROW K. and ROGER W. (1999), "The Economic Consequences of Ageing: a Comparison of the EU, US and Japan", Economic Papers N°138, Directorate General for Economic and Financial Affairs, European Commission.

OECD (1998b): *Maintaining Prosperity in an Ageing Society*, Paris.

ROSEVEARE D., LIEBFRITZ W., FORE D. and WURZEL E. (1996): "Ageing Populations, Pension Systems and Government Budgets: Simulations for 20 OECD Countries", Economics Department Working Paper N°168, Paris.

RICHARD DISNEY

# HOW SHOULD WE MEASURE PENSION LIABILITIES IN EU COUNTRIES?

## 1. INTRODUCTION

How pension liabilities are measured is central to our understanding of the long-run sustainability of European social security programmes. Better data and forecasting procedures are an integral part of any attempt to understand the magnitude of these pension liabilities. Measures of pension liabilities are highly susceptible to both measurement error and to misinterpretation. Moreover, misjudgement of future costs are exacerbated by accounting measures that tend both to understate the extent of future liabilities and to overstate the potential costs of some reform strategies.

Proper measurement of pension liabilities in European economies requires three inputs. First it requires common assumptions, time horizons and forecasting procedures across European governments. These parameters must be agreed on a common, pan-European, basis and forecasts must be provided on actuarial assumptions and not be subject to political expediency.

Second, measurement requires appropriate data: data that permit actuaries to utilise accurate forecasts of key economic parameters, such as labour force participation rates and earnings growth rates. It will be suggested below that the standard approach, of using cross section data with assumed growth factors, may generate very misleading projections.

Third, the measurement of pension liabilities must be on an agreed, transparent, basis. There are important conceptual issues here, arising from whether official financial accounts are provided on a cash flow basis or an accrual basis, on how projected liabilities are assumed to be financed, and so on. Most of all, it is important to ensure that the measures that are used answer the questions being posed: in this case, what are the existing and projected liabilities of the programme under reasonable assumptions. There are few cross-country measures of pension liabilities, and those that exist tend to suffer from the often *ad hoc* principles on which they are constructed. The result is that the relative ordering of countries in terms of projected liabilities, fiscal deficits, required fiscal adjustments, and so on, tends to be arbitrary, varying from study to study and often flying in the face of common sense.

The purpose of this essay is to examine these three issues in the European context. The nature of the pension reform process, and in particular the relative



*T.Boeri, A.Börsch-Supan, A.Brugiavini, R.Disney, A.Kapteyn and F.Peracchi (eds.), Pensions: More Information, Less Ideology, 95—111.*

merits of different types of reforms, lies outside its scope. I have written on these issues elsewhere.[1] Nevertheless, it would be naïve to pretend that the nature of what is feasible in the way of pension reforms is a separate issue to that of how pension liabilities are measured.

Specifically, if the accrued pension liabilities arising from existing unfunded (PAYG) social security programmes are not explicitly presented in government balance sheets, then there is a clear bias against any form of reform which involves making these accrued liabilities explicit (for example, a transition to a partially funded scheme). Governments that wish to go down such a reform 'route' may resort to, effectively, subterfuge (for example, by treating accrued liabilities not as future expenditure flows but as reductions in future tax receipts) in order to avoid increased 'measured' debt-GDP ratios. Indeed, there are strong pressures on EU governments, via the convergence criteria, to avoid *any* measure of additional liabilities that may affect debt-GDP ratios. This issue has to be tackled head on, at an EU-wide level.

Of the three issues to be tackled here – common forecasting procedures and assumptions, data issues, and the appropriate measure of pension liabilities – I give increasing weight, in terms of length, from the first to the third. Although the issues are all of major importance, other essays in this volume pay greater attention to the first two. Much of the present focus is therefore on the issue of the measurement of pension liabilities. As will become clear, this issue is very far from a simple technical issue, and understanding of alternative measures, and the consequences of adopting alternative measures, is central to the pension reform process.

## 2. COMMON ASSUMPTIONS

Most EU governments, although by no means all, have regularly undertaken simulations of projected pension costs as a percentage of GDP. Typically, however, countries have adopted their own methodologies, assumptions and time horizons. Predictive success has often been poor.[2] Few countries provide comprehensive simulations of pension liabilities for all their unfunded schemes – notably those covering public sector workers are often left out of the calculations.

In recent years, the European Commission has taken a more active role in commissioning and providing common features to these projections. In March 2000, the Special European Council in Lisbon asked the Economic Policy Committee to prepare a progress report on the sustainability of the member states' public pension systems. The simulations underpinning this progress report were run under two assumptions: on employment and unemployment data provided by member states, and on the basis of convergence of employment and unemployment rates on EU 'best practice' as well as convergent productivity growth arising from the Lisbon targets. The Commission provided common macroeconomic and demographic assumptions in both cases.

The details and ensuing projections are discussed in the contribution of Buti and Costello to this volume. For all countries bar the United Kingdom, rising pension expenditure as a percentage of GDP is predicted, with all but the UK and Ireland requiring a double digit share of GDP to be spent on public pensions by 2020. Italy and Austria currently have the highest shares of GDP devoted to public pensions, but Italy is overtaken by Finland, France, Portugal and Spain (and probably Greece) by 2040. Some countries stabilise by 2020 (for example Denmark) but for many other countries, the pension/GDP ratio continues to rise into the second quarter of the century.

Even so, these common simulations are of limited value and incorporate political considerations. It should be borne in mind that once such projections are incorporated into the macroeconomic EU-wide agenda, countries still have an interest in downplaying their own potential pension liabilities. First, note that individual countries are still relied on to produce much of the data, such as 'average retirement age' and scheme rules. These data need not be derived from a common 'template' (for example, by using country-specific household level data sets) and the scope for understating eligibility (for example, for early retirement benefits, disability benefits etc.) is considerable. Second, the ECOFIN projections are far from a 'worst case scenario' – they assume rising fertility, slowing improvements in longevity, a stabilisation of male participation rates and slowly falling unemployment rates. Although some sensitivity analysis is provided assumption by assumption, it would be useful to see projections on a 'worst case' basis – which, for example, assumed constant fertility, a constant rate of improvement in longevity, continued (but decelerating) falls in male participation and constant unemployment.

Third, while useful as an 'outcome measure', the 'Lisbon scenario' simulations conflate policy and projection. While it is still an open question as to *how* EU countries will be able to achieve convergence targets in terms of employment and unemployment rates, as well as productivity growth, it seems largely meaningless to use achievement of such targets as a benchmark on which to base projections of pension liabilities. This is putting the cart before the horse – the outcome before policy implementation. Ideally, simulations and projections should be detached both from country-specific interests and from policy considerations, and in this respect 'external' calculations by such bodies as the IMF and the OECD offer greater scope for objective projections and simulations.[3] Thus the marriage of 'external' calculation and common data sources should provide a balanced account of pension liabilities across EU member states.

## 3. APPROPRIATE DATA

Actuarial forecasts require assumptions as to future labour force participation rates, retirement behaviour, unemployment, prices and earnings growth and so on. As with demographic calculations, these forecasts rely on techniques for projecting future pension payments from available data on current and past trends. Calculation of three key variables, over and above the basic forecasts of future longevity, are the 'building blocks' of this process. These are: projections of the numbers in employment relative to the number of pensioners (the 'support ratio'), of the future time path of average value of pensions in payment relative to the average wage (the 'replacement rate'), and of the rate of real earnings growth (the difference between the expected growth of earnings and of prices).

Typically, forecasts of support ratios use a combination of survey and census data. First, estimates of the population in each age group, typically from census data, are combined with survey data concerning the fraction of each working age group that are in paid employment relative to the fraction of each age group that are inactive (and, in some age groups, retired and eligible for a public pension). Second, projected age-specific mortality rates are combined with assumptions as to how activity rates within each age group will change in the future.

Data are readily available from both cross sections of households and surveys of employers that give 'snap shots' of the fraction of each age group that are economically active at a point in time, and such fractions are typically combined with demographic data to extrapolate the future support ratio. 'Panel' data, which track the economic activity and inactivity of successive birth cohorts of individuals, are much rarer, but will give a better guide to future numbers of employed and pensioners if each cohort has a specific age-activity profile. Indeed, in such circumstances, the use of cross section data will give misleading forecasts of the future support ratio.

One short-run solution, if no panel exists but if there are long runs of an existing cross section survey, is to construct a 'pseudo panel'. In this case, a series of repeated cross sections are used to construct cohort averages of the key variables, such as activity ratios by age group, which can be tracked through successive cross sections as each age group 'ages' over time. Such 'pseudo panels' will give a guide as to the likely errors, if any, arising from using age-activity rates from a cross section of households at a point in time rather than cohort-specific age activity rates. However the construction of 'pseudo panels' itself requires that the cross section surveys have been undertaken for a number of years, such as the United Kingdom's *Family Expenditure Survey*.

By way of example, the difference in age-employment rates that are calculated by using cross sections rather than cohort data derived from 'pseudo panels' is illustrated by Banks, Disney and Smith (2000) using the UK *Family Expenditure Survey*. Figure 1A and Figure 1B show, for men and women respectively, the age employment rates that are obtained taking 1978 as the base from the cross section (that is, across all age groups in 1978) as against the cohort profile (that is, by ageing each cohort over time and tracking cohort-specific average age employment rates). It is clear from the Figures that the cross section data do not give a bad 'fit' for the cohort employment rates for women, but systematically understate the decline in participation among older male workers observed in the cohort averages. Use of cross section employment rates to calculate support ratios for men would therefore sharply underestimate the decline in the support ratio over that period.

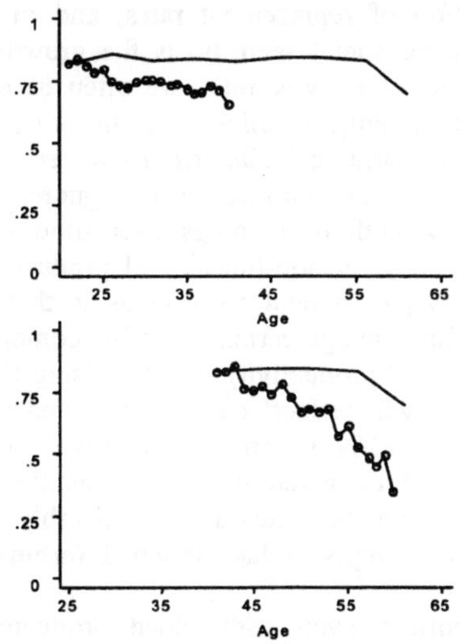


*Figure 1A. Cross-sectional and life-time profiles,*
*Male employment rates, 1978–96, Cohorts born 1955-59, 1945-49 & 1935-39*

*Source: United Kingdom Family Expenditure Survey, 1978-96*

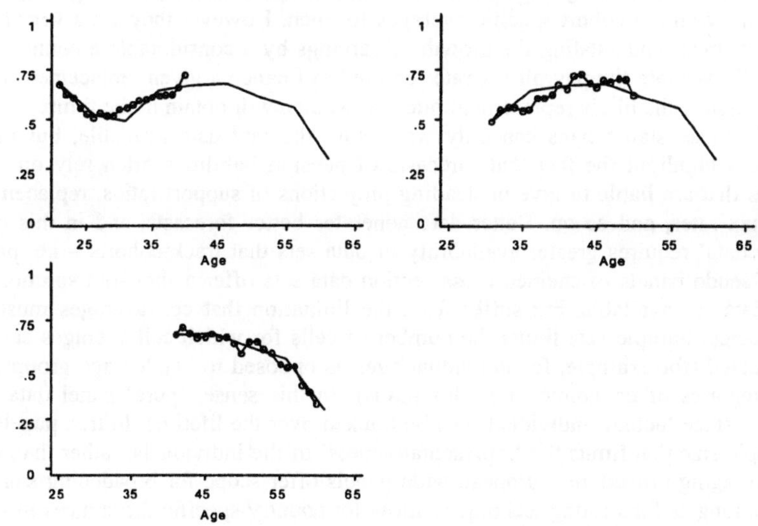


*Figure 1B. Cross-sectional and life-time profiles,*
*Female employment rates, 1978–96, Cohorts born 1955-59, 1945-49 & 1935-39*

*Source: United Kingdom Family Expenditure Survey, 1978-96*

A key 'building block' in the calculation of replacement rates, and in the calculation of equilibrium payroll tax rates for social security, is the growth of earnings over time. So, just as cross sections of activity rates are often used to calculate support ratios, cross section age earnings profiles form the basis of projections of earnings growth in official actuarial calculations. However, it is widely accepted that the use of the cross section age earnings profile ignores real productivity growth and that the assumed growth of earnings over time must combine life cycle earnings growth (which may be non-linear) and productivity growth. This is usually taken into account by government statisticians so that the most sophisticated calculations use as a baseline the age-earnings profile, combined with the projected age activity rates and assumed productivity growth. Using these proportions, a weighted lifecycle earnings growth 'effect' can be combined with assumed productivity growth (typically, say, 1 to 2% per annum) to derive overall growth rates of earnings over time. It should be noted that some calculations underpinning future replacement rates and payroll tax rates are considerably less sophisticated than those described here, and simply utilise assumed (arbitrary) growth rates of earnings.

Nevertheless, cross-section earnings profiles, even with added productivity growth, may still not track actual cohort-specific earnings growth rates. Again, we can utilise the UK's *Family Expenditure Survey* pseudo panel to examine whether biases arise. Figures 2A and 2B chart the 1978 cross section age earnings profile (labelled 'X-section') and the cross section with assumed 1% productivity growth against the cohort-specific age earnings profile. And here, the findings in Figure 1 are reversed. Productivity-augmented cross section age earnings profiles give quite a good 'fit' with the cohort-specific averages for men. However they are a very poor fit for women, understating the growth of earnings by a considerable amount. This bias will overstate the payroll tax rate required to finance a given replacement rate, but understate the likely replacement rate that women will obtain in the future.

Of course, statisticians can only work with the raw data available, but these examples highlight the fact that forecasts of pension liabilities often rely on data sources that are liable to give misleading projections of support ratios, replacement rates, tax rates, and so on. Better data generates better forecasts, and in this case 'better data' requires greater availability of data sets that track cohorts – i.e. panel data. Pseudo panels of chained cross section data sets offer a short-run solution, if such data are available, but suffer from the limitation that cell averages must be constructed. Sample size limits the number of cells for which cell averages can be constructed (for example, for individual ages as opposed to banded age groups, or for categories of economic or health status). In this sense, 'pure' panel data are superior since 'actual' individuals can be tracked over the lifetime. In true panels, it is sample size that limits the 'representativeness' of the individuals, rather than this cell averaging procedure. European-wide panels offer scope for broadening sample size, as long as forecasting techniques allow for country-specific differences in age-earnings profiles.

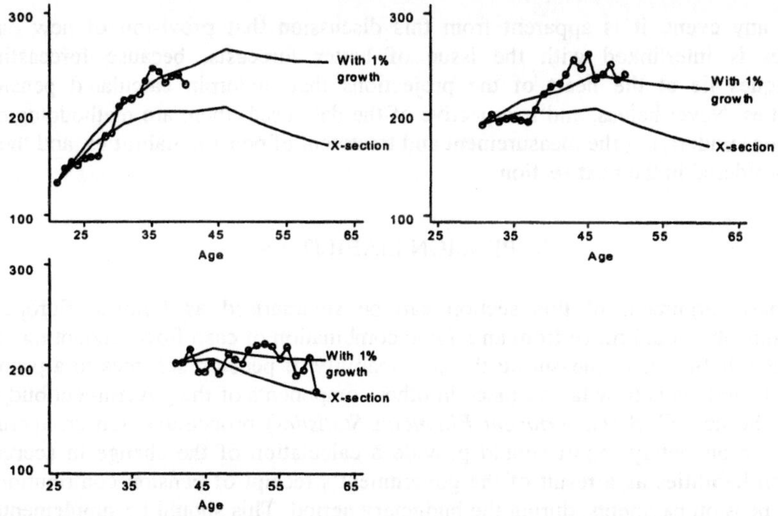


*Figure 2A. Cross-sectional and life-time profiles*
*Male earnings, 1978–96, Cohorts born 1955-59, 1945-49 & 1935-39*
*Source: United Kingdom Family Expenditure Survey, 1978-96*

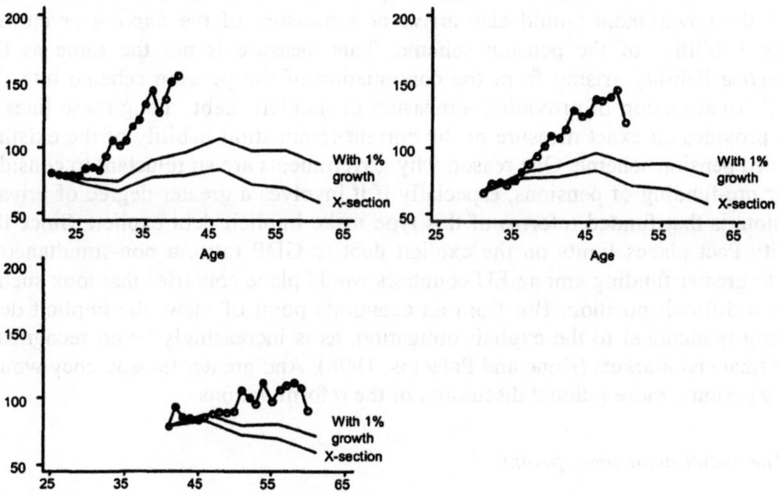


*Figure 2B. Cross-sectional and life-time profiles*
*Female earnings, 1978–96, Cohorts born 1955-59, 1945-49 & 1935-39*
*Source: United Kingdom Family Expenditure Survey, 1978-96*

In any event, it is apparent from this discussion that provision of new data sources is interlinked with the issue of better forecasts, because forecasting techniques lie at the heart of the projections that underpin calculated pension liabilities. Nevertheless, and irrespective of the data used, there are methodological questions underlying the measurement and treatment of pension liabilities, and these are considered in the next section.

## 4. PENSION LIABILITIES

The basic argument of this section can be summarised as follows. European governments should move from an *ad hoc* combination of cash flow accounting and projected liabilities in measuring the sustainability of pension schemes to a proper accrual basis, as is now taking place in other components of the government budget under the new GFS (*Government Financial Statistics*) procedures. On an accrual basis, the budgetary report should provide a calculation of the change in accrued pension liabilities as a result of the government's receipt of pension contributions, net of pension payments, during the budgetary period. This should be supplemented by, but not confused with, additional analyses including actuarial confirmation that, at current contribution rates, *current* pension expenditure is indeed covered by current contribution receipts, and by actuarial projections of future liabilities with, perhaps, some calculation of the contribution rates required to finance these prospective liabilities.

By cumulating the accrued liabilities up to the end of the current accounting period, the government would also arrive at a measure of the *implicit* or current accrued liabilities of the pension scheme. This measure is not the same as the *prospective* liability arising from the continuation of the pension scheme into the future.[4] An attraction of providing a measure of implicit 'debt' along these lines is that it provides an exact measure of the current termination liability of the existing unfunded pension scheme. One reason why governments are so reluctant to consider greater pre-funding of pensions, especially if it involves a greater degree of private provision, is that funded reforms of this type make implicit debt explicit. Since the Stability Pact places limits on the explicit debt to GDP ratio, a non-simultaneous move to greater funding among EU countries would place countries that took such a step in a difficult position. But from an economic point of view, the implicit debt overhang is identical to the explicit obligation, as is increasingly being recognised by the financial markets (Kane and Palacios, 1996). And greater transparency would thereby permit a more rational discussion of the reform options.

### *4.1 The social insurance 'promise'*

As is well known, most European public pension programmes are financed largely by earmarked payroll taxes (public, or social, insurance) contributions. These schemes are generally 'pay as you go' (PAYG) financed: current contributions are immediately paid out to finance current pension expenditure to existing claimants.

So although public schemes generally maintain a fund sufficient to finance a few months' payments, the fund is generally much less than even the annual total of pension expenditure, let alone the prospective liabilities generated by accrued 'claims' on future tax payments (see, for example, Chand and Jaeger, 1996, Table 2). This is in stark contrast to a *funded* scheme, where, at least in principle, a stock of assets is built up to match the prospective liabilities arising from the payment of contributions to the pension scheme.

Although most European public pension systems have operated on a PAYG basis for many years, most were also constructed as 'social insurance' schemes, in which eligibility for future pensions was made conditional on previous payments of contributions (as opposed to, say, need or a residency requirement). Such schemes are popularly perceived as giving participants future pension 'rights', based on those individual contributions. Governments have in generally been happy in their public discourse to let contributors to public pension schemes continue to believe that these 'rights' are indeed an inviolate claim on future taxpayers. This leads to much anger and resentment when these 'promises' are broken as a result of the twin pressures of overgenerous pension formulae and demographic ageing.

### *4.2 Pension accounting*

The standard basis for accounting for contribution receipts and expenditures in PAYG schemes is on a *cash flow* basis: that is, public budgets typically provide statements of contribution receipts and pension expenditure over the accounting period. In a PAYG scheme, these should normally approximately balance, since the contribution rate should have been set to achieve this aim. This accounting procedure, of course, provides no means of judging the sustainability of the future liabilities generated by those current contributions to the public scheme, which are paid on the understanding that they will generate *future* pension rights, to be covered by later generations of taxpayers. Most governments typically therefore provide separate statements of the time path of this stream of future public pension liabilities with, it is hoped, some statement of how they (or, rather, future generations of taxpayers) intend to pay for them.

But, not only are these estimates often incomplete and inaccurate, but the *projected* liabilities are themselves presented on an *ad hoc* basis which would gain few marks in any examination in accountancy. A key point is that the means of financing these liabilities (usually, future payments of contributions) themselves generate further liabilities, and so on, *ad infinitum*. Thus the only consistent means of presenting these liabilities is on an *accrual* basis, which permits a measure of the change in these future liabilities arising from the contributions paid in the current accounting period. The *accrued liability* (sometimes known as the implicit pension debt) is then the accumulated pension rights that would exist were the public scheme to be notionally wound up.

Now commentators have often argued that a cash flow basis is indeed the appropriate accounting procedure for public pensions. Pension schemes, they argue, are no different from other public transfers and expenditures (such as health and education) – in all these spheres the government is likely to incur future liabilities which should be forecast. Therefore, they argue, if pension liabilities are included in the budgetary measure, why not include other projected expenditures?

However this is to miss the point of the difference between accrued and projected liabilities, which is the essential difference between a 'pseudo insurance' scheme and other public schemes such as health and expenditure provision. In other spheres of public provision, current payment of taxes does not normally generate a perception of future individual 'rights'. Individuals who pay taxes may expect the public health programme to cover their current health needs and, they hope, later tax receipts will do so in the future. In similar vein, they may expect their contribution to the tax burden to cover educating their children, now and in the future. But it is publicly accepted that in these spheres, taxation, whether hypothecated or not, is a *social* burden – better quality public services, now and in the future, will, *ceteris paribus*, require higher tax rates on everyone than will lower quality provision. Individual payment of taxes does not in and of itself guarantee either current or future provision of the public service to the level that the individual would wish. Of course the same is also true of public pension rights in a social insurance system, but public perception treats these 'rights' very differently from other forms of public spending, and it is logical that our accounting measures should reflect these accrued liabilities more realistically.

A more pertinent critique is that measuring accrued liabilities explicitly would 'set in stone' commitments which are not, in fact, effective commitments. Future pension liabilities can be, and indeed have been, changed by government *fiat* (Bohn, 1992). But it should be noted that, while *projected* liabilities are indeed subject to this argument (which is another reason for being sceptical about using only projected liabilities rather than an accrual measure), it is relatively rare for governments to change already-accrued pension rights retrospectively – most pension reform in recent years has been about cutting back the value of future rights by raising retirement age, changing eligibility conditions, benefit rules etc. The important exception to this generalisation is in the case of post-retirement indexation of benefits, which have typically been changed from indexation to pre-tax earnings to post-tax earnings or to price inflation. This represents a cut-back in accrued rights insofar as individuals expected existing indexation arrangements to continue forever. However, if people expected to at least receive an annuity which is maintained in real terms, no OECD pension reform has so far reneged on this 'promise'.

### *4.3 Measures of budgetary stance and pension rights*

As Blejer and Cheasty (1991) point out, measures of budgetary stance (such as the 'public sector borrowing requirement' or PSBR) are never quite consistent in treating flows of expenditure and liabilities on a cash flow basis or an accrual basis. For example, when the government borrows money, interest payments can be measured as they accrue, or when they are actually paid. If the former is adopted, as is often the case, an accrual basis is being used. In contrast, tax revenues, including contribution receipts, are generally measured as a cash flow, ignoring any future liabilities that may thereby arise.

In terms of pensions, therefore, there is a parallel with government borrowing. The public sector is in effect borrowing from the private sector by levying pension contributions (often at a negative rate of interest, if internal rates of return on pension contributions are measured)[5] and 'repaying' the contributions later in the form of public pensions. An accrual basis to budgeting would take the change in prospective liabilities as the appropriate measure of expenditure in the period, being equivalent to the future change in interest payments in the previous case. Note however that this measure of the change in accrued liabilities, whilst perhaps being a better guide to future sustainability than current outgoings (which arose from past decisions) is not the same as PAYG equilibrium, which intrinsically operates on a cash flow basis (Valdes-Prieto, 1999). It is important not to confuse the two concepts.[6]

It might seem confusing for governments to offer two measures concerning public pension scheme finances. But greater confusions already abound – for example in measuring scheme liabilities by combining cash flow measures of current budgetary stance with *ad hoc* calculations of prospective liabilities (see the next section). In contrast, measuring on an accrual basis would be consistent with the current shift in reporting practice within the GFS away from a cash basis. It would require that the government present an annual measure of the change in accrued pension liabilities over the financial period, unsullied by irrelevant projections of future contribution receipts. In addition, the government actuary might be required both to provide two pieces of information: first, to show that the PAYG condition was satisfied, i.e. that current receipts did in fact cover current outgoings; and secondly, to provide regular projections of future liabilities under reasonable assumptions as to future macroeconomic and demographic trends, and some suggestion as to what contribution rate would be required to finance the most likely scenarios.

### *4.4 Pension projections*

How does this stylised model compare with typical projections of pension expenditure, costs and net financial balances? An influential paper from the International Monetary Fund by Chand and Jaeger (1996) uses a generic pension projection approach to consider the relative merits of a so-called 'parametric' reform of PAYG pension programmes in a number of OECD countries (meaning, structural alterations to the PAYG itself, such as raising retirement age, cutting replacement rates etc.), which is contrasted (favourably) with an alternative reform strategy, of partial or complete 'privatisation' of the programme. The issue of which reform strategy is best in any institutional setting is finely balanced of course, but it is important nevertheless that the economic considerations underlying such a choice are not concealed by potentially misleading 'pension accounting', of which this is, unfortunately, in my view, a good illustration.

Chand and Jaeger (1996) calculate three types of discounted pension liabilities: current accrued rights of pensioners, current accrued rights of workers, and future prospective rights were the scheme to continue up to a time horizon (the year 2050). These rights, of course, exceed the implicit pension liabilities so far discussed since they include prospective liabilities that will be accumulated in the future. The authors assume that contribution (payroll tax) rates will remain at their current level up to this time horizon. Given scheme maturation and demographic ageing, which imply rising contribution rates for PAYG equilibrium, they therefore project increasingly negative 'pension fund balances' to the time horizon for the countries that they consider (the G7 and Sweden).

They then calculate the 'primary balance' required to pay for these projected liabilities on a year-on-year basis. This can be interpreted as the annual budget surplus (as a percentage of GDP) that would be needed to finance these projected pension liabilities. The calculation, using macroeconomic forecasts, also calculates the surplus required to maintain the existing ratio of existing debt to GDP. This combined 'per cent of GDP' is denoted as the 'sustainable primary balance'. Finally, this is contrasted with the existing primary balance (basically, the cash budget deficit or surplus currently observed in 1995) in order to calculate the fiscal adjustment. The results are given in Table 2.

There are several difficulties in the approach adopted by the IMF authors. First, Table 2 conflates calculations on an accrual basis (column 1) with projections (column 2) and cash flows (column 3). The projected net liabilities, as suggested previously, incorporate future flows of contributions that will generate further liabilities. On the other hand, instead of solving for the 'equilibrium' PAYG contribution rate required to finance future expenditures, the contribution rate is arbitrarily fixed at its current level (which may or may not be fiscally sustainable). This generates an arbitrary 'net pension liability' which is added to an existing accrued liability (net public debt). Finally, to compound the confusion, the 'sustainable primary balance' is then added to a cash flow measure, the current budget surplus or deficit, to generate a fiscal adjustment. The 'proof of the pudding', in the light of all this, is whether the projected cross-country fiscal adjustments seem plausible. Thus Sweden, which has made a sustained effort to put its pension scheme into actuarial balance, is shown to require a fiscal adjustment 470% of that of Italy, which has wrestled with an unsustainable pension programme for several years. It is clear that the *current* balance (column 3) dominates the ordering of countries, rather than the projected liabilities, perhaps reflecting the IMF's short term goals in macroeconomic stabilisation.

What would be a superior way of presenting these liabilities and adjustments, in line with our earlier discussion? A natural method would be to start with net public debt (column 1) and add to it a 'net pension liability' based on *accrued* pension liabilities to date. We could then ask: what 'primary balance' (fraction of GDP) is required to service a debt of this magnitude (abstracting from contribution flows, which simply add to the liability)?[7] Under alternative assumptions, it would be possible to generate projections both of the path of public debt, and of accrued pension liabilities, so that both the *changes* in the debt and the *changes* in the fraction of GDP required to finance it, are calculated.

*Table 1: Measures of accrued public pension rights as % of GDP, OECD, 1990*

| | Accrued rights as % of GDP, 1990 *(Source: van der Noord and Herd, 1994)* | | | | Accrued rights as % of GDP, 1990 *(Kune, 1996, as from Holzmann, et al., 2000)* | *Memo item:* General gross debt as % of GDP, 1994 *(IMF data)* |
|---|---|---|---|---|---|---|
| Country | Total (3)+(4) (5) | Present retired | Present workforce | Existing assets | Total | Total |
| Belgium | - | - | - | - | 75 | 136 |
| Canada | 105 | 42 | 71 | 8 | - | 96 |
| Denmark | - | - | - | - | 87 | 69 |
| France | 216 | 77 | 139 | - | 83 | 48 |
| Germany | 157 | 55 | 102 | - | 138 | 50 |
| Greece | - | - | - | - | 185 | 114 |
| Ireland | - | - | - | - | 55 | - |
| Italy | 259 | 94 | 165 | - | 157 | 129 |
| Japan | 145 | 51 | 112 | 18 | - | 83 |
| Luxembourg | - | - | - | - | 156 | - |
| Netherlands | - | - | - | - | 103 | 79 |
| Portugal | - | - | - | - | 93 | 71 |
| Spain | - | - | - | - | 93 | 63 |
| UK | 139 | 58 | 81 | - | 68 | 46 |
| US | 89 | 42 | 70 | 23 | - | 69 |

*Notes on Table 1:*

1) Accrued liabilities constitute the sum of obligations to current pensioners and accrued-to-present rights of workers, less pension scheme assets if any.
2) The OECD study discounts accrued rights at 4%, falling to 3% after 2050. It assumes benefits are accrued in line with earnings growth but are price indexed after retirement (in this simulation). Various additional financial obligations (for example, unfunded supplementary schemes for public sector workers) are ignored.
3) The study by Kune assumes 4% discount rates, ignores all complementary schemes (e.g. French supplementary schemes, Spanish and Portuguese schemes for public workers) and takes no account of longevity improvements. The maturation of the State Earnings Related Scheme (SERPS) in the UK is ignored.
4) Each study relies on simulation models from published data, coupled with projections of economic assumptions, rather than actual administrative microdata, to calculate liabilities.

*Table 2: Net Pension Liabilities and Sustainability of Fiscal Stance: 1995*

| | Net public debt, end 1994<br>(1) | Net pension liability 1995-2050<br>(2) | Sustainable primary balance to stabilise debt (1+2) as % GDP<br>(3) | Primary balance 1995 as % of GDP<br>(4) | Adjustment to primary balance for fiscal sustainability (3 4)<br>(5) |
|---|---|---|---|---|---|
| United States | 63.3 | 25.7 | 1.9 | 0.4 | 1.5 |
| Japan | 33.2 | 106.8 | 3.6 | 0.2 | 3.8 |
| Germany | 52.5 | 110.7 | 4.5 | 2.4 | 2.1 |
| France | 42.4 | 113.6 | 4.0 | 0.3 | 4.3 |
| Italy | 112.9 | 75.5 | 4.6 | 3.3 | 1.3 |
| UK | 37.7 | 4.6 | 0.8 | 0.4 | 0.4 |
| Canada | 71.6 | 67.8 | 4.7 | 0.2 | 4.5 |
| Sweden | 54.5 | 20.4 | 1.0 | 5.1 | 6.1 |

*Source: Chand and Jaeger (1996), Table 8.* See the text for details about the method used to calculate net pension liabilities and sustainability of primary balance.

How difficult is it to calculate implicit pension liabilities? One response is that it is no more difficult than other pension projections, as described in Section 2. The calculations described in Table 1 are 'external' calculations based on published data, typically in age bands, in order to calculate projections of pension entitlements under different assumptions. However, one method that is far superior is to utilise the actual administrative procedures used to calculate individuals' ongoing accruals of pension entitlements. For example, the UK government now has an 'annual pension statement' providing details of an individual's ongoing accrued rights (presented as an accumulated pension entitlement per week) derived from the social security programme. It is actively considering ways of extending this statement to include rights accruing through membership of private pension schemes (Department of Social Security, 1998). Grossing up these accumulated pension rights, and adding the total value of existing pensions paid out, could be used as the basis of an exact (rather than simulated) account of pension liabilities, subject to assumptions concerning age-specific mortality and the future path of real earnings growth. At present, many European governments may not have the administrative capacity to provide such information to individuals, but they should surely have the administrative capacity to make such calculations on an ongoing basis, and to sum them subject to actuarial calculations. If they do not, a high priority is to install such capacity if any meaningful pension projections are to be made.

*4.5 Pre-funded public pensions*

It is sometimes argued that some degree of pre-funding of public pensions is innately superior to both PAYG financing and to private funding which, it is asserted, may involve a greater degree of individual risk. This is not the place to go into these arguments in detail. Indeed Blejer and Cheasty argue that the degree of pre-funding is irrelevant to the issue of cash flow or accrual basis, as discussed previously. However accounting procedures utilised in pre-funded public pension schemes are also open to misuse and misinterpretation. At the crudest level, some degree of pre-funding implies that pension contributions will be higher than they would be in a wholly PAYG financed scheme, since some contributions will presumably be diverted to finance current pension expenditure while some are allocated to a notional 'fund' that will be used to finance in part the future pension liabilities generated by current contributions. Since contribution revenues are therefore higher than they would be on a pure current-financed basis, simplistic measures of the government budget stance may appear to reveal a surplus, or lower deficit, than would otherwise exist. This can lead to a good deal of political confusion concerning fiscal stance including, at its extreme, attempts to 'double count' the budget surplus and the pension 'surplus' or even to suggest using the pension 'surplus' to pay off other public debts.

This last suggestion is not, in practice, as bizarre as it might appear as a *de facto* government policy. Even if the component of pension liabilities that is pre-funded is 'deposited' in a separate 'trust fund' as in the United States, these accumulated contributions may be used to offset government liabilities, for example, by using them to buy government securities. It is easy to demonstrate that, if these purchases allow the government to soften its 'budget' constraint, the generational incidence of a policy of pre-funding is likely to be identical to that of a pure tax-financed scheme. Indeed Kotlikoff (1992) demonstrates that a number of seemingly different government accounting conventions may be associated with the same generational incidence of government spending.[8] This is not to suggest that pre-funding is a good or bad policy *per se*, merely that it raises other, equally problematic, accounting issues.

## 5. CONCLUSION

Better pension forecasting and transparent measures of pension liabilities are essential prerequisites to the development of pension reform strategies. This essay has considered how to improve pension forecasting in European countries. It focuses on three issues: improved forecasting, better data, and on the appropriate measures of pension liabilities.

The conclusions are straightforward. First, whilst countries need to develop their own capacities for projections of pension liabilities, the variety of methods employed in practice and the scope for political intervention in order to 'downsize' unpleasant deficits and debts requires that some simulations are undertaken on a comparable and consistent basis across countries.

Second, better data are needed in order to underpin projections. The paper illustrated how 'representative' profiles of employment and earnings drawn from cross-section data sets may give a misleading guide to future 'economic' assumptions. There is a need to use microdata on a consistent basis to motivate such projections, and furthermore a panel element to such data is essential.

The third issue considered was that of the appropriate measure of pension liabilities. In the typical format of a 'pay-as-you-go' (PAYG) 'social insurance' scheme, the essay suggested that two broad measures of 'the pension finances' were needed. The first was simply a cash flow-based calculation of how existing outgoings would be financed. This could be supplemented by projections of future pensioners, contributors, earnings etc., in order to give some guide as to the future path of the payroll tax rate that would be needed to finance expenditure on pensions in each period. However, this should be clearly separated from a measure of pension *liabilities*, in which governments should calculate both the accrued liability of the pension programme to date and also the change in liability within each period implied by receipt of social insurance contributions in that period.

This accrual basis to 'pension accounting' should not be confused with the forecasts of tax rates, projections of liabilities on various assumptions, and so on, used to simulate future tax rates in a constant policy scenario. It was argued that these accrued liabilities are exactly consistent with, and represent a similar burden to, other forms of government debt, given the 'pension promise' inherent in social insurance. Calculation of such a measure should form the basis of any coherent discussion of 'sustainability' (for example, of the amount of GDP that needs to be devoted to 'servicing' it), and also of the costs of alternative pension reforms. Without clear data and measurement along these lines, however, the scope for rational discussion of pension reform in Europe will continue to be impeded.

## NOTES

1. See Disney (1996, 1999, 2000a, 2000b).
2. For examples, see Disney (2000a).
3. As we shall see, however, some of these 'external' studies also raise major issues concerning the appropriate measure of pension liabilities.
4. An intermediate calculation between the accrued liability and the prospective liability from the ongoing PAYG scheme is to calculate the liabilities if no new entrants were allowed into the scheme but where existing contributor-pensioners remained in the scheme until their death (Holzmann, *et al.*, 2000). An alternative 'intermediate' calculation is where existing contributors are attached a probability of leaving the scheme before reaching 'full' pension entitlement – see Disney and Whitehouse (1996).
5. See, for example, Disney and Whitehouse, 1993a.
6. Schemes which offer contracting-out of contribution requirements by private schemes, such as in the UK, can therefore be regarded as the public sector loaning cash to the private sector to take other future pension obligations. The 'return' on this transaction for the private sector therefore depends on the terms of this rebate (see Hemming and Kay, 1981; Disney and Whitehouse, 1992, 1993b).
7. Of course, the official actuary would also have to confirm that current outgoings (payments of pensions) are matched by current contribution receipts (PAYG equilibrium).
8. This raises the issue of whether permitting the trust fund to invest in other assets, such as private equity, changes the generational incidence. However, switching the portfolio strategy in this manner

may be entirely neutral if the supply of government debt and private equity remain the same as before.

## REFERENCES


BANKS J., DISNEY R. and SMITH, Z. (2000), 'What can we learn from Generational Accounts for the United Kingdom?', *Economic Journal Features*, 110 (November), F575-F597.

BLEJER M. I. and CHEASTY A. (1991), 'The measurement of fiscal deficits: Analytical and methodological issues', *Journal of Economic Literature*, XXIX (December), 1644-1678.

BOHN H. (1992), 'Budget deficits and government accounting', in Meltzer A. and Plosser C. (eds.) *Carnegie-Rochester Conference Series on Public Policy*, 36, July, 1-84.

CHAND S. and JAEGER A. (1996), 'Aging populations and public pension schemes', *Occasional Paper*, 147, The International Monetary Fund, Washington.

COMMISSION OF THE EUROPEAN COMMUNITIES (2000), 'Progress report to the ECOFIN Council on the impact of ageing population on public pension systems', *mimeo*, Economic Policy Committee, EPC/ECFIN/581/00-EN-FINAL, Brussels, 26 October.

DEPARTMENT OF SOCIAL SECURITY (1998), *A New Contract for Welfare: Partnership in Pensions*, Cm 4179, HMSO, London.

DISNEY R. (1996), *Can We Afford To Grow Older? A Perspective on the Economics of Aging*, MIT Press, Cambridge, Mass.

DISNEY R. (1999), 'Notional Accounts as a pension reform strategy: An evaluation', *SP Discussion Paper*, No. 9928, HDSP, the World Bank, Washington.

DISNEY R. (2000a), 'Crises in public pension programmes in OECD: What are the reform options?', *Economic Journal Features*, 110, February, F1-F23.

DISNEY R. (2000b), 'Declining public pensions in an era of demographic ageing: Will private provision fill the gap?', *European Economic Review*, 44:4-6 and 957-973.

DISNEY R. and WHITEHOUSE E. (1992), *The Personal Pension Stampede*, Report Series, Institute for Fiscal Studies, London.

DISNEY R. and WHITEHOUSE E. (1993a), 'Will younger cohorts obtain a worse deal from the UK pension scheme?', 85-103, in Creedy J. and Casson M. (eds.) *Industrial Concentration and Economic Inequality: Essays in Honour of Peter Hart*, Edward Elgar, Aldershot.

DISNEY R. and WHITEHOUSE E. (1993b), 'Contracting-out and lifetime redistribution in the UK state pension system', *Oxford Bulletin of Economics and Statistics*, 55 (February), 25-41.

DISNEY R. and WHITEHOUSE E. (1996), 'What are occupational pension plan entitlements worth in the Britain?', *Economica*, 63 (May), 213-238.

HEMMING R. and KAY J. (1981), 'Contracting out of the State Earnings Related Pension Scheme', *Fiscal Studies*, 2 (February), 20-28.

HOLZMANN R., PALACIOS R. and ZVINIENE A. (2000), 'On the economics and scope of implicit pension debt: An international perspective', *mimeo*, HDSP Department, the World Bank, Washington.

KANE C. and PALACIOS R. (1996), 'The implicit pension debt', *Finance and Development*, June, 36-38.

KOTLIKOFF L. (1992), *Generational Accounting*, Free Press, New York.

KUNE J. (1996), 'The hidden liabilities: Meaning and consequences', *mimeo*, CBP seminar Series, Den Haag, Netherlands.

VALDES-PRIETO S. (1999), 'The financial stability of notional account pensions', *mimeo*, Catholic University of Chile.

VAN DEN NOORD P. and HERD R. (1994), 'Estimating pension liabilities: A methodological approach', *OECD Economic Studies*, 23:131-166.

AXEL BÖRSCH-SUPAN

# WHAT WE KNOW AND WHAT WE DO NOT KNOW ABOUT THE WILLINGNESS TO PROVIDE SELF-FINANCED OLD-AGE INSURANCE

## 1. INTRODUCTION

The point of departure for this chapter is the current flurry of pension reforms in Europe, actually, around the world. The reason for these reforms are well known, and it is no surprise that they are particularly debated in Europe: of the world regions, Europe has the highest proportion of population aged 65 or over (NAS, 2001). Within Europe (and hence in the world), Italy has the highest proportion of people aged 65 or over (18% in 2000), but Belgium, Sweden and Greece also score very high (17% or more). Outside Europe, only Japan has a similar age structure (about 17% of the population is 65 or over). In Europe, the ratio of persons aged over 65 as a percentage of the working age population 20-64 (the dependency ratio), is expected to increase from about 27% in 2000 to 39% in 2025, and to 53% in 2050 (European Commission, 2000). This increase of the dependency ratio in itself places a heavy financial burden on society.

In addition, Europeans retire much earlier than inhabitants of other developed countries (for instance, in Belgium only a quarter of all males are still in the labour force at age 60, compared to three quarters in Japan, see NAS, 2001), and replacement rates of public pensions are quite generous, requiring a large volume of benefits to be financed by the taxes and contributions of the younger generations. Thus, everything else being equal, ageing places a much higher burden on the sustainability of income maintenance systems in Europe than elsewhere in the world.

No wonder then that governments rediscover the virtues of self-financed old-age insurance in order to relieve the pressure from state-financed retirement income maintenance systems. While this author shares the view that we have no choice but to base a significant part of future retirement income on self-provision (Börsch-Supan, 1999, 2000), designing such a transition is not an easy task. This paper addresses some of the issues involved in such a transition. It focuses on the willingness of individuals to participate in voluntary and/or mandatory saving schemes for retirement. Essential to understanding this willingness is the various interactions between private saving behaviour and state rules. So we begin this paper with a rough estimate of how much self-financing has to be done in order to stabilise



*T.Boeri, A.Börsch-Supan, A.Brugiavini, R.Disney, A.Kapteyn and F.Peracchi (eds.), Pensions: More Information, Less Ideology, 113—135.*

the state-financed pension systems. We then provide a short review of what we know about private saving behaviour over the life cycle, both in theory and as evidenced in Europe. We then look at the various interactions: how have the generous public pension systems changed saving behaviour? Have they completely replaced the necessity to provide for self-financed old-age insurance? What will happen when the replacement rates of public pensions declines? Do workers start by themselves to save for retirement – or do we have to provide strong incentives to prevent old-age poverty? Or even stronger ones – do we need to make self-financed old-age provision mandatory? If we do so, and workers are actually not willing to save, what is the effect of forcing them? Finally, if workers spend a larger proportion of their income on self-financed old-age provision, what is the effect on consumption and other savings? Will housing prices decline because more savings will be channelled into retirement consumption and less into housing?

As it turns out, we know shamefully little about all these important questions. This begins with the astounding insight that we do not even have reliable evidence to describe how saving behaviour looks like over the life cycle, and thus much less on its policy determinants. While we have some (my reading is: convincing) evidence that there is substitution between public and private old-age insurance, the extent of potential crowding out is very much disputed. We have some direct evidence for the workers' willingness to self-insure rather than to rely on public pensions, but the evidence for additional savings is contradictory and scant. We also have some indirect evidence for flight mechanisms like migration into the shadow economy – direct evidence may be too much to ask for in this case. Finally, portfolio choice between pension and other assets, such as housing, is very little understood. We argue that a major reason for this lack of knowledge is lack of suitable data from which to derive such knowledge.

The following paper is structured as follows. Section 2 sets the stage by estimating the volume of self-financed old-age insurance necessary to stabilise a typical European pension system. Section 3 sketches our main theory of savings and the implications that have been drawn by academics and international organisations from this theory on order to make long-run predictions about private saving and its reaction to policy changes. Section 4 collects the available – and contradictory – empirical evidence about actual saving behaviour and interprets these findings in the light of self- and state-financed old-age provision. Section 5 attempts a synthesis of the contradictions between Section 3 and Section 4. Section 6 is devoted to the issue of substitution and crowding out. Section 7 cites survey evidence for whether workers prefer voluntary or mandatory self-financed old-age insurance. Finally, Section 8 discusses whether tax incentives work to generate the retirement savings needed.

Section 9 then summarises what we know and what we do not know, and where it would be quite crucial to have better data in order to anticipate future problems.

## 2. HOW MUCH SELF-FINANCED OLD-AGE INSURANCE IS NEEDED TO STABILISE THE STATE-FINANCED OLD-AGE INSURANCE SYSTEMS?

Pension reform is a major policy issue in the countries of Continental Europe. As pointed out in the introduction, they face a common problem: their populations are ageing, and this especially quickly from the year 2010 on. The dependency ratios – the demographic parameter of most importance for the old-age pension systems – will about double, particularly so in Italy and Germany, thereby also more or less doubling the financial burden of the PAYG pension systems. Since solutions within the PAYG systems are limited in light of this doubling of the burden, almost all pension reform attempts in Europe try to make use of self-financed old-age provision. How much saving for old age is necessary to stabilise the PAYG fiscal burden?[1]

We use Germany as an example for a numerical calculation of the volume of pre-funding necessary to stabilise the PAYG contribution rate. Of course, this depends on the policy scenario and a host of other assumptions. We carry out a partial equilibrium analysis and build on the following "natural" policy scenario which we dub the "freezing model" (Birg and Börsch-Supan, 1999). First, within the PAYG system the effective retirement age will be increased by 3 years and the contribution rate frozen. Second, a pre-funded second pillar finances the emerging ageing burden. Concretely, at the end of 2001, it is announced that the contribution rate will be frozen from year 2008 on at the then current level. Because population ageing increases the dependency ratio, this implies a reduction in the replacement rate – a "pension gap" will emerge. We assume that this pension gap will be completely filled by pre-funding such that the sum of future reduced PAYG pension benefits and new funded pensions will remain equal to the current PAYG pension benefits.[2]

This bookkeeping exercise implies that in response to the increasing dependency ratio, the benefits provided by the frozen PAYG system will shrink to two-thirds of what they are now. Hence, new funded pensions eventually have to provide for about one third of current PAYG benefits. Adding the other existing sources of retirement income, the balance between PAYG and other sources will create a mix in Germany similar to what it is now in the Netherlands and Switzerland. In countries that age less than Germany (e.g. France), the funded share will be lower, while in countries that age more (e.g. Italy), the funded share will be higher if such a freezing policy is applied.

How much new saving is needed in order to provide a third of current pension income? This mainly depends on the instruments used and their rates of return. We design an instrument similar to a group life insurance which covers all three biometric risks (longevity, disability and survivorship) and is paid out on retirement as an annuity. For the sake of simplicity our computations are based on a standardised life course, in which gainful employment begins at age twenty and ends at age 60 (in 2000), the latter gradually increasing to age 63 (in the year 2035). We apply the upper variant of the life expectancy projections used by the most recent government computations. Hence, this insurance covers the individual risk of longevity as well as this projected aggregate increase of longevity. Early disability occurs between age 45 and 60 with an increasing probably averaging 15 percent, the current frequency. Survivor benefits are paid in accordance to the average current probabilities which is likely to be an overestimate because an increasing share of women will have their own pensions.[3]

The pension or insurance company is investing the accumulated capital in the market using a broad portfolio of stocks, bonds, direct placement and real estate. We assume that this portfolio generates the average gross rate of return that prevailed between 1980 and 1995 in the industry. This was 6.5% in real terms – however, we will also vary this rate in our projections. We subtract administrative costs of 6% of contributions, the average for group insurance policies.[4] Here enters the significance of the group policy: past experience has shown that individual accounts tend to have higher administrative costs. Group policies and a universal spread of pre-funding "enforced" by the notional account mechanism also minimises the costs of adverse selection in the annuity market. We do not propose additional incentives or mandatory contributions but a consistent taxation of all retirement benefits together with tax deductibility of all pension contributions.

The resulting net rate of return to the customer is 4.5% in real terms. One may find this overly optimistic, but we think that the experience between 1980 and 1995 is a fairly good indicator of the future – it includes the "golden years" of the mid-1990s as well as the Asian and other financial crises. Nevertheless, we also present simulations with a slightly higher (5.5%) and a substantially lower real rate of return (3.0%). We assume that this rate will decline in the wake of population ageing to 4.2% in 2035, and then remain constant. This estimate is based on a growth model taken from Börsch-Supan, Heiss und Winter (2001) that simulates the effect of population ageing and the feedback of a partially funded pension system on capital intensity and the rate of return.

Figure 1 shows the path of savings and PAYG contributions under the proposed mixed and under the current pure PAYG system for a representative worker. For each birth cohort, it compares the total contributions in the transition scenario – the frozen contributions to the remaining PAYG system (the lower part of the bars, denoted by 1) plus the savings invested in the group account (upper part of the bars, denoted by 2) – with the contributions in a continued PAYG system (3, solid line). The transition smoothens the increase of the total contribution rate relative to the PAYG system, and prevents the total contribution rate from reaching the peak burden of the PAYG system after the year 2035 without changing pension benefits. For cohorts born after about 1970, the transition results in substantially lower total contributions than under the PAYG system.

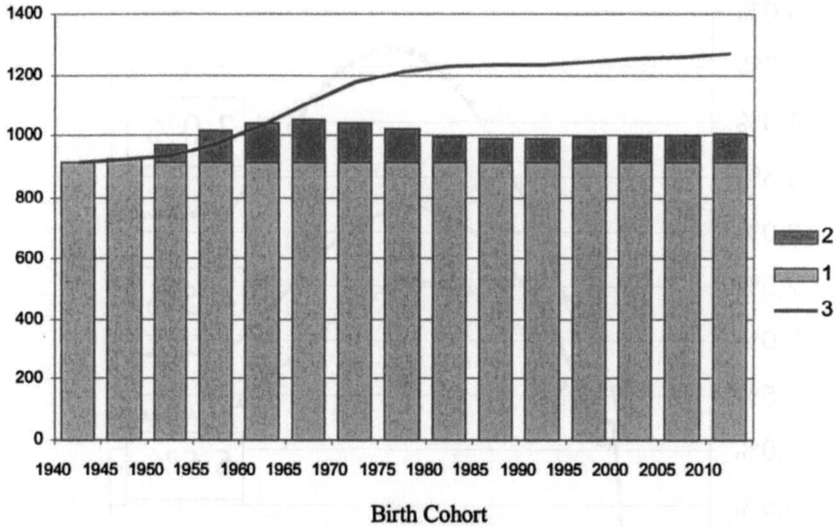


*Figure 1: PAYG Contributions and Savings Implied by Pension Reform (DM/month at the average wage) - Source: Birg and Börsch-Supan (1999)*

*Note: 1000 DM are approximately 500 US$ at PPP. The Figure shows PAYG (1) and savings (2) contributions to the mixed system and the PAYG contribution to the old pure PAYG system (3). Replacement rate fixed at the level of 1997. Real rate of return is 4.5%.*

Note the cohort dependency of savings in Figure 1. Unlike the current government proposals or the Swedish model, the freezing model implies a higher savings rate for the cohorts born around 1965 than earlier or later cohorts. This is most clearly shown in Figure 2. The earlier cohorts need to fill a smaller gap, while the later cohorts have more time to exploit the force of compound interest. The implied saving rate (i.e., contributions to new pension accounts, expressed as a percentage of gross wages to be compatible to the PAYG contribution rates) is highest for the 1965 cohort and reaches about 3.2%.

These simulations are sensitive with respect to the assumed rate of return. Figure 2 shows the variation. If rates of return are lower, saving rates need to make up and increase. The peak rate will reach 4.7% at a 3% real rate of return, but is only 2.5% at a 5.5% rate of return.

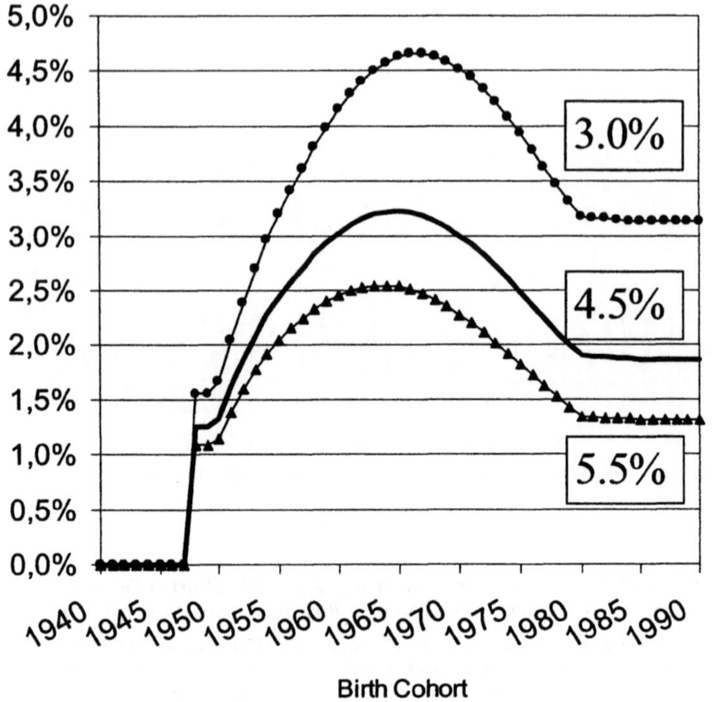


*Figure 2: Saving Necessary to Fill Pension Gap (% of gross income, by rate of return)*

*Source: Birg and Börsch-Supan (1999)*

The upshot of this simulation is that the private saving rate has to increase by 1.8 percentage points in the long run if the creation of a pre-funded second pillar is the main policy response to population ageing (in addition to an increase in the retirement age by 3 years). If one believes in lower future rates of return, say, 3% rather than the 4.5% assumed, the private saving rate has to increase by slightly more than 3.2 percentage points. Applied to the 1965 cohort, the saving rate has to increase from some 12.1% (1998) to 13.9% or 15.3%, depending on the rate of return.

Extrapolating this simulation to France and most other European countries will generate a smaller gap to be filled than in Germany because Germany is projected to experience one of the highest increases in the dependency ratio in Europe. It will, however, be surpassed by Italy. In this country, households will have to save more than the Germans in order to fill the corresponding pension gap.

We conclude from this stage-setting section that the volume of saving necessary to fill the pension gap which emerges from a population-ageing stable PAYG system is not trivial but well in the realm of the historical variation in German household saving rates. Our estimates are of course subject to parameter criticism. The "freezing model" is in our eyes a "natural" transition model but the reader might like other policy scenarios better. More important, however, is the fact that our simple bookkeeping exercise ignores all potential feedback mechanisms. It is not based on a behavioural model of saving.

## 3. THE LIFE-CYCLE HYPOTHESIS AND ITS IMPLICATIONS FOR SAVINGS

Will the workers actually save as much as postulated in the bookkeeping model of the preceding section? Will they do it voluntarily? In order to answer, we need to understand the saving behaviour of workers. In the next three sections, we show that we have such a model. However, it is too simple yet to describe the actual saving patterns observed in Europe. Extensions to make it more realistic, however, require better data which we are lacking in Europe.

The main work-horse for studying savings from a theoretical point of view is based on Franco Modigliani's seminal work (Modigliani and Brumberg, 1954). The life-cycle hypothesis supposes that households look forward in order to smooth consumption. Hence, households save when income is high and dissave when income is low. A household just as impatient as the average household will smooth consumption to be constant, and its level is determined only by the total income over the life cycle (the permanent income), not its fluctuations. In fact, saving reflects such fluctuations (positive transitory income), while dissaving reflects transitory income losses.

This theory has strong predictions. First, during a stylised life cycle, in which individuals earn wage income until retirement and then receive a much lower retirement income (in the form of an annuity), individuals will save until retirement and then dissave. Hence, life-cycle saving profiles should be first positive, then drop to negative values after retirement. Second, as long as retirement income is lower than earnings, asset profiles over the life-cycle saving profiles should be strongly hump-shaped: assets increase until retirement and then decrease during the dissaving period after retirement. Third, in a life course with reasonably steady earnings and substantially lower pension income, retirement saving is by far the most important motive for saving. This is simply due to the large volume of income maintenance necessary after retirement.

The life-cycle theory of saving also has a strong prediction for our crowding-out questions posed in the introduction and to which we will return in Section 6. Substitution between state-provided old-age insurance (a pension annuity) and self-provided retirement income (also received as an annuity) should be exactly one-to-one. Each Euro of benefits provided by a state pension should crowd out exactly one Euro in self-financed insurance benefits.

There may be other reasons to save than for retirement, e.g., to smooth over short-run earnings fluctuations, to finance large indivisible consumption goods (homes, cars), to buffer against uncertainty, and/or to leave bequests. Modigliani's theory can be extended to accommodate these additional saving motives. We can draw a fifth prediction, however, and again it is a strong one: these other saving motives should be unaffected by any change in the ratio between self- and state-provided retirement income – as long as all else (e.g., total disposable income) remains unaffected. There may be second-order feedback effects (e.g., pension policy changes affect risk and uncertainty) but they should be small.

A sixth prediction concerns population ageing and it is no less crisp than the other ones. Future saving rates will decline in response to population ageing because elderly households who dissave become a larger proportion of the population.

Because Modigliani's life-cycle theory of savings is the only workable theory we have so far, most policy analyses which require a behavioural model of saving use this theory more or less implicitly. Examples are the earlier analyses on the effect of population ageing on saving conducted by the IMF and the OECD (Heller, 1989; Auerbach and Kotlikoff, 1987; Auerbach *et al.*, 1989). They use the hump-shaped life-cycle saving patterns and it comes as no surprise that they conclude that future saving rates will strongly decline in response to population ageing. Policy makers took these predictions as a strong warning for capital shortages in the 1920s and 1930s. Some quoted these predictions to advocate stronger tax subsidies to saving in order to foster the willingness to save, especially through tax-preferred retirement saving vehicles such as individual retirement accounts (so-called "IRAs") and employer-sponsored retirement saving plans (so-called "401(k) plans") in the United States.

## 4. EVIDENCE ON LIFE-CYCLE SAVINGS BEHAVIOUR

Are these strong predictions correct? This is not only an academic question but has strong policy implications, as we made clear at the end of the preceding section. Will people automatically and voluntarily fill any pension gap created by the retrenchment of public pay-as-you-go pension systems with self-provided old-age insurance (prediction 4)? Will other savings, and therefore corresponding prices and returns, e.g., in the housing market, be unaffected by a fundamental change in pension policy (prediction 5)? Will we need to take expensive measures to prevent future capital shortages (prediction 6)?

Here, we quickly reach the limits of our current knowledge. We have little direct evidence, at least for Continental Europe, because pension systems have stayed fairly unaltered during the last few decades. Our line of argument will therefore be: if predictions 1 through 3 about life-cycle saving behaviour hold, we might be in a good position to also believe the other three more policy-relevant predictions 4 through 6. If not, we obviously need to be careful.

It is not straightforward to measure life-cycle savings. First, saving is a complicated concept that has to be measured carefully – as a change in assets, a difference between income and consumption, taking care of inflation as well as potential unrealised capital gains. Second, to understand how saving changes over the life-cycle, one needs to observe households as they age – a single observation in time will not provide that information. Comparing individuals of different ages is not sufficient since these individuals have been born at different times and experienced different earnings and policy histories (Brugiavini and Weber, 2001).

We do not have such data. Hence, we must resort to a mixture of genuine and pseudo-panel data in order to derive a pure life-cycle savings profile. Figure 3 below presents saving rates in Germany, Italy and the Netherlands. These were derived from reasonable (although by no means perfectly) comparable saving definitions which makes the following results preliminary (Börsch-Supan, 2001a). The figures show the fitted values by age in each observed year together with the upper and the lower point of a 95% confidence interval. They therefore offer a visual impression of the stability and precision of these age profiles – stability in terms of changes from year to year, and precision in terms of estimated standard deviations.

Figure 3 gives a good impression of the diversity of age-saving profiles. First, levels are very different: Italian households have a high saving rate that exceeds the age-specific saving rates of Dutch households at all ages, with German households in between. Second, Italian households have experienced quite different saving rates over time (and possibly cohort) while the savings behaviour of Dutch and German households was much more stable. Third, the saving rates of Dutch and Italian households can be fairly precisely measured in a statistical sense. This is also true for German households who are in the middle age groups, while sampling errors are large for young and elderly households. Fourth and finally, the life-cycle patterns are rather different: In Italy, a decline in saving rates comes late (after age 60). In Germany, households save less after about age 40 but savings rates appear to slightly (not significantly) increase at old age again. The median elderly household in Germany and Italy does not dissave – in Germany, the saving rate stabilises at around 4% and in Italy it remains even higher in old age as well. This is quite different in the Netherlands where the median saving rate is about zero for elderly households and slightly negative for the oldest.

The German and Italian saving patterns look quite different from what the life-cycle hypothesis would predict. Even the Dutch households dissave only very little. Obviously, we cannot use the textbook life-cycle theory naively in a prediction model. This puts a big question mark over the predictions about future capital shortages based on the textbook life-cycle model presented in the previous section. In order to use the life-cycle model, we need to extend it in such a way that it will predict the patterns observed in Figure 3.

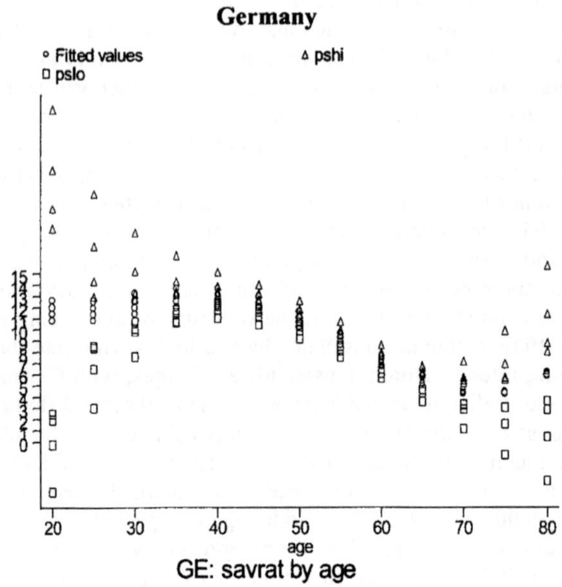


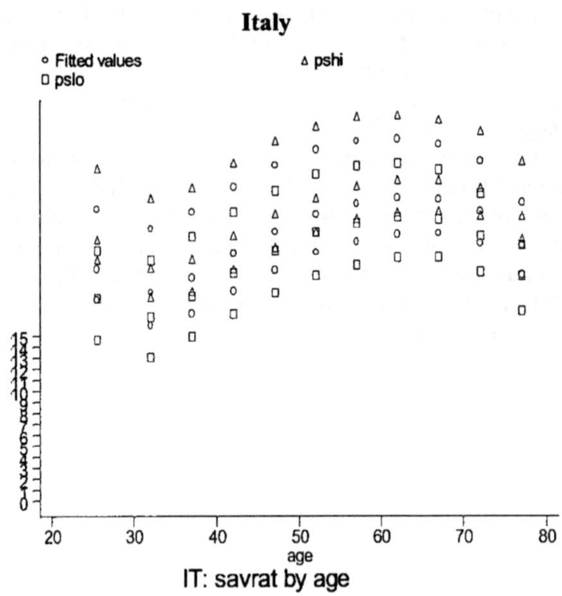


*Figure 3: Cohort-corrected saving rates by age (medians)*

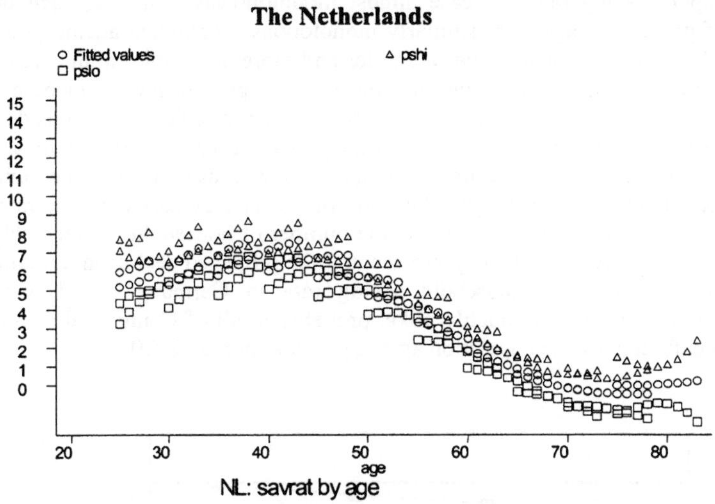


*Figure 3 (continues): Cohort-corrected saving rates by age (medians)*

*Sources: Germany: Börsch-Supan, Reil-Held, Rodepeter, Schnabel and Winter (2001); Italy: Brugiavini and Padula (2001); Netherlands: Alessie and Kapteyn (2001).*

Using the actual life-cycle profiles of Figure 3, we do not predict a strong decline in saving rates (see Figure 4). Actually, we predict an increase for a country with demographics like Japan, a slight decline in a country with demographics like the US, and we do not really know for countries with demographics like Germany and Italy. The methodology ("shift-share analysis") is simple (see Börsch-Supan, 1996): we apply the age and cohort specific saving rates of Figure 3 to projections of population size by age group and of income growth. It is noteworthy that for the purpose of projecting future savings, the high saving rates among households aged 45-64 are significant because the baby boom generation will soon be entering these ages, and because income is highest during those ages. The decline after age 65, which is stronger in the cohort-corrected data than in the raw data, is an interesting puzzle in itself (e.g., see Banks, Blundell and Tanner, 2000; Börsch-Supan, 2001b), however, for a projection of total saving it turns out to be less significant because the population weights decrease with age due to mortality and because retirement income is lower than income at age 45-64.

In addition to Germany, we will also undertake this exercise for Japan and the United States. This is helpful because the underlying age-specific saving rates and speed and extent of population ageing are different across countries.

In the United States, population ageing during the next 15 years shifts more weight to the high saving ages 45-64. After 2010, the numerous baby boom generation enters the low saving ages 65+. Hence, as can be seen in Figure 4, American saving rates increase by 0.5 percentage points from 1990 to 2010, then fall almost to the 1990 level during the following 10 years.

In Japan, saving rates increase almost monotonously with age, such that the effect of population ageing is similarly monotonous. Population ageing puts fewer households in the low saving age categories and more households in the high saving age categories, resulting in higher saving on an aggregate level. Japanese saving rates are projected to increase from 14.3% to 15.8% during the period considered.

In Germany, the overall effect is ambiguous. Population ageing reduces the relative proportion of households below age 37, but it also increases the number of households in the "saving trough" after retirement. The increase in saving rates after age 75 is of smaller relevance because the number of households of very old age is relatively small even after taking into account the projected decline in mortality. As a result, the aggregate household saving rate in Germany – and, since the demographic changes are roughly alike, probably in all of Continental Europe – is almost unaffected by the population ageing process through 2020.

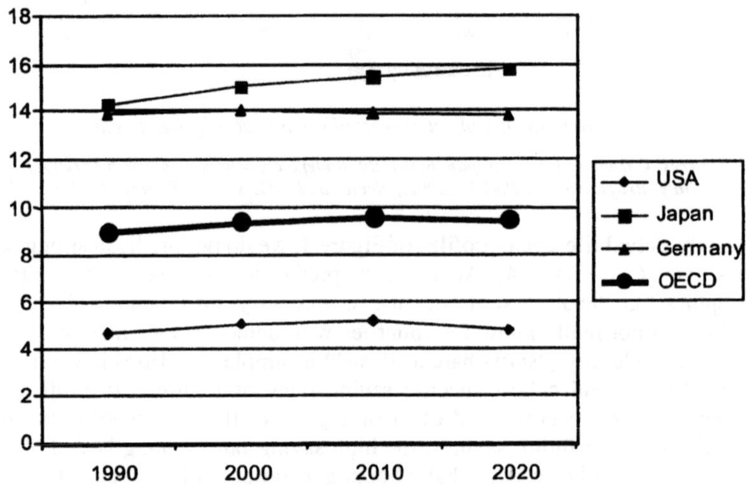


*Figure 4: Age-Composition Effect in OECD Saving Rates*

*Source: Börsch-Supan (1996)*

The results in Figure 4 are in sharp contrast to the projections by Heller (1989), Auerbach and Kotlikoff (1987), and Auerbach *et al.* (1989), which rest on the theoretical life-cycle profile of saving rates presented in Section 2. Using the actual saving rates depicted in Figure 3, we cannot find an indication for serious capital shortages. Our results rest on the combination of high saving rates and high incomes of the baby boom generation in the year 2010. In 1990, the leading edge of the US baby boom generation was age 44, while the youngest baby boomers were 27 years old. In 2010, the baby boomers are between 47 and 64, exactly in their peak saving and peak income ages.

## 5. WHAT DO WE KNOW ABOUT FUTURE SAVINGS RATES?

Sections 3 and 4 leaves us puzzling: what is now true as a prediction of future savings? Strong decline with potential need for policy intervention, or essentially unchanged such that one does not even have to contemplate policy action?

The honest answer is that we do not know. The popular projections in Section 3 are based on a model that predicts a much simpler saving behaviour than observed in the data. One feels uncomfortable. However, the projections of aggregate saving on the basis of a current description of behaviour, as in Section 4, are subject to what is called the "Lucas-critique": how do we know that current behaviour will remain stable? Why shouldn't changes in public policy feed back and change saving behaviour? This critique makes us feel equally uncomfortable about the predictions of Section 4. Specifically, pension provisions and transfer habits may well be adapted in the wake of population ageing when pension systems are adapted to remain financially sustainable. Hence, we realise how central the question is, how self-provided old-age insurance (i.e., retirement saving) will react to changes in state-provided pension income.

We come back to the insight that we need to extend the life-cycle model of Section 3 in a way that enables it to predict the saving patterns observed in Figure 3. The simple textbook model is obviously mis-specified. Only the knowledge of the correct model, however, enables us to escape the Lucas-critique. Crucial for the construction of the correct model is longitudinal data, covering several countries with comparable data definitions. Why longitudinal? Because saving is a choice over time, shifting resources from fatter to leaner years. Cross-sectional data will not uncover how people do this shifting over time. Why cross-national? Because in a single country, policy rarely changes, and especially pension policy. Cross-national variation is then the only way to include policy variation. And without variation no influence can be measured, no behaviour identified, therefore no new model constructed.

The following may exemplify how we would use such data, using the preliminary saving profiles from Figure 3 with all their measurement problems as a departure to predict what might happen in the future.

Consider the pension systems in those three countries as a working explanation for the strong differences between Germany and Italy on the one hand, and the Netherlands on the other hand. Germany and Italy have PAYG financed public pensions with very high replacement rates. They generate net retirement incomes that are approximately 70% of pre-retirement net earnings in Germany and may even exceed 100% in Italy.[5] In addition, the public pension systems in Germany and Italy provide generous survivor benefits that constitute a substantial proportion of total unfunded pension wealth, and disability benefits at similar and often even higher replacement levels than old-age pensions. As a result, public pensions are by far the largest pillar of retirement income in these countries and constitute more than 80% of the income of households headed by persons aged 65 and older, while funded retirement income, such as asset income from private saving or firm pensions in which the employer saves on behalf of the worker, plays a much smaller role. This is quite different from the Netherlands which only provides a flat base pension on a PAYG basis with a replacement rate that is very low for households above median income. All other retirement incomes are withdrawals from mandatory occupational and individual pension accounts.

Hence, a crucial difference between Germany and Italy on the one hand, and the Netherlands on the other, is that saving for old age is unlikely to be the main savings motive in Germany and Italy, while it is necessary for Dutch households. The famous hump shape of savings predicted by the life-cycle hypothesis therefore applies better to Dutch households, while (physical) savings are relatively flat in Germany and Italy – in turn, "notional" social security wealth increases and decreases faster in Germany and Italy than in the Netherlands (see the individual country studies in Börsch-Supan, 2001a).

Figure 5 tries to make the point clearer by extracting the average profile from Figure 3 (using regression analysis) and indexing the saving rates to 100% at age 40. The saving rates in old age very well reflect the replacement rates from PAYG-financed public old-age insurance: about 45% in the Netherlands, 60% in Germany and 80-120% in Italy.

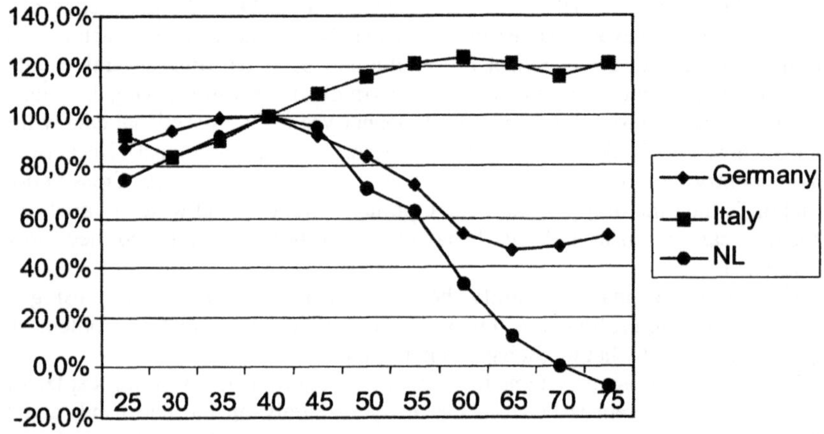


*Figure 5: Life-cycle saving patterns*

*Source: Börsch-Supan and Winter (2001)*

If this explanation of the observed cross national saving differences were correct, it has important implications for the future. If indeed most of the saving patterns currently observed in Germany and Italy are caused by generous retirement benefits from their PAYG pension systems, we should expect distinct changes in saving patterns when the pension reforms in these countries are put in place. The introduction of multi-pillar systems with a substantial portion of funded retirement income will revive the retirement motive for saving. In fact, these reformed systems will look very similar to the current Dutch system. Hence, it is likely that saving rates among the young will increase (to accumulate retirement savings), and saving rates among the elderly will decline sharply (because they will dissolve their retirement savings).

Using the same logic, we should add PAYG contributions to the savings visible in Figure 5 (as additions to pension wealth), and subtract pension receipts (as withdrawals from pension wealth) in order to do justice to Modigliani's life-cycle theory, as has been done by Jappelli and Modigliani (1998). This would rescue the predictions 1 through 3 in Section 3 but it does not help us much in explaining what will happen in the future. Why do Dutch households have a lower saving rate even though we need to add less PAYG contributions to other Dutch savings? Why do Germany and Italy have such high saving rates even though the pension system takes care of their retirement savings? To answer these questions, we need to understand the entire variety of saving motives, not only retirement saving. And in order to do this, we need to observe how people over their life-courses adapt their savings to changed circumstances. We do not have such panel data in Europe. Hence, we are left with applying predictive models explicitly or implicitly using Modigliani's life-cycle theory, even though we do know that it cannot answer all our questions on saving behaviour.

## 6. SUBSTITUTION AND CROWDING OUT

Adding PAYG contributions to other savings in Figure 5 amounts to the assumption that there is no feedback effect of retirement saving to other saving, and that substitution between contributions and saving for self-provided old-age insurance is one-to-one – as postulated in the life-cycle hypothesis.

It is not clear, however, whether this assumption holds. Going back to Section 2, not all of the additional saving depicted in Figure 2 will be new saving since some other saving will be "crowded out" by the new saving for self-financed retirement income. For example, people may buy smaller homes (and thus save for a smaller down payment) when they have to pay more for their retirement.

One has to distinguish carefully between two kinds of substitution: (1) substitution between bequeathable wealth and wealth that is annuitised for retirement, and (2) substitution within "retirement wealth".[6] Both substitution mechanisms are important in the pension reform discussion. In fact, while all forms of private saving (whether annuitised or not) constitute private wealth accumulation, and are usually recorded that way in national accounts, the difference between bequeathable (fungible) wealth and retirement wealth rests on the basic motives for saving. Hence, in theoretical models or in simulation exercises one is usually concerned with describing changes in total capital accumulation (i.e. total private wealth even if annuitised), but in the empirical work the extent of substitutability is usually assessed by comparing bequeathable wealth on the one hand and retirement wealth (or just public retirement wealth) on the other.

Section 2 has addressed the question of how much private saving needs to be substituted for PAYG-financed retirement income provision in order to stabilise the current PAYG system contribution rates (this is the second substitution mechanism). In this section, we review what we know about possible crowding-out effects *vis-à-vis* other savings (the first substitution mechanism). Buying smaller homes, the example that we mentioned in the outset of this section, is the most probable avenue for the first of the two substitution mechanisms.

Crowding out is an important policy issue for two reasons. First, a central argument put forward in pension reform discussions is the macroeconomic superiority of a funded system *vis-à-vis* a PAYG system.[7] This argument is valid only to the extent that new savings is created which adds to the capital stock and therefore promotes economic growth. This requirement holds *a fortiori* when the transition costs of a pension reform are considered. Second, if pre-funding is incensed by tax relief, full crowding out implies that these subsidies are merely windfall gains that shift existing savings from one form to another. We discuss the first point here and the second in the following subsection.

The extent of crowding out is the subject of the famous debate between Feldstein (1974) and Barro (1974). Our reading of the controversy is that we do not have reliable estimates of the quantitative extent, but that the evidence supports a positive effect on *total* savings when the PAYG system is reduced, e.g., in a partial transition as described in the previous subsection. We do not have reliable econometric estimates because crowding out takes place through the behavioural adaptation of generations, thus requiring long periods of time in which many other macroeconomic circumstances change.

Auerbach and Kotlikoff (1983) pioneered the discussion on the difficulties associated with the identification of the substitution parameters both in time series and cross sectional studies for the US. The structural instability of the parameters is due to the changes in population structure and to the fluctuations in interest rates as well as contribution rates during the transition after the introduction of a new pension system.

For Europe the empirical evidence is scanty and there exists a wide variety of results, making it particularly hard to reach any conclusion. To our knowledge time series studies include Rossi and Visco (1994)[8] for Italy, who are able to attribute part of the decline that occurred during the 1980s in the saving rate to the increased generosity of social security in the 1970s. In other countries the relationship between pension wealth and private fungible wealth emerging from time series data is poorly determined[9]. Cross sectional analysis based on Italian micro data (Brugiavini, 1987; Jappelli, 1995) obtain low estimates of the substitution parameter. Recent studies for the Netherlands obtain mixed results. In particular, by using the Dutch Socio Economic Panel (SEP) data on private wealth and (constructed) data on social security wealth and pension wealth, Alessie, Kapteyn and Klijn (1997) and Kapteyn, Alessie and Lusardi (1999) have investigated the question of whether or not there exists displacement between discretionary private wealth on the one hand and social security and pension wealth on the other. For pension wealth they do not find any evidence of displacement, while for social security wealth they find full displacement[10].

Clear-cut "experiments" in which the pension system changes but everything else remains constant are hard to come by. Attanasio and Brugiavini (1997) rely directly on a test of how changes in saving rates are related to changes in pension wealth following the 1992 Reform of the Italian Social Security System in a "quasi-natural-experiment" setting. They find that households whose public pension wealth was substantially curtailed by the reform show a marked increase in their private saving rate.

Given this lack of conclusive econometric evidence, one can infer the extent of crowding out from an overlapping generations (OLG) model. Börsch-Supan, Heiss and Winter (2001) calibrate such a model to German data and conclude that substitution amounts to about one third, leaving two thirds new saving. This estimate is fairly robust for a reasonable variation in the underlying parameters, so it is probably a good guess for other countries as well. However, it is based on the tight structure of an OLG model and thus only a last resort in the search for a sorely-needed number.

How could we get better information? The crowding-out issue is a prime example of the virtues of observing policy variation in cross-national data. Only different mixtures of public and private pension systems can identify how people react with their saving behaviour to those different mixes. Europe is a great laboratory in this respect, and particularly these days with many different approaches to pension reform under way. We need to collect data during the initial phases in order to predict the future better. Currently, we are not only not really able to anticipate problems, but we also risk missing a golden opportunity to exploit the "European Laboratory".

## 7. WILL WORKERS SAVE VOLUNTARILY?

Closely related to the question of substitution is the question of whether workers will save voluntarily for self-financed old-age insurance – or whether it is necessary to make self-financed old-age insurance mandatory. This is a hotly-debated issue in the policy arena, particularly in the current pension reform processes in Germany and Italy. The pro-mandatory-savings argument is mainly the need to cover all persons in order to avoid pockets of poverty and to prevent moral hazard. The arguments against mandatory savings essentially rest on the well-known economic efficiency arguments against taxation. One advantage of private savings for old age as opposed to PAYG contributions is that the latter mainly have a tax character (Börsch-Supan and Reil-Held, 2000) therefore creating dead weight losses, while private saving does not. Making saving mandatory, however, introduces an element of force, thus shifting savings understood as voluntary insurance premiums towards mandatory taxes.

The issue is complicated by moral hazard. As long as the government provides last-resort pension income, voluntary saving is a waste – from the individual point of view, at least among those in the lowest parts of the earnings distribution – if one can just as well apply for social assistance. People may therefore opt for mandatory savings in order to reduce moral hazard.

How do you find out? Asking workers directly provides unreliable and potentially strategic answers. There are also strong framing effects. It does not surprising if workers are reported to fervour self-provided old-age insurance when surveys are conducted by pension funds and insurance agencies, while they prefer state-provided old-age insurance when asked by the unions. Besides framing, respondents usually have no realistic alternatives from which to choose – with all their costs and benefits clearly stated. Pure intentional questions tend to give misleading answers.

Boeri, Börsch-Supan and Tabellini (2001) used a different approach and asked if workers would like to partially opt out of the public pension system. They formulated this question so as to mean that they and their employer would only pay half the contributions in the future, but they would also receive only half of the pension rights once they opt out. Past contributions would be valued at their old benefit levels. This question clearly states costs and benefits, although workers may simply not know the contributions and benefits of their pension system. The questions were posed to a large sample of French, German, Italian and Spanish workers.

In order to shed light on the issue at hand – voluntary or mandatory? – the opting-out proposal was presented in several versions. In the first version, the amount saved by the reduced contributions was simply added to net income. In this case, the employee had the free choice of how to dispose of this money. In a follow-up question, the employee was constrained to invest the amount rebated in an old-age fund of his own choice, either private or employer-based. A third version, asked to those who agreed to the first opting-out proposal, imposed a transition burden in the form of a lower valuation of future pension rights.

In all four countries only a small fraction does not know or refuses to answer, but nowhere was an absolute majority willing to opt out. In Germany and Italy, about 47% of those who give a valid answer would like to opt out of the public pension systems, while some 48% would prefer to remain in it. In France and in Spain, the approval of an opting-out deal is much lower, about 24% and 19% respectively. The rate of acceptance decreases with age and rises with income and education. Males are more likely to accept. More informed individuals (about pension system features) are also more likely to accept the proposal.

Workers who wanted to opt out were also asked what they would do with the money. Interestingly, most workers would indeed use the money for self-provided old-age insurance. One might be tempted to conclude that there is some, albeit not overwhelming, empirical support for voluntary self-insurance.

It is more complicated, though. The second version of the opting-out proposal constrains individuals to invest the rebated contributions. One might expect that this would reduce the willingness to opt out relative to the previous question. But one finds the opposite: if the money saved has to be invested in a private old-age provision of one's own choice, the acceptance rate of the proposal *rises* from 47% to 67-71% in Italy and Germany, from 19% to 63% in Spain, and from 24% to 50% in France. A mandatory private pillar has more supporters than a voluntary supplemental provision, although most respondents who would accept the unconditional opting-out proposal, would in any case invest in old-age provision.

To make matters even more complicated, shifting the financial burden of old-age insurance from state to self-financing incurs a transition burden. Opting out of the

PAYG system is only feasible if someone bears additional contributions: those who have already retired need to be financed through the existing PAYG system, while at the same time future retirees have to save for themselves. This transition burden can be financed either by cutting existing pension benefits thereby lowering the PAYG contributions of current workers and making room for savings, or by adding savings to the current contributions. Both options are unattractive and are likely to reduce the political support for a fully-funded system.

With a third version of the opting-out proposal, Boeri *et al.* (2001) intended to find out to what extent individuals are willing to pay for the transition burden in order to get out of the PAYG system. All those who had accepted the (unconditional) opting-out proposal were asked whether they would still accept a less favourable proposal, offering the same tax rebate but a smaller future pension. Not surprisingly, the acceptance rate is considerably lower than without a burden. But the extent to which opting-out is rejected may surprise and suggests that perhaps the question was not fully understood. In Germany and Italy, only a quarter of those who accept the previous proposal are still willing to opt out. In France and Spain, where fewer people accept the unconditional opting out proposal, the decline is less pronounced: 40-50% still want to opt out even under a transition burden. Altogether, these numbers convey a similar negative result: in all four countries only little more than 10% of the respondents are willing to opt out if that entails bearing the transition burden envisaged in our question.

The exercise by Boeri *et al.* (2001) was a first and promising step and conveys an important methodological insight: they needed new data to get new insights. More experimentation with such complicated questions, however, is needed. In particular, we need data collection that mixes the experience and insights of economists and social scientists in this important area.

## 8. WHAT KIND OF INCENTIVES MAY INDUCE SAVING?

Section 7 suggests that workers, at least in France, Germany, Italy and Spain, prefer mandatory saving for self-financed old-age insurance, and given the necessity of a transition burden, a voluntary transition may not work at all. Most economists, however, do not like such mandatory saving plans because they resemble mandatory contributions to PAYG pension systems. These latter contributions are well-known to have the character of taxes and thus discourage labour supply. Isn't it possible to have it both ways, and that is to encourage savings by tax incentives so that everybody voluntarily does what is required? There are also technical reasons to study the effects of tax incentives on savings: in most pension system transitions that have occurred in recent history, the governments wanted to speed up the transition through tax relief for private old-age provision.

Economic theory is ambiguous regarding the effect of tax subsidies on the volume of private savings because the substitution effect (higher after tax returns make saving more attractive than consumption) has an impact opposite to that of the income effect (the subsidy increases total income which increases consumption in all periods). Moreover, the interpretation of the available evidence is hotly debated (see especially the controversy between Venti and Wise (1990) on the one hand, and Gale and Scholz (1994) and Attanasio and De Leire (1994) on the other) in reference to the effects of tax subsidies on American households' retirement saving and in discussing the "creation" of new saving. The issues are summarised by Skinner and Hubbard (1996) for the US, and by Attanasio and Banks (1998) for a comparison of the US and the UK.

In Continental Europe, this debate is complicated by the fact that in some cases households seem to be "overannuitised". Evidence by Börsch-Supan and Stahl (1991) and Börsch-Supan (1992, 1994) shows that the annuity income of a majority of pensioners (mostly PAYG income provided through the public system) by far exceeds consumption expenditures. The next generation of pensioners appears to be aware of this fact, since saving rates in Germany drop for the now middle-aged cohorts. Given this trend, a reduction in public pension wealth may not necessarily be channelled into new savings, or only after a transition period of new costly learning. At the same time, these households, if left to their own devices, may also shun pension assets because they do not want to lock their wealth into long-term saving for retirement.

This debate teaches us two lessons. First, we do not really know whether saving-related tax relief or similar subsidies increase total saving. Second, we do know that subsidies strongly increase saving in the specific form that is subsidised, possibly to the detriment of other saving forms (see Section 6).

Obviously, we again have a case for cross-national data collection. We need policy variation – and we have policy variation across the European countries. The sheer variety of tax treatment of private pensions across Europe generates the "European Laboratory" that helps us to detect which type of taxes encourage or discourage different types of assets.[11]

## 9. CONCLUSIONS

We have surveyed the ongoing debate on the role of self-financed versus state-financed old-age insurance. From simulation studies calibrated on German data we have learned that freezing current PAYG contributions requires a funded component of about one third of the existing benefits. This corresponds to an increase in the saving rate between 1.8% and 3.2% of the current rate. It is much harder to judge how much of this is "new saving" or whether it simply crowds out other forms of capital accumulation. In fact, the econometric evidence does not allow us to draw firm conclusions on the degree of substitutability between public pension "mandatory saving" and private saving. The picture is further blurred by tax incentives provided in some countries to some forms of capital accumulation, hence making it even harder to reach a conclusion on whether tax incentives on pension assets will encourage this form of saving and contribute to the creation of new saving.

Hence, while we find that in studying saving behaviour and the effects of public policy on it, theoretical models and simulation studies deliver useful information and qualitative policy prescriptions, we cannot provide reliable information that helps governments reliably anticipate problems. The lack of good quality longitudinal data on European households strongly impedes empirical research that could deliver quantitative results and permit judgements on the dominance of opposing effects.

Longitudinal data is essential here because saving takes place over the life-cycle. Cross sectional data – i.e., data for just one point of time – are obviously unable to identify life-cycle behaviour. Only longitudinal data can enable researchers to draw conclusions on the effects of pension reforms and welfare reforms on saving, on the interaction of credit markets arrangements and liquidity constraints, and on the role of precautionary and bequest motives alongside the traditional life-cycle motives in explaining choices.

Equally essential is cross-national data, collected under strict comparability. Only cross-national data provide the necessary policy variation – only different mixtures of public and private pension systems can identify how people react with their saving behaviour to those different mixes. Europe is a great laboratory in this respect, and particularly these days with many different approaches to pension reform under way. We need to collect data during the initial phases in order to predict the future better. Currently, we are not only ill-positioned to anticipate problems, we may also risk missing a golden opportunity to exploit the "European Laboratory".

## NOTES

1. Parametric reform steps within the PAYG system, particularly an increase in the retirement age, can go a long way in stabilising future contribution rates. Unlike the UK, however, they cannot absorb all the burden in the countries most affected by population ageing. Germany, for example, would need a shift of the average retirement age by 9.5 years in order to fully compensate the increase in the dependency ratio. See Börsch-Supan (2000).
2. Hence, we only look at the 85% of retirement income that is currently provided for by the first pillar (see Table 2.1). Details of this and related transition models can be found in Birg and Börsch-Supan (1999).
3. In this case, Germany has a partial offset rule which reduces total claims.
4. Administrating individual policies is more expensive. This is why we choose group policies that can be bundled by employers, as is done in the Netherlands or, in a slightly modified form, through the US 401(k) plans.
5. See Gruber and Wise (1999) for a comparable description of the Dutch, German and Italian pension systems.
6. Bernheim (1987a and b) first addressed this issue.
7. Macroeconomic superiority refers to a *de novo* system. Welfare superiority *including transition costs* requires additional effects over and above this capital accumulation, strengthening the necessity of *new* saving. See Börsch-Supan (1999), Breyer (2000) and Sinn (2000) for an exchange on this point.
8. The studies are based on long-run relationships between saving, growth and changes in public pension wealth.
9. See Kohl and O'Brien (1998) for a detailed survey.
10. See also Euwals (2000). The evidence based on cross-sectional data for the USA (Hubbard, 1986) and Canada (King and Dicks-Mireaux, 1982) is also rather mixed.
11. See Dilnot (1992), World Bank (1999) and Börsch-Supan and Lührmann (2000) on the variety of pension taxation rules in Europe and elsewhere.

## REFERENCES


ALESSIE R., and KAPTEYN A. (2001), "Household Savings in the Netherlands", *Research in Economics*, forthcoming.

ALESSIE R., KAPTEYN A. and KLIJN F. (1997), "Mandatory pensions and personal savings in the Netherlands", *De Economist*, 145, no. 3:291-324.

ATTANASIO O. and DE LEIRE T. (1994), "IRAS and household saving revisited: some new evidence", *NBER working paper* 4900.

ATTANASIO O. and BRUGIAVINI A. (1997), "L'effetto della Riforma Amato sul risparmio delle famiglie italiane", *Ricerche Quantitative per la Politica Economica-1995*, Banca d'Italia-CIDE (eds.), Rome.

ATTANASIO O., and BANKS J. (1998), "Trends in household saving don't justify tax incentives to boost saving", *Economic Policy*, October.

AUERBACH A.J. and KOTLIKOFF L.J. (1987), *Dynamic Fiscal Analysis*, Cambridge University Press, Cambridge, England.

AUERBACH A.J., KOTLIKOFF L.J., HAGEMANN R.G. and NICOLETTI G. (1989), "The Economic Dynamics of an Ageing Population: The Case of Four OECD Countries", *OECD Economic Studies*, No. 12.

BANKS J., BLUNDELL R. and TANNER S. (1998), "Is There a Retirement-Savings Puzzle?", *American Economic Review* 88(4):769-88.

BARRO R. J. (1974), "Are Government Bonds Net Wealth?", *Journal of Political Economy*, 82, 5:1095-117

BERNHEIM B. D. (1987a), "The Economic Effects of Social Security: Toward a Reconciliation of Theory and Measurement", *Journal of Public Economics*, 33:273-304.

BERNHEIM B. D. (1987b), "Dissaving After Retirement: Testing the Pure Life Cycle Hypothesis", in Bodie Z., Shoven J. and Wise D. (eds.), *Issue in Pension Economics*, NBER, The University of Chicago Press, Chicago.

BIRG H. and BÖRSCH-SUPAN A. (1999), *Für eine neue Aufgabenteilung zwischen gesetzlicher und privater Altersversorgung*, GDV, Berlin.

BOERI T., BÖRSCH-SUPAN A. and TABELLINI G. (2001), "Would you Like to Shrink the Welfare State? The Opinions of European Citizens", *Economic Policy*, 32, in press.

BÖRSCH-SUPAN A. (1992), "Saving and consumption patterns of the elderly: the German case", *Journal of Population Economics*, 5:289-303.

BÖRSCH-SUPAN A. (1994), "Savings in Germany - Part II: Behavior", in Poterba J. (ed.), *International Comparisons of Household Savings*, University of Chicago Press, Chicago and London, pp. 207-236.

BÖRSCH-SUPAN A. (1996), "The Impact of Population Ageing on Savings, Investment and Growth in the OECD Area", in OECD, *Future Global Capital Shortages: Real Threat or Pure Fiction?*, Paris, OECD, 103-141.

BÖRSCH-SUPAN A. (1999), "Zur deutschen Diskussion eines Übergangs vom Umlage- zum Kapitaldeckungsverfahren in der Gesetzlichen Rentenversicherung", in *Finanzarchiv*, 55 (3):400-428.

BÖRSCH-SUPAN A. (2000), "A Model under Siege: A Case Study of the Germany Retirement Insurance System", *The Economic Journal*, 110 (461):F24-45.

BÖRSCH-SUPAN A. (ed.) (2001a), *International Comparisons of Household Saving: A Study of Life-Cycle Savings in Seven Countries*, Academic Press, New York.

BÖRSCH-SUPAN A. (2001b), "The German Savings Puzzle", *Research in Economics*, 55, in press.

BÖRSCH-SUPAN A. and LÜHRMANN M. (2000), *Prinzipien der Renten- und Pensionsbesteuerung*, Frankfurter Institut, Bad Homburg.

BÖRSCH-SUPAN A. and STAHL K. (1991), "Life-cycle savings and consumption constraints", *Journal of Population Economics*, 4:233-255.

BÖRSCH-SUPAN A. and REIL-HELD A. (2001), "How much is Transfer and how much Insurance in a Pay-As-You-Go System? The German Case", *Scandinavian Journal of Economics*, in press.

BÖRSCH-SUPAN A. and WINTER J. K. (2001), "Population Aging, Savings Behavior and Capital Markets", Universität Mannheim, Sonderforschungsbereich, 504.

BÖRSCH-SUPAN A., HEISS F. and WINTER J. K. (2001), "Pension Reform, Capital Markets, and the Rate of Return", mimeo, University of Mannheim and Herbert-Giersch-Stiftung, Magdeburg.

BÖRSCH-SUPAN A., REIL-HELD A., RODEPETER R., SCHNABEL R. and WINTER J. (2001), "The German Saving Puzzle", *Research in Economics*, forthcoming.

BREYER F. (2000), "Kapitaldeckungs- versus Umlageverfahren", *Perspektiven der Wirtschaftspolitik*.

BRUGIAVINI A. (1987), "Empirical Evidence on Wealth Accumulation and the Effects of Pension Wealth: an Application to Italian Cross Section Data", *Financial Markets Group*, D. P. 20, LSE, London.

BRUGIAVINI A. and PADULA M. (2001), "Too much for Retirement? Saving in Italy", *Research in Economics*, forthcoming.

BRUGIAVINI A. and WEBER G. (2001), "Household Savings: Concepts and Measurement", in Börsch-Supan A. (ed.), *International Comparisons of Household Saving*, Academic Press, New York.

DILNOT A.W. (1992), "Taxation of Private Pensions: Costs and Consequences", in OECD, *Private Pensions and Public Policy*, OECD, Paris.

EUROPEAN COMMISSION (2000), *The Contribution of Public Finances to Growth and Employment: Improving Quality and Sustainability*, Communication from the European Commission to the Council and the European Parliament.

EUWALS R. (2000), "Do Mandatory Pensions Decrease Household Savings: Evidence for the Netherlands", *De Economist*, 148:643-670.

FELDSTEIN M. (1974), "Social Security, Induced Retirement and Aggregate Capital Accumulation", *Journal of Political Economy*, 82 (5):905-926.

GALE W. J. and SCHOLZ J. K. (1994), "IRAs and household saving", *American Economic Review*, 84:1233-1260.

GRUBER J. and WISE D. (eds.) (1999), *Social Security and Retirement Around the World*, The University of Chicago Press, Chicago.

HELLER P. (1989), "Aging, Savings and the Sustainability of the Fiscal Burden in the G7-countries: 1980-2025", IMF.

HUBBARD R.G. (1986), "Pension wealth and individual saving, some new evidence", *Journal of Money Credit and Banking*, 18:167-178.

JAPPELLI T. (1995), "Does social security wealth reduce the accumulation of private wealth? Evidence from Italian survey data", *Ricerche Economiche*, 49:1-31.

JAPPELLI T. and MODIGLIANI F. (1998), "The Age-Saving Profile and the Life-Cycle Hypothesis", CSEF Working Paper No. 4, University of Salerno.

KAPTEYN A., ALESSIE R. and LUSARDI A. (1999), "Explaining the wealth holdings of different cohorts: productivity growth and social security", mimeo, Tinbergen Institute.

KING M. and DICKS-MIREAUX L. (1982), "Asset Holding and the Life Cycle", *Economic Journal*, 92.

KOHL R. and O'BRIEN P. (1998), *The Macroeconomics of Ageing, Pensions and Savings: A Survey*, OECD Working Paper AWP1.1, Paris.

MODIGLIANI F. and BRUMBERG R. (1954), "Utility Analysis and the Consumption Function: An Interpretation of Cross-section Data", in Kurihara K. (ed.), *Post-Keynesian Economics*, Rutgers University Press, New Brunswick, NJ.

NATIONAL ACADEMY OF SCIENCES (NAS, 2001), *A Research Agenda and New Data for An Aging World*, forthcoming.

ROSSI N. and VISCO I. (1994), "Private Saving and the Government Deficit in Italy", in Ando A., Guiso L. and Visco I. (eds.), *Saving and the Accumulation of Wealth*, Cambridge University Press, Cambridge.

SINN H. W. (2000), "Why to Fund and Why Not to Fund", mimeo, CES, Munich.

SKINNER J. and HUBBARD R. G. (1996), "Assessing the Effectiveness of Saving Incentives", *Journal of Economic Perspectives*,10(4):73-90.

VENTI S. and WISE D. (1990), "Have IRAS increased U.S. Savings? Evidence from consumer expenditure surveys", *Quarterly Journal of Economics*, 105:661-98.

WORLD BANK (1999), "The Tax Treatment of Funded Pensions", *World Bank Pension Reform Primer*, 2.3, Washington, D.C.

JAMES Y. NAZROO AND MICHAEL G. MARMOT

# HEALTH AND SOCIAL WELFARE IMPLICATIONS OF AN AGEING POPULATION: WHAT ARE THE UNCERTAINTIES?

## 1. INTRODUCTION

The rapid increase in life expectancy over the last century, as well as the 'demographic shift', has led to concerns about dependency ratios, population trends in disability, and the impact of these on the use of health and social services. Beyond the older age profile of populations in Europe, central elements of the contemporary demographic shift in industrialised countries are changes in family formation and household structure, increasing labour force participation among women, and decreasing labour force participation among older workers (as described by Boeri, Brugiavini and Maignan in this volume). These changes appear to be resulting in significant decreases in the level of informal care, received from relatives and friends, and, coupled with an ageing and possibly more dependent population, consequent greater dependency on formal, state-funded, care – for example long term care and help at home. So, in addition to concerns over the provision of state pensions, there are major concerns about the sustainability of government funded health and social services, and the economic impact of increasing demand on these services as the population ages (Hurd 1998, Townsend 1981, Walker 1981).

However, a focus on the dependency ratio can easily lead to a premise that ageing represents an undifferentiated experience of increasing physical and financial dependency. This ignores growing evidence that the ageing process cannot be so easily demarcated. The equation of old age with either a specific biological age or a statutory social or economic transition, such as the age at which an individual becomes eligible for a state retirement pension, is no longer adequate. For example, not only are large numbers of people choosing to retire at earlier ages, but the gradual phasing of redundancy into retirement has lessened the impact of what was once a phenomenon of mass retirement at statutory ages (Disney 1996). Likewise, the impact on morbidity of an increasing life expectancy depends on both the rate of change of the incidence of disabling conditions and the rate of survival with such conditions. While there has been some controversy surrounding the evidence on this, for example the debate about the compression of morbidity (Fries 1980, Fries and Crapo 1981, Fries 1989), to which we will shortly return, it is possible that there is a



*T.Boeri, A.Börsch-Supan, A.Brugiavini, R.Disney, A.Kapteyn and F.Peracchi (eds.), Pensions: More Information, Less Ideology, 137—152.*

reduction of disability over time (Bebbington 1991, Manton *et al.* 1997, Singer and Manton 1998, Waidmann and Manton 1998). This evidence, coupled with evidence on the relative affluence of some of those in retirement, has led to the recognition that some older people could be living in what has been called a 'third age' – a period of self-fulfilment, rather than physical decline, starting at the point that the individual relinquishes work and parenting roles (Laslett 1989, The Carnegie Inquiry 1992). While the 'third age' may be a newly-identified phenomenon in Europe, its central components are familiar in the US where there has been extensive discussion of 'successful ageing', a closely related concept (Rowe and Kahn 1987 and 1998).

In this chapter we will discuss the evidence on changes in life expectancy and levels of disability. We will examine variations in levels of disability and life expectancy across Europe, and the implications of these, and relate these population level data to inequalities within populations in life expectancy and rates of disability. We will discuss the implications of this for a conceptualisation of older ages as a third age, made up of self-realised active consumers, or a fourth age, made up of those who are truly dependent.

## 2. CHANGES IN LIFE EXPECTANCY

The large increase in life expectancy across Europe during the last century has been documented extensively (see also Anderson, Tuljapurkar and Li in this volume). As the progressive rectangularisation of the survival curves in Figure 1 shows, underlying this increase in life expectancy are dramatic shifts in age specific mortality rates at particular points of the life course. Of course, the observation that there is an association between age and risk of dying is a truism (although this was first systematically observed as recently as the 19th century by the actuary Gompertz – see Shroots and Birren 1993). Nevertheless, the risk of mortality can be characterised by three phases. A rapid decrease in risk during early childhood, which is followed by a slow increase during early adulthood and middle adulthood, with the final phase being an exponential increase in the death rate at older ages. In most countries, this final phase is characterised by a doubling in death rates every eight years. And it is the increase over time in the age at which this phase begins, together with a reduction in mortality rates during infancy, that underlies the rectangularisation of the survival curves shown in Figure 1.

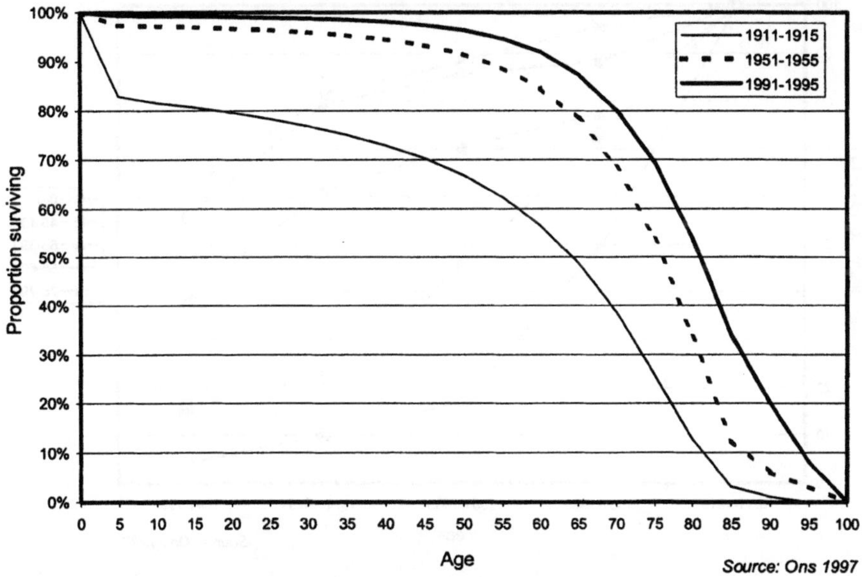


*Figure 1. Patterns of survival for females born in the UK*

This shift in the survival curve in part reflects a shift in the main causes of mortality from infectious diseases to chronic degenerative diseases, as a consequence of population level improvements in nutrition and public health measures, such as the construction of safe water supplies and sewerage systems. As recent World Health Organisation discussions show (e.g. WHO 2000), current improvements in mortality would depend on reductions in cardiovascular disease (including hypertension, ischaemic heart disease and stroke), chronic obstructive airways disease, diabetes and cancers. However, the implication of the above, that we have seen rapid declines in mortality rates in childhood and early to mid adulthood, with only small declines at older ages, is only true of the first half of the 20th century. This is illustrated in Figures 2 and 3, which show for the UK the change over time in mortality rates at specific ages relative to the period 1911-1915 (arbitrarily set at 100). While in earlier years the decline in mortality rates was much steeper for children and young adults, in the period 1951 to 1995 the relative rate of decline for these age groups had decreased, while that for all of the older age groups has continued to increase sharply.

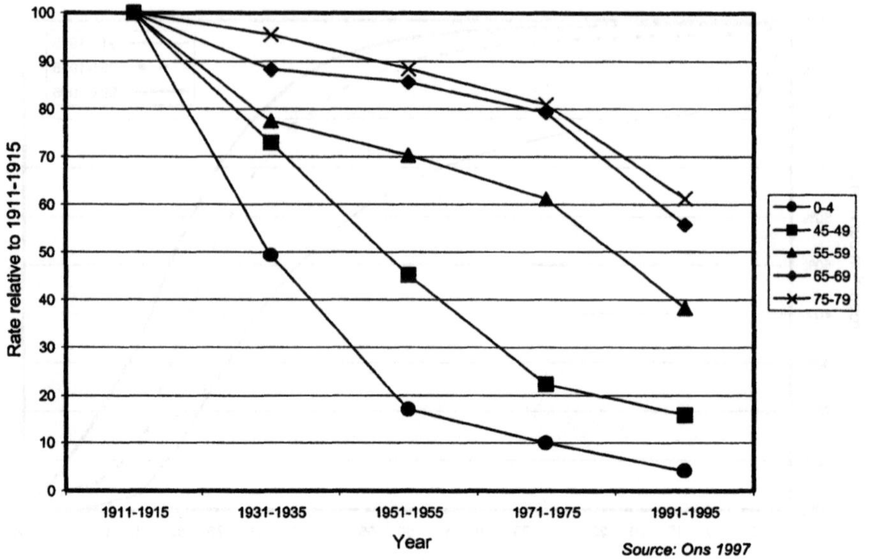


*Figure 2. Changes in age-specific relative mortality rates in the UK – men*

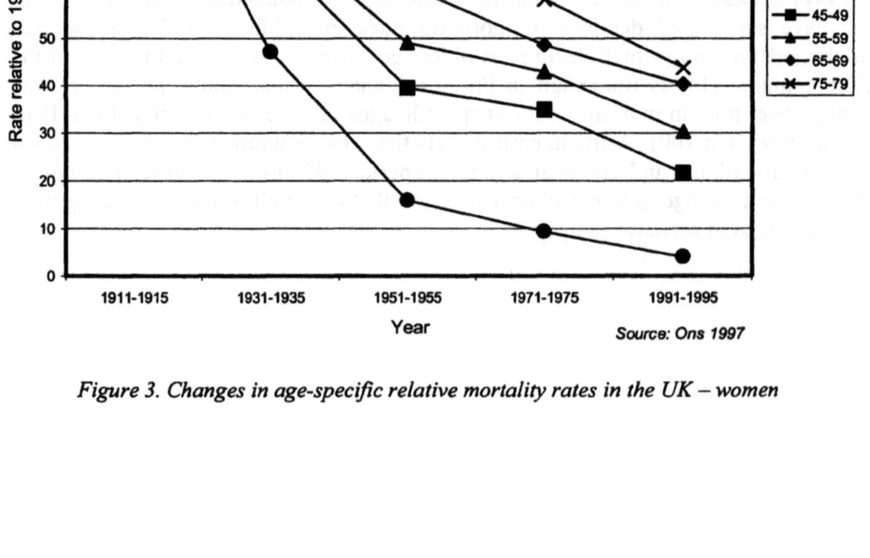


*Figure 3. Changes in age-specific relative mortality rates in the UK – women*

One can only speculate about this shift in decline in mortality rates across the life-course: it could be a consequence of recent improvements in health technologies that are having an impact on the older population, or it could be that those generations who benefited from improvements in nutrition and public health in the early parts of the 20th century are now continuing to reap the benefits at older ages, a possible 'health capital' effect. Without longitudinal data it is difficult to progress our understanding of this, and there are important implications. The former explanation suggests significant illness and disability, and the need for investment in health and social care, while the later suggests a healthy older population. The relationship between mortality and morbidity is a theme that we will return to later.

## 3. VARIATIONS IN LIFE EXPECTANCY ACROSS EUROPE

Given the increasing rectangularisation of survival curves in Europe (shown for women in the UK in Figure 1), it might be expected that there would be little variation in life expectancy across European countries. Figures 4 and 5 show relative life expectancy by age across eight European countries, compared with the European average (arbitrarily set at the value of 100). Both figures show an increasing variation in relative life expectancy with age. Differences at birth are relatively small compared with those at ages 65 and older. Although there is widening of the gap between countries at younger ages, the gap seems to widen particularly from middle age. Interestingly, for both men and women at older ages the same four countries have a better (France, Sweden, Spain and Italy) and worse (Denmark, UK, Germany and Holland) life expectancy than average. And across the age spectrum there is little movement across the line marking the average rate (i.e. from a worse than average to better than average life expectancy, or *vice-versa*). Importantly, given that life expectancy is rapidly increasing across European countries, this suggests country-specific contexts that have influenced the rate of increase, particularly at older ages.

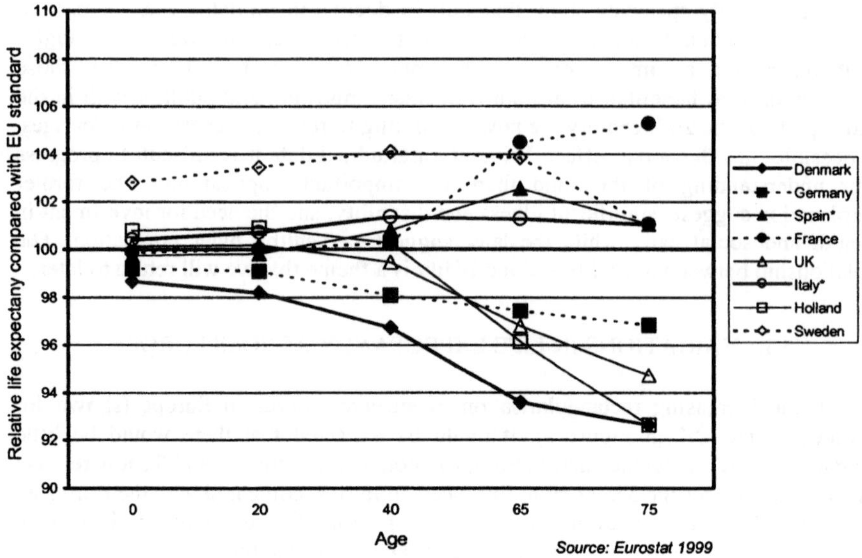


*Figure 4. Relative life expectancy by age – men*

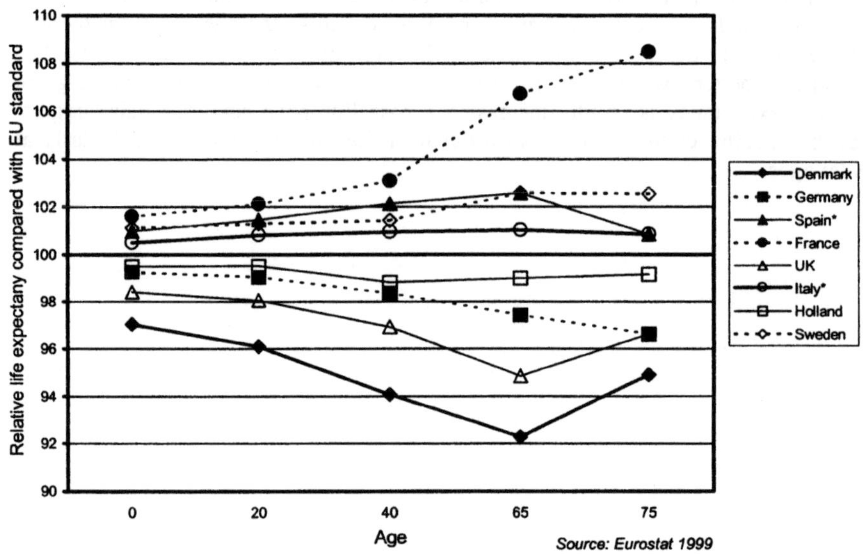


*Figure 5. Relative life expectancy by age – women*

## 4. MORBIDITY AND DISABILITY

Of course, the mortality data presented in survival and life expectancy figures only partly reflect underlying health and morbidity. An examination of health at older ages must cover chronic illnesses that are not necessarily fatal, such as arthritis, falls and fractures, visual and hearing impairments, mental illness and cognitive function. As we described in the introduction, it is the possibility that increasing life expectancy will result in increasing numbers of older, frail and dependant people, who will require state provided health and social services, that is a central policy concern (particularly as changes in household structures and working patterns mean that younger people will be less willing and less able to provide the care themselves). In fact, there are three possible scenarios relating to the relationship between the rectangularisation of the survival curve and underlying morbidity. First, levels of morbidity could also fall, but more slowly than those for mortality rates, resulting in both an absolute and a relative increase in the number of older people with poor health. Second they could fall at a similar rate, resulting in an absolute increase in older people with poor health, but no proportionate increase. And third, they could fall more rapidly, resulting in an older, but more healthy, population.

The final scenario relates to the compression of morbidity hypothesis, developed by Fries (1980 and 1989) and Fries and Crapo (1981). This has been the subject of much debate, with some cross-sectional data supporting this possibility (Bebbington 1991, Manton *et al.* 1997, Singer and Manton 1998, Waidmann and Manton 1998). For example, Figure 6 shows data from work by Manton *et al.* (1997), charting actual and projected absolute numbers of disabled Americans aged 65 or more. Starting from the assumption that the disability rate remains constant (scenario two above) one line in the chart shows the rapid rise in the actual number of disabled Americans. The second line, based on actual falls in the proportion of disabled Americans aged 65 or more, and projected to 1996, shows an initial rise in the number of disabled people, with a subsequent plateauing, reflecting a fall in the proportion disabled. The implication is clear, if health is improving alongside mortality rates, i.e. if we are seeing a compression of morbidity, implications for health and social welfare costs are very different than those that might occur if disability rates did not fall. However, without longitudinal data it is impossible to do more than speculate on changing patterns of disability and the causal factors that might underlie cross-sectional shifts.

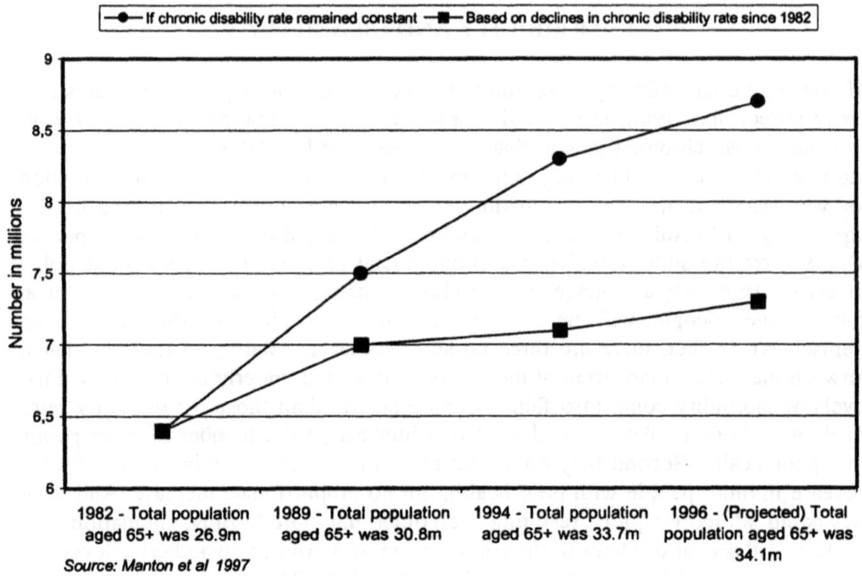


*Figure 6. Number of chronically disabled Americans aged 65 plus*

Indeed, the shortage of data with which we can explore patterns of disability and how they vary across countries, time, generation and age, greatly hampers any attempt to predict future use of services, levels of disability and dependency, let alone the factors that might increase disability-free life expectancy. Figure 7 gives an indication of the kinds of data that we have available. It shows self-reported levels of any and severe disability for the adult population in six of the eight European countries shown in earlier figures (there are no comparable data for Holland and Sweden). Again the rates are expressed as a relative risk standardised to the European average (arbitrarily set at 100). The figure shows a large variation in rates of disability across the countries reported, that for some countries the relative rates for any and severe disability are inconsistent (Germany, France and the UK), and that for some countries the reported relative levels of disability are not consistent with the relative life expectancy data shown earlier. For example, Figure 7 suggests that Denmark has low rates of both any and severe disability and the UK has low rates of severe disability, while the life expectancy data shown in Figures 4 and 5, demonstrated high rates of mortality in both Denmark and the UK. It is likely that such inconsistencies are at least partly a consequence of the poor measures of disability that we currently have available.

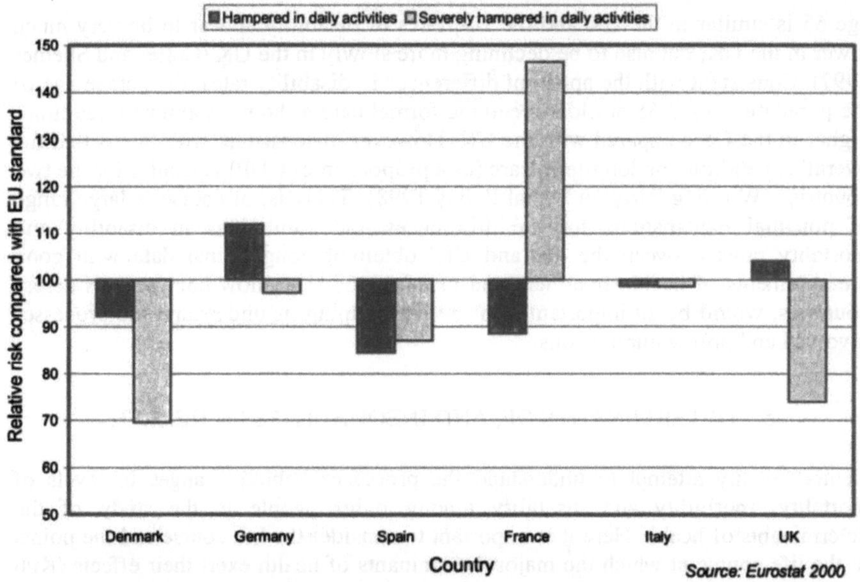


*Figure 7. Level of disability, men and women aged 16 or older*

A more useful framework than self-reported data within which to tackle both the assessment of disability and changes in levels of disability is the US Institute of Medicine model of disability. This argues that disability is a consequence of the ecological gap between individual functional ability and environmental demands (Waidmann and Manton 1998). For example, the drop in levels of disability that has been reported in the US (Manton *et al.* 1997, Singer and Manton 1998), could be a consequence of declines in the prevalence of functional impairment, or the result of interventions that modify the experience of the environment. Indeed, it has been suggested that the drop in disability in the US is a consequence of both the adoption of healthy lifestyles, which have reduced impairment, and the rational implementation of health care interventions, which have reduced the impact of impairment (Singer and Manton 1998), and they could, of course, also be a consequence of environmental modifications that have reduced environmental demands. If we are to understand more about the impact of disability on both individuals and the community, it will be important to obtain data on the development and extent of functional impairment in individuals, the sources of their functional impairment, and the treatments and environmental modifications that reduce the disabling impact of any impairment. This requires longitudinal data sources that contain a combination of: direct measures of functional impairment, reports of impairment, assessment of the environment and evaluation of treatment.

Of course, if such data were available it would be possible to draw comparisons across countries, which would give important insights on contextual effects that may influence levels of impairment and disability. For example, while life expectancy at age 65 is similar in the UK and the US, rates of disability appear to be very much lower in the UK, but also to be declining more slowly in the UK (Cutler and Sheiner 1997). Consistent with the apparent differences in disability rates, the percentage of the population aged 65 or older receiving formal care at home is almost three times higher in the US compared with the UK. However, inconsistent with this is that the overall expenditure on long-term care (as a proportion of GDP) is similar for the two countries (Working Party on Social Policy 1998). There is, of course, a large range of potential explanations for the differences and similarities in disability and mortality rates between the US and UK, obtaining longitudinal data with good measurements of health, treatment and context, and that allow comparisons across countries, would be an important step towards helping us understand the processes involved and policy implications.

## 5. DETERMINANTS OF, AND INEQUALITIES IN, HEALTH

Central to any attempt to understand the processes behind changes in levels of mortality, morbidity and disability among older people is the study of the determinants of health. Here it is important to consider the life course and the points in the life course at which the major determinants of health exert their effects (Kuh and Ben-Shlomo 1997). As the earlier discussion of the possible interpretations of Figures 2 and 3 suggested, here we need to explore whether circumstances currently impinging on the elderly, or whether circumstances from earlier in life are more important determinants of health status. In practice, of course, there will be interactions between early and current factors. Research on the British birth cohorts and the Whitehall II study have led to the identification of at least three models of the relation between earlier life influences and health in older adults. First, a latency effect, whereby exposures early in life have later effects. This fits with the series of studies conducted by Barker (1995), but can only be directly explored using appropriate information from early life. Second, later health could be a consequence of the accumulation of advantage and disadvantage throughout the life course (Power and Hertzman 1997) a possibility that can be explored by examining social and economic conditions, changes in these through the life course and subsequent health outcomes (Brunner *et al.* 1998). Third is the pathway model, which suggests that there is no direct effect of social circumstances from earlier life on health in later life, but that such circumstances determine the social and economic position that a person reaches in later life, and it is the factors attendant on this contemporary position, acting concurrently, that affect health (Marmot *et al.* 2001). All three possibilities suggest the need for complex longitudinal studies of individuals.

We have already pointed to differences in health outcomes across countries, and introduced the need to examine variations in outcomes within the older population. In particular, how health outcomes, and the underlying causal pathways, might vary according to economic position and social status would be relevant to any investigation of health and mortality among the older population. Although economic position and health have been shown to be related over the long-term (Drever and Whitehead 1997, Independent Inquiry into Inequalities in Health 1998), much of the research has been conducted using studies of younger populations (typically those below statutory retirement age). Indeed, socioeconomic differences in health status are sometimes thought to diminish with age, perhaps as a result of selective survival of the 'fittest' (Arber and Ginn 1993). The evidence, however, suggests continuing and, possibly, increasingly large socioeconomic inequalities in self-reported health and mortality into older ages, even at those ages where rates of morbidity and mortality are very high (Marmot and Shipley 1996, Grundy *et al.* 1997, Breeze *et al.* 1999). Such studies have shown that as people move into, through and past retirement, inequalities in health continue. However, the full nature of the social, psychological and biological causal links between social and economic position and health are still to be established (Kaplan *et al.* 1996, Wilkinson 1996, Kawachi *et al.* 1997, Independent Inquiry into Inequalities in Health 1998). Here studies of the older population will yield important insights. For example, the period around retirement provides a point at which we can begin to measure how changing physical and psychological health interacts with transitions in social and economic position.

The investigation of endogenous economic position effects for older people is clearly crucial, not least because such effects have been found in the US (Smith 1999). For example, decreasing functional ability and cognitive functioning pre-retirement may be related to job changes, part-time working and early retirement. But the situation is unlikely to be straightforward, such changes in economic activity may be more likely to occur to those who are in particular occupational positions. And in an examination of the relationship between economic position and health, it will be important to have data that allow for a comparison of the impact of the different policy contexts across Europe. For example, the costs of a 'health shock' and the extent of welfare available following a deterioration in health differ greatly across countries. Similarly, the relationship between decreasing economic resources and deteriorating health may be a consequence of falling economic resources as a direct cost of poor health, or a consequence of spending down alongside deteriorating health in anticipation of increasing dependency. And the relationship will be mediated by factors such as the extent and cost of state-provided health and social welfare. The nature of state support (with safety nets set at particular levels of wealth or income) might both promote spending down, leading to a deterioration in economic position, and/or might protect against economic hardship among those with less wealth and poor and deteriorating health. Similarly, for those with poor or deteriorating health, the existence of a social network of support might protect against economic hardship directly (through the provision of economic support), or indirectly (through the provision of services). Central to this, therefore, is the possibility that social position mediates the relationship between health and economic position – those in particular occupations may be protected from health-related downward social mobility, those who are married may have less incentive to spend down and a lower dependency on formal health care, and those who have good social support may receive economic support and care improving their ability to protect their economic position.

## 6. MOVING BEYOND HEALTH

We have outlined the evidence suggesting that social and economic position is an important predictor of adverse health outcomes at older ages. But there is also an accumulating body of evidence suggesting that past social and economic position is also relevant to other outcomes at older ages, such as social participation and movement into institutional care. So, while only a minority of older people move into institutional care at older ages, this risk has increased substantially over time (and the proportion of older people moving to live with relatives has declined) – estimates for the UK suggest that the risk of moving into an institution increased by over a third between 1981 and 1991 (Grundy *et al.* 1997, Grundy and Glaser 1997). Although the increase in the number of older people living in institutions is likely to partly reflect increased availability of places, the risk of moving into an institution is not uniform across the population. Women, those who are single (particularly those who have never married), those who are tenants rather than owner-occupiers, those who are in lower economic positions, and those who appear to have suffered downward economic mobility, are far more likely to move into an institution (Vicente *et al.* 1979, Branch and Jette 1982, Grundy 1992, Grundy *et al.* 1997, Breeze *et al.* 1999). Interestingly, the relationship between prior self-perceived health and a subsequent move into an institution for older people is less clear (Branch and Jette 1982). That those who are in the least privileged economic positions have the greatest risk of moving into an institution (as they do for poor health and mortality) is a cause for concern. Those with the least resources will be consuming the most health and social care, with a consequent large personal economic burden, some of which will be transferred to the state.

Of course, older people have traditionally been viewed as passive and grateful recipients of state-provided health and social services (Breemhar *et al.* 1990), rather than as consumers making choices about the services they wish to purchase. Central to this is a conception of older people as dependent, perhaps as a consequence of their position within social structures, a conceptualisation that is in contrast to more recent approaches informed by the theory of the third age (Laslett 1989). In part, the third age approach reflects the growing economic wellbeing of and consumption by older people (Gilleard and Higgs 1998), portraying later life as a period of self-fulfilment where individuals are freed to plan their lives and pursue their plans – the 'crown of life' (Laslett 1989). Such a position can, however, only be realised from a position of relative wealth and good health, and theories of the third age (and the US equivalent, successful ageing) do not fully acknowledge the extent of economic and health inequality among older people (Bury 1995). The position of people in a 'fourth' age, with chronic illness, few economic and social resources, and using scarce and targeted state-provided services, is a sharp contrast to that of third age consumers.

Within the contemporary economic context, the provision of health and social care has involved a shift from an ideology of universal state provision to one of individual (and family) responsibility for the provision of care. Individuals can, in theory, afford this because of increasing accessibility to private health insurance and returns from investments in pension funds and other forms of financial planning. So, a growing number of people in the third age have a choice-based alternative to an uncertain, dependent, future relying on state funded care (Gilleard and Higgs 1998). Indeed, the shift in emphasis from universal provision to more limited targeted support may in part have been a consequence of a desire to see services organised in a way that allowed them to be responsive to individual, consumer, choices. But, in such a situation, those in less advantaged situations in the consumer market may find themselves placed at considerable disadvantage compared with those who are better off. Without the financial and health resources to consume, they are left to rely on more basic, targeted, levels of care, and to support their receipt of care with whatever wealth they still possess.

Such possibilities raise a number of crucial questions about quality of life in older ages, the extent to which older people might actively participate in consumption, and implications for the provision and cost of health and social care. And, importantly, how, as for health, social inequalities at older ages might be related to economic and social position throughout the life course. But they remain questions that cannot be adequately addressed without longitudinal data, and comparisons across a number of countries will allow an exploration and evaluation of the impact of national policies.

## 7. CONCLUSION

To summarise, we have seen a progressive increase in life expectancy, which in the first half of the 20th century was largely due to declines in mortality rates in childhood, but more recently has been equally driven by declines in mortality rates among older people (see Figures 2 and 3). Accompanying this have been declines in labour force participation among older workers – leading to concerns about increasing dependency ratios – and changes in family formation and household structure and increasing labour force participation among women – leading to concerns about possible drops in levels of informal care and greater dependency on state or privately-funded formal care.

On the other hand, there remains great uncertainty about the extent to which an increasing proportion of older people will result in greater numbers of disabled, or dependent, older people. In particular, there has been considerable debate about the possibility that increasing life expectancy is associated with reductions in morbidity among older people, with the compression of morbidity hypothesis suggesting that the older population may be becoming healthier (and wealthier) and consequently less dependant. We may be seeing a redefinition of old age as a third age of wellbeing and self-fulfilment (Laslett 1989).

Associated with this possibility, and general increases in life expectancy, is the observation that not all sections of the population are equally benefiting from improvements in health and associated financial and social wellbeing. Figures 4 and 5 show differences in life expectancy across Europe, and how these differences increase with age. And socio-economic inequalities in health within national populations have been consistently documented for some time. What is less clear is whether socio-economic inequalities increase or decrease with age, how far they are a consequence of early or accumulated economic and social disadvantage, or how far they are a consequence of (or contribute to) contemporary socio-economic disadvantage.

Addressing such questions is far from straightforward using currently available data sources. Longitudinal studies are vital to understanding ageing processes. Such studies will enable the separation of age and cohort effects and the investigation of health, social and economic trajectories. From the point of view of health outcomes, longitudinal data are essential to identify risk factors for downward health trajectories, and the factors and interventions that mitigate downward trajectories and that may be associated with a compression of morbidity. And such data will give us a greater opportunity to understand the processes involved in determining socio-economic inequalities in health, helping us to identify causal directions and endogenous effects (Smith 1999).

However, the greatest benefit will undoubtedly come from investing in longitudinal studies that will allow cross-national comparisons. Such a strategy will both expand the variation of outcomes to be investigated, and allow a comparison of the effect of varying institutional systems. One can evaluate what common outcomes and effects emerge despite differences in systems and investigate how systems modify outcomes. Cross-national comparisons offer extended possibilities for the evaluation of institutional effects and policy reforms, a need that the debate around the importance of relative deprivation to health inequalities has illustrated (Wilkinson 1996).

## REFERENCES


ARBER S., GINN J. (1993), "Gender and inequalities in health in later life", *Social Science and Medicine*, 36:33-46.

BARKER D. J. (1995), "Foetal origins of coronary heart disease", *British Medical Journal*, 311:171-174.

BEBBINGTON A. (1991), "The expectation of life without disability in England and Wales", *Population Trends*, 66:26-29.

BRANCH L. G., JETTE A. M. (1982), "A prospective study of long-term-care institutionalization among the aged", *American Journal of Public Health*, 72:1373-9.

BREEMHAAR B., VISSER A. and KLEIJEN J. G. (1990), "Perceptions and behaviour among elderly hospital patients: description and explanation of age differences in satisfaction knowledge, emotions, and behaviour", *Social science and Medicine*, 31:1377-85.

BREEZE E., SLOGGETT A., and FLETCHER A. (1999), "Socioeconomic and demographic predictors of mortality and institutional residence among middle aged and older people: results from the Longitudinal Study", *Journal of Epidemiology and Community Health*, 53:765-774.

BRUNNER E. J., SHIPLEY M. J., BLANE D., DAVEY SMITH G., MARMOT M. G. (1998), "Past and present socioeconomic circumstances and cardiovascular risk factors in adulthood", *Journal of Epidemiology and Community Health*.

BURY M. (1995), "Ageing, gender and sociological theory" in Arber S. and Ginn J. (eds.) *Connecting Gender and Ageing*, Open University Press, Buckingham.

CUTLER D. M., and SHEINER L. (1997), "Demographics and Medical Care Spending: Standard and Non-Standard Effects", paper delivered at the Conference on Demographic Change and Fiscal Policy, October.

DISNEY R. (1996), "Can we afford to grow older?", in Juster F. T., Smith J. P., and Stafford F. (eds) *The Measurement and Structure of Household Wealth*, MIT Press, Cambridge Mass.

DREVER F, WHITEHEAD M. (1997), *Health Inequalities: Decennial Supplement*, Series DS No.15:1-257.
EUROSTAT (1999), *Demographic Statistics.*
EUROSTAT (2000), *A Statistical Eye on Europe.*
FRIES J. F. and GRAPO L. M. (1981), *Vitality and Aging*, Freeman, San Francisco.
FRIES J. F. (1980), "Aging, Natural Death, and the Compression of Morbidity", *New England Journal of Medicine*, 303:130-135.
FRIES J. F. (1989), "The Compression of Morbidity: Near or Far?", *The Millbank Quarterly*, 67, 2:208-232.
GILLEARD C. and HIGGS P. (1998), "Old people as users and consumers of healthcare: a third age rhetoric for a fourth age reality?", *Ageing and Society*, 18:233-248.
GRUNDY E. (1992), "Socio-Demographic variations in rates of movement into institutions among elderly people in England and Wales: An analysis of linked census and mortality data 1971-1985", *Population Studies*, 46:65-84.
GRUNDY E. and GLASER K. (1997), "Trends in, and transitions to, institutional residence among older people in England and Wales, 1971-1991", *Journal of Epidemiology and Community Health*, 51: 531-40.
HURD M. (1998), "Symposium on Assets, Incomes and Retirement", *Fiscal Studies*, 19, 2:141-151.
*Independent Inquiry into Inequalities in Health Report*, The Stationary Office, London, 1998.
KAPLAN G. A., PAMUK E. R., LYNCH J. W., COHEN R. D. and BALFOUR J. L. (1996), "Inequality in income and mortality in the United States: analysis of mortality and potential pathways", *British Medical Journal*, 312:999-1003.
KAWACHI I., KENNEDY B. P., LOCHNER K. and PROTHROW-STITH D. (1997), "Social capital, income inequality, and mortality", *American Journal of Public Health*, 87:1491-1498.
KUH D. and BEN-SHLOMO Y. (1997), *A Life Course Approach to Chronic Disease Epidemiology*, Oxford University Press, Oxford.
LASLETT P. (1989), *A Fresh Map of Life*, Weidenfield and Nicholson, London.
MANTON K. G., CORDER L. and STALLARD, E. (1997), "Chronic disability trends in elderly United States populations: 1928-1994", *Proceedings of the National Academy of Science Medical Sciences*, 94:2593-2598.
MARMOT M., SHIPLEY M., BRUNNER E. and HEMINGWAY H. (2001), "Relative contribution of early life and socioeconomic factors to adult morbidity in the Whitehall II study", *Journal of Epidemiology and Community Health*, 55:301-307.
MARMOT M. and SHIPLEY M. (1996), "Do socioeconomic differences in mortality persist after retirement? 25 year follow-up of civil servants from the Whitehall Study", *British Medical Journal*, 313:1177-80.
*OPCS Mortality Statistics*, General Series DH1 no. 28, HMSO, London,1997.
POWER C. and HERTZMAN C. (1997), "Social and biological pathways linking early life and adult disease", *British Medical Bulletin*, 53:210-221.
ROWE J. W. and KAHN R. L. (1987), "Human ageing: usual and successful", *Science*, 237:143-149.
ROWE J. W. and KAHN R.L. (1998), *Successful Aging*, Pantheon, New York.
SCHROOTS J. J. F. and BIRREN J. E. (1993), "Theoretical issues and basic questions in the planning of longitudinal studies of health and aging", in Schroots J.J.F. (ed.), *Aging, Health and Competence*, Elsevier Science Publishers.
SINGER B.H. and MANTON K. G. (1998), "The effects of health changes on projections of health service needs for the elderly population of the United States", *Proceedings of the National Academy of Science*, 95:15618-15622.
SMITH J. P. (1999), "Healthy Bodies and Thick Wallets", *Journal of Economic Perspectives*, Spring.
THE CARNEGIE INQUIRY INTO THE THIRD AGE. *Life work and livelihood in the Third Age*, 1992 (Abstract).
TOWNSEND P. (1981), "The Structured Dependency of the Elderly", *Ageing and Society*, 1:5-28.
VICENTE L., WILEY J. A. and CARRINGTON R. A. (1979), "The risk of institutionalization before death", *Gerontologist*,19:361-7.
WAIDMANN T. A. and MANTON K. G. (1998), "International Evidence on Disability Trends among the elderly", US department of Health and Human Services (Abstract).
WALKER A. (1981), "Towards a Political Economy of Old Age", *Ageing and Society*, 1:73-94.

WORLD HEALTH ORGANISATION (2000), "Global strategy for the prevention and control of noncommunicable diseases", A53/14, WHO, 22nd March.
WILKINSON R. G. (1996), *Unhealthy Societies: the Afflictions of Inequality*, Routledge, London.
WORKING PARTY ON SOCIAL POLICY. "The health of older persons in OECD countries: Is it improving fast enough to compensate for population ageing?", Directorate for Education, Employment, Labour and Social Affairs, Employment, Labour and Social Affairs Committee, 17th Meeting October 1998, Paris.

CHETI NICOLETTI AND FRANCO PERACCHI

# AGEING IN EUROPE: WHAT CAN WE LEARN FROM THE EUROPANEL?

## 1. INTRODUCTION

This paper describes what the European Community Household Panel (ECHP) can tell us about health status, labour force behaviour, income and wealth of the elderly across the European Union (EU). Information of this kind is very important for public policy given the rapidly increasing share of the elderly in the European population.

The ECHP is a standardised annual longitudinal survey carried out throughout the EU. Its main purpose is to collect comparable information on demographic characteristics, income (especially earnings and public transfers), labour force behaviour (including job search activities), health, education and professional training, housing, migration and geographical mobility, at both the household and the personal level.

The paper exploits the high level of comparability of the survey across countries, and is close in spirit to the first part of the country studies in the volume edited by Gruber and Wise (1998). The novelties are the use of a comparable data source with a longitudinal dimension, and the inclusion of information on health status, home ownership and ownership of durables.

The remainder of this paper is organised as follows. Section 2 describes the data and some of their problems. Section 3 compares the European countries using the evidence provided by the ECHP on some basic trends associated with ageing. The next four sections focus on health status (Section 4), labour market activity (Section 5), income (Section 6) and wealth (Section 7). Finally, Section 8 offers some conclusions.

## 2. THE DATA

This paper uses the anonymised microdata from the first three waves of the ECHP. After a brief description of the survey, we discuss a number of issues that ought to be taken into account when analysing the sample evidence, namely the types of response patterns, construction of the survey weights and representation of the target



*T.Boeri, A.Börsch-Supan, A.Brugiavini, R.Disney, A.Kapteyn and F.Peracchi (eds.), Pensions: More Information, Less Ideology, 153—187.*

population, item nonresponse and income imputation, and the anonymisation criteria adopted by Eurostat.[1]

*2.1. Brief description of the ECHP*

The target population of the ECHP consists of all individuals living in private households within the EU. In its first wave (1994), the ECHP covered about 60,000 households and 130,000 individuals in 12 countries of the EU (Belgium, Denmark, France, Germany, Greece, Ireland, Italy, Luxembourg, the Netherlands, Portugal, Spain and the UK). Austria, Finland and Sweden began to participate in the ECHP later, respectively from the second, third and fourth wave. Table 1 presents, for each country, the achieved sample size in the first three waves.[2] The table also presents additional detail for two age groups, those aged 50-69 and those aged 70 or older (70+), which represent the focus of this paper. The largest sample size is for Italy and Spain, the smallest for Luxembourg and Denmark. The wide variation across countries reflects both differences in the planned sample size in the first wave and differential nonresponse and attrition rates across waves. As the table makes clear, the loss of sample units has been substantial in some countries, especially Ireland and the UK.

*Table 1. Achieved sample size by age group in the first 3 waves of the ECHP.*

| | 1994 | | | 1995 | | | 1996 | | |
|---|---|---|---|---|---|---|---|---|---|
| | 50-69 | 70+ | Total | 50-69 | 70+ | Total | 50-69 | 70+ | Total |
| Austria | | | | 2066 | 859 | 7436 | 2025 | 838 | 7269 |
| Belgium | 1666 | 815 | 6710 | 1578 | 800 | 6456 | 1498 | 787 | 6151 |
| Denmark | 1523 | 775 | 5903 | 1406 | 672 | 5503 | 1273 | 612 | 4994 |
| Finland | | | | | | | 2297 | 598 | 8173 |
| France | 3774 | 1612 | 14333 | 3389 | 1492 | 13305 | 3331 | 1492 | 13049 |
| Germany | 3009 | 895 | 9490 | 2844 | 911 | 9002 | 2779 | 923 | 8746 |
| Greece | 3853 | 1592 | 12492 | 3697 | 1601 | 12271 | 3529 | 1587 | 11605 |
| Ireland | 2486 | 975 | 9904 | 2170 | 870 | 8531 | 1946 | 773 | 7487 |
| Italy | 4877 | 1724 | 17729 | 4891 | 1781 | 17780 | 4915 | 1834 | 17736 |
| Luxembourg | 532 | 160 | 2046 | 523 | 168 | 1968 | 511 | 172 | 1914 |
| Netherlands | 2295 | 953 | 9407 | 2252 | 914 | 9151 | 2336 | 942 | 9277 |
| Portugal | 3619 | 1610 | 11621 | 3649 | 1656 | 11858 | 3468 | 1664 | 11706 |
| Spain | 5016 | 2265 | 17893 | 4337 | 2158 | 16263 | 4099 | 2120 | 15643 |
| UK | 2960 | 1445 | 10517 | 2304 | 1161 | 8386 | 1918 | 962 | 6940 |

The ECHP divides sample participants into sample and nonsample persons. Sample persons are all individuals belonging to the sample drawn for each country in the first year of participation, plus children born after the first wave to a sample woman. Nonsample persons are all other individuals. Sample and nonsample persons may or may not be eligible for interview. Sample persons are eligible if they belong to the target population (that is, they live in a private household within the EU) and are aged 16+. In addition, eligibility of nonsample persons also requires them to live in a household containing at least one sample person.

Sample persons who are ineligible (those who are homeless, institutionalised or living outside the EU) are "traced" and interviewed again if they return to the target population. Ineligible nonsample persons are not traced. Sample and nonsample persons whose refusal to respond is considered "final" or did not return a complete questionnaire in two consecutive waves are dropped from the sample. Households not interviewed in two consecutive waves are also dropped.

The ECHP is carried out by National Data Collection Units (NDUs) with Eurostat providing centralised support and coordination. The NDUs are responsible for sample selection, adaptation of the questionnaire, fieldwork, basic data processing and editing, and initial weighting of the data. Although Eurostat sets general guidelines in order to ensure comparability of survey results, the NDUs largely rely on their normal rules and routines.

In Belgium and the Netherlands, the ECHP was linked from the outset to already existing national panels. In Germany, Luxembourg and the UK, instead, the first three waves of the ECHP ran parallel to existing panels with similar content, namely the German Social Economic Panel (GSOEP), Luxembourg's Social Economic Panel (PSELL), and the British Household Panel Survey (BHPS). Starting with the fourth wave (1997), it was decided to merge the ECHP into the GSOEP, the PSELL and the BHPS.

All national samples are selected through probability sampling. Sampling frames and sampling procedures are not standardised across countries, however, and each NDU relies on its own methods. In most countries, the sampling frame is either the population register or a master-sample created from the latest population census. Depending on the sampling frame, we may have noncoverage of small portions of the target population, such as households that recently arrived in a country (Ireland, Italy) or nonresidents unable to speak the national language (Greece, the Netherlands). The most common sampling procedure is two-stage sampling, with geographical areas (usually the municipalities) as primary sampling units, and households or addresses as secondary sampling units.

An essential feature of the ECHP is the adoption of a common questionnaire centrally designed by Eurostat. The questionnaire consists of a household register, mainly for record keeping and control of the sample, a household questionnaire submitted to a "reference person" (usually the household head or the spouse/partner of the head), and a personal questionnaire submitted to all eligible household members.

The interviewing method recommended by Eurostat is face-to-face personal interviewing, but other interviewing methods have also been used (e.g. telephone or proxy interview). In Greece, the Netherlands, Portugal and the UK, interviews are carried out, at least partly, using computer-assisted personal interviewing (CAPI). All other countries rely instead on the conventional "paper and pencil" method.

After going through standard checking routines, the microdata files collected by the NDUs are sent to Eurostat and stored in the so-called Production Data Base

(PDB). Because the PDB contains information considered confidential according to EU Statistical Law and has a rather complex structure, access to the data is limited to Eurostat and the NDUs.

People interested in the ECHP may negotiate with Eurostat the purchase of the User Data Base (UDB), which is an anonymised and user-friendly version of the data. The UDB has been made available only recently. The first longitudinal UDB, covering waves 1 and 2, was released in December 1998, three years after completion of fieldwork for wave 2. A longitudinal UDB covering the first three waves was released in December 1999, and the one covering the first four waves is expected in 2001.

## 2.2. *Response patterns*

A person is said to be unit nonrespondent in a given wave if her/his personal questionnaire is not available. We are interested in analysing cross-country differences in sample dynamics caused by unit nonresponse, disregarding the dynamics due to ineligibility.

The causes of ineligibility may be classified into two broad categories: demographic events (death or person younger than 16, the age of eligibility for a personal interview) and other causes, which we lump together into the single category "out of the scope" (for example, people who are homeless, institutionalised or move outside the EU). For unit nonresponse we distinguish between lack of cooperation by the individual and absence of contact. The latter may be due to data collection problems or absence of the person.[3]

Let $D_j$ be a 0-1 indicator of unit response in wave $j$ ($D_j$ = 1 for sample respondents). Since only 3 waves of the survey are currently available, a response pattern is described by the triple $D = (D_1,D_2,D_3)$. The seven possible response patterns may be classified into four types:

1. Always responding: $D = (1, 1, 1)$,
2. Monotone attrition: $D = (1, 0, 0)$ or $(1, 1, 0)$,
3. New entry: $D = (0, 1, 1)$ or $(0, 0, 1)$,
4. Irregular response patterns: $D = (1, 0, 1)$ or $(0, 1, 0)$.

The pattern (1, 1, 1) is the most frequent at all ages.[4] The frequency of the irregular response pattern and of new entry is very low, with the exception of new entry of people younger than 30 in the Netherlands. The frequency of monotone attrition is lower than 10% only in Germany, Italy and Portugal. It is higher than 10% in all other countries, reaching 28% in Ireland and 34% in the UK. In general, the frequency of attrition shows no clear relation with age except in Denmark and the Netherlands, where it sharply increases after age 70, and in Ireland and the UK, where it is higher for people younger than 25.

## 2.3. *Weighting*

Issues of sampling design and nonresponse affect the quality of the inference that can be drawn from survey data. If the sampling design is such that individuals in the target population have different probabilities of sample participation, then selection probabilities should be explicitly taken into account. The ECHP provides a specific set of weights for this purpose.

The ECHP also deals with three distinct types of nonresponse. The first is household nonresponse, that is, the household interview is not completed. The second is unit nonresponse, that is, the personal interview is not completed. The third is item nonresponse at either the household or the personal level, that is, the household or the personal interview are completed but there is missing information on some questions. The ECHP provides weights to take into account household and unit nonresponse, and deals with item nonresponse by applying an imputation procedure described in the next section.

We remark that nonresponse may not only cause efficiency losses relative to the complete-data case, but may also bias inference. As shown by Horowitz and Manski (1998), the seriousness of the problem is directly proportional to the amount of nonresponse.

The ECHP provides three types of weights: (i) "design weights" to take into account sampling design, (ii) "base weights" for household nonresponse, and (iii) "cross-sectional weights of interviewed persons" for unit nonresponse. The basic idea is to assign to each unit a weight inversely proportional to the probabilities for an individual to belong to the sample, to be resident in a responding household, and to return the personal questionnaire. The weights, however, are not simply the product of these inverse probability factors. Their computation is complicated by a post-weighting or "calibration" procedure to reflect the population structure by sex and age, and the marginal distributions of a number of variables (household size, tenure, number of economically active persons and region).[5]

To check for over- or under-representation of the population, we compare the unweighted and the weighted distributions by sex and age from the pooled personal files (P-files) of the ECHP, with the population distribution obtained from the annual population-weighted data of Eurostat's Labour Force Survey (LFS). The comparison is carried out by using both the base weights, which take into account sampling design and household nonresponse, and the cross-sectional weights, which also take into account unit nonresponse in responding households. To ensure full comparability between the age distributions in the ECHP and the LFS, we confine ourselves to the 17-69 age range.

As a summary of the differences with respect to the population age distribution, Table 2 presents the value of the statistic $\delta = \sum_a | w_a - \omega_a |$, where $w_a$ is the sample frequency of age $a$ in the ECHP (weighted or unweighted) and $\omega_a$ is the corresponding frequency in the LFS data, computed separately by country and sex. The weights succeed in correcting, at least in part, the distribution by age and sex. In general, the differences between the ECHP and the LFS are smaller when using the weights. There are important exceptions however for Greece, Portugal and Spain, where the use of the weights does not lead to improvements.

*Table 2. Sum of the absolute deviations between the age distributions in the ECHP and the LFS. Age range 20-69.*

| | Unweighted | | Base weights | | Personal weights | |
|---|---|---|---|---|---|---|
| Country | Men | Women | Men | Women | Men | Women |
| Austria | .141 | .129 | .101 | .098 | .100 | .102 |
| Belgium | .134 | .111 | .107 | .078 | .103 | .074 |
| Denmark | .103 | .096 | .098 | .091 | .087 | .087 |
| Finland | .161 | .199 | .168 | .155 | .169 | .147 |
| France | .066 | .064 | .070 | .059 | .059 | .054 |
| Germany | .097 | .083 | .067 | .054 | .071 | .049 |
| Greece | .064 | .044 | .076 | .080 | .082 | .064 |
| Ireland | .116 | .107 | .083 | .071 | .080 | .070 |
| Italy | .070 | .079 | .063 | .052 | .059 | .054 |
| Luxembourg | .150 | .136 | .120 | .115 | .130 | .114 |
| Netherlands | .145 | .118 | .094 | .094 | .089 | .092 |
| Portugal | .097 | .089 | .102 | .075 | .113 | .075 |
| Spain | .054 | .046 | .080 | .074 | .074 | .072 |
| UK | .112 | .098 | .066 | .074 | .062 | .067 |

### *2.4. Item nonresponse and income imputation*

In general, the ECHP deals differently with unit (or complete) nonresponse and item nonresponse. The first is dealt with by weighting, the second by imputation. In this section, we describe the procedure used to compute total household income when some household members are unit nonrespondents, and the imputation procedure used for item nonresponse to income variables at the individual level.

Computation of total net household income starts by summing the personal incomes of responding household members. The ECHP corrects for unit nonresponse in responding households by multiplying this sum by an inflation factor greater or equal to 1. To construct the inflation factor, individuals are divided into classes (depending on auxiliary variables, such as sex and age) and a weighted average of income is computed for each class. This class average is then assigned to all individuals belonging to the class, whether respondents or not. Finally, the inflation factor of a household is computed as the ratio between the sum of the personal incomes assigned to all its members and the sum of the personal incomes assigned only to the responding units.

The ECHP distinguishes among the following income components:

1. wages and salaries,
2. income from self-employment or farming,
3. pensions (old-age related benefits and survivors' benefits),
4. unemployment/redundancy benefits,

5. any other social benefits or grants (family-related allowances, sickness/invalidity benefits, education-related allowances, any other personal benefits, assigned social assistance, assigned housing allowance),
6. nonwork private income (capital income, property/rental private transfers received).

The same inflation factor used for total household income is also used for single components of household income.

The income imputation procedures in case of item nonresponse at the individual level have changed through time. The first wave of the ECHP uses random hotdeck imputation within classes (RHWC) and predictive mean matching (PMM). Starting from the second wave, a variant of the EM algorithm is used.

Both RHWC and PMM first divide the sample of respondents into groups, then they match each nonrespondent to a group of respondents, and finally they use a randomly drawn respondent from the matched group as a "donor" for the nonrespondent. In RHWC, respondents are grouped on the basis of the value of a set of auxiliary variables. Each nonrespondent is matched to the group of respondents for whom the auxiliary variables assume the same values, and the missing value is imputed using the value observed for a randomly drawn respondent from the matched group. In PMM, however, a linear regression model is used to predict the missing variable, say $Y$, given a set $X$ of observable covariates. The respondents are divided into classes on the basis of the predicted value of $Y$, and each nonrespondent is associated with the class with the closest mean predicted value of $Y$. Finally, a randomly drawn respondent from the matched class is used as a "donor" for the nonrespondent. Since linear regression is adequate only to predict continuous variable, PMM is not used for the imputation of discrete variables.

The procedure used from the second wave, called IVE (Imputation and Variance Estimation), may be viewed as a variant of the EM algorithm because it iteratively repeats the imputation of missing values until convergence.[6] In the first step of the IVE algorithm, imputation is carried out for variables with a low fraction of missing cases using the information from variables without missing data. In the second step, imputation is carried out for variables with more severe problems of missingness, conditioning both on variables without missing data and variables imputed in the first step; and so on. The specific model used for the imputation depends on the type of variable to be imputed. For example, it is a linear regression model when the target variable is continuous and a logistic regression model when the target variable is binary.[7]

### 2.5. *Anonymisation criteria*

Construction of the UDB required extensive negotiations with the NDUs and various bodies of the European Commission. The anonymisation criteria adopted restrict the information available on age, occupation and industry of employment, income, health status, and geographical mobility and region of residence. The criteria are not the same for all countries and are generally more severe for Germany and the Netherlands.

Specifically, information on the upper end of the age distribution has been restricted by bottom-coding year of birth at 1909 (1924 for Germany). Information on school attainments has been collapsed to the very coarse three-category ISCED level. Occupational codes and sector of activity are restricted to a level of aggregation intermediate between 1 and 2 digits.

Income components are aggregated at an intermediate level and converted to annual net amounts. In particular, most of the detail about pensions is lost in the UDB, which only distinguishes between three aggregates: old-age related benefits, survivor pensions and sickness/invalidity benefits. Notice that old-age related benefits, survivor pensions and sickness/invalidity benefits are not separable in Germany and the UDB only reports the sum of old-age related benefits and survivor pensions. Problems of identification of the different types of pensions also arise in Ireland.

Comparability of incomes across countries is affected by two further problems: in France all income variables (except total household income) are collected as gross instead of net, whereas in Belgium income data are still provisional and the impact of the revision cannot be anticipated.

Concerning health, the first wave only provides the total number of visits to a doctor, optician or dentist for all countries, whereas the information on the number of nights spent in a hospital as in-patient is always available for all countries except Germany.

No information on migration trajectory is available for Germany, whereas the information on foreign country of birth and last foreign country of residence is not available for Germany, Greece and the Netherlands. Finally, no regional information is available for Germany and the Netherlands, whereas for all other countries, except Finland and Portugal, the breakdown is at the coarse level of NUTS 1.

## 3. BASIC TRENDS BY AGE

This section compares basic trends associated with ageing across European countries using the evidence provided by the ECHP. For each country, we pool all the available waves and compute weighted statistics (frequencies, means and quantiles) using the cross-sectional personal weights. As discussed in Section 2.3, these weights are introduced to correct for sampling design, household nonresponse, and unit nonresponse within responding households. We focus on individuals born after 1909 (after 1924 for Germany) and the households they live in.

Figure 1 shows the average size (number of persons in the household) and the average number of adults (persons aged 16+) in households that contain at least one adult by the age of that person. The difference between the two curves is just the average number of household members aged less than 16. Already at age 50, the household size and the number of adults almost coincide in all countries except Ireland and the Southern European countries (Greece, Italy, Portugal and Spain). This difference mainly reflects the demographic structure of the population.

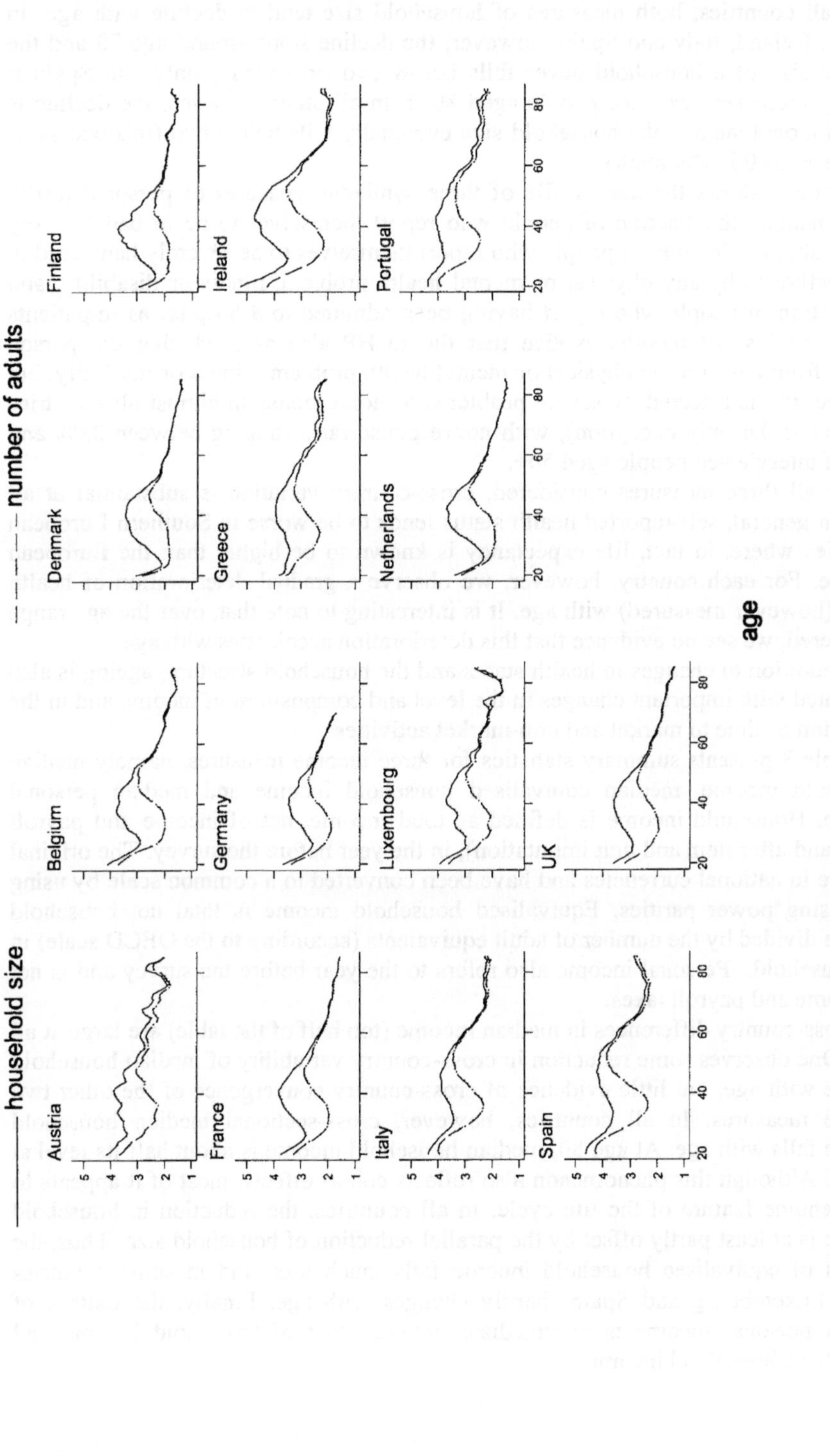


*Figure 1. Average size and average number of adults in households that contain at least one person aged 16+ by country and age of that person.*

In all countries, both measures of household size tend to decline with age. In Greece, Ireland, Italy and Spain, however, the decline stops around age 70 and the average size of a household never falls below two (in Ireland, Italy and Spain it actually increases again for people aged 80+). In all other countries, the decline is instead monotone and the household size eventually falls below two (this occurs as early as age 60 in Denmark).

Figure 2 shows the age profile of three synthetic measures of personal health status, namely the fraction of people who report themselves to be in bad (or very bad) health, the fraction of people who report themselves to be severely hampered in daily activities by any physical or mental health problem, illness or disability, and the fraction of people who report having been admitted to a hospital as in-patients during the last 12 months. Notice that the ECHP also asks whether the person suffers from any chronic physical or mental health problem, illness or disability, but this question is affected by severe problems of nonresponse in almost all countries (Finland is the only exception), with nonresponse rates ranging between 33% and 45% of interviewed people aged 50+.

For all three measures considered, cross-country variation is substantial at all ages. In general, self-reported health status tends to be worse in Southern European countries where, in fact, life expectancy is known to be higher than the European average. For each country, however, we observe a gradual deterioration of health status (however measured) with age. It is interesting to note that, over the age range considered, we see no evidence that this deterioration accelerates with age.

In addition to changes in health status and the household structure, ageing is also associated with important changes in the level and composition of income and in the allocation of time to market and non-market activities.

Table 3 presents summary statistics for three income measures, namely median household income, median equivalised household income and median personal income. Household income is defined as total income, net of income and payroll taxes (and after item and unit imputation), in the year before the survey. The original data are in national currencies and have been converted to a common scale by using purchasing power parities. Equivalised household income is total net household income divided by the number of adult equivalents (according to the OECD scale) in the household. Personal income also refers to the year before the survey and is net of income and payroll taxes.

Cross-country differences in median income (top half of the table) are large at all ages. One observes some reduction in cross-country variability of median household income with age, but little evidence of cross-country convergence of the other two income measures. In all countries, however, cross-sectional median household income falls with age. At age 80, median household income is about half its level at age 50. Although this phenomenon also reflects cohort effects, most of it appears to be a genuine feature of the life cycle. In all countries, the reduction in household income is at least partly offset by the parallel reduction of household size. Thus, the median of equivalised household income falls much less, and in some countries (Italy, Luxembourg and Spain) hardly changes with age. Finally, the pattern of median personal income is intermediate between that of household income and equivalised household income.

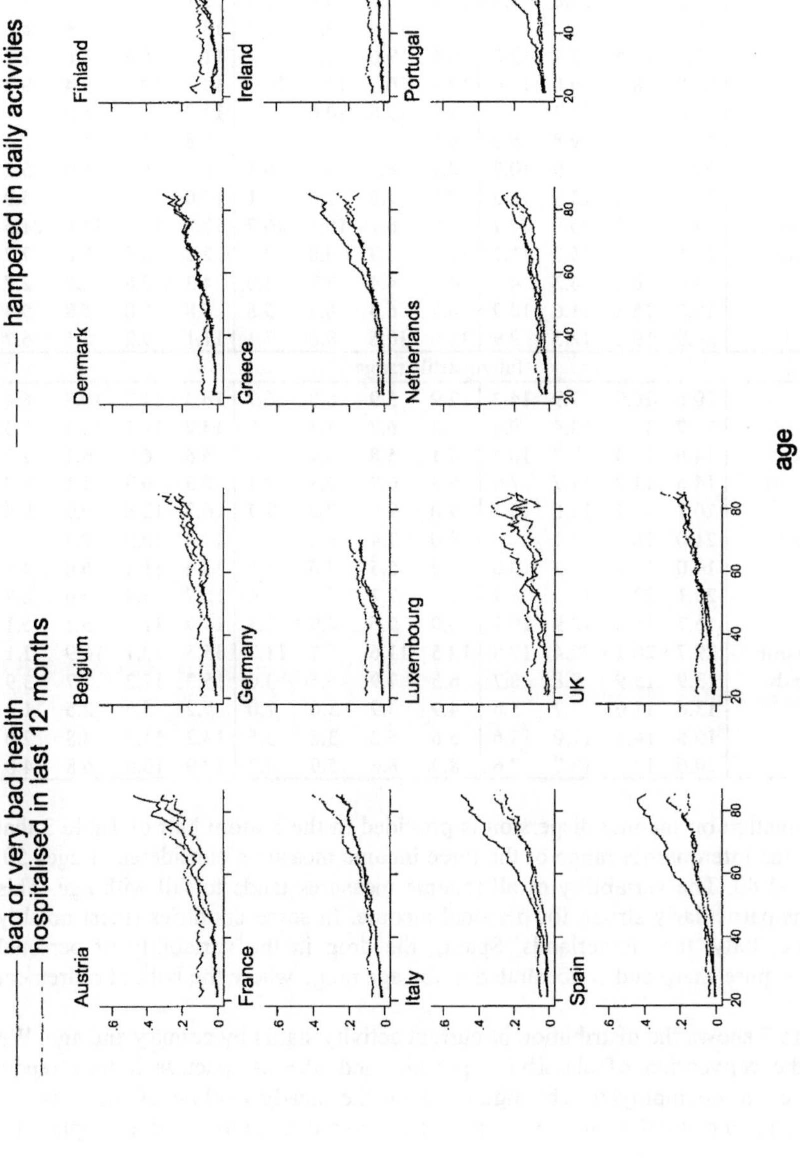


*Figure 2. Fraction of people with poor health by country and age.*

*Table 3: Median and interquartile range of income (in thousands of purchasing power parities) by age.*

| Country | Household income | | | | Equiv. hh. income | | | | Personal income | | | |
|---|---|---|---|---|---|---|---|---|---|---|---|---|
| | 50 | 60 | 70 | 80 | 50 | 60 | 70 | 80 | 50 | 60 | 70 | 80 |
| Median | | | | | | | | | | | | |
| Austria | 31.6 | 24.0 | 20.2 | 14.8 | 12.3 | 10.8 | 11.0 | 10.7 | 11.7 | 8.7 | 9.9 | 9.1 |
| Belgium | 30.2 | 19.2 | 15.6 | 11.4 | 12.8 | 10.2 | 9.9 | 8.9 | 15.1 | 9.0 | 9.8 | 8.7 |
| Denmark | 27.5 | 21.0 | 13.3 | 12.4 | 12.9 | 12.4 | 9.1 | 9.9 | 12.9 | 11.2 | 7.8 | 8.3 |
| Finland | 21.9 | 17.5 | 13.4 | 12.0 | 9.6 | 9.6 | 7.9 | 7.2 | 11.0 | 8.6 | 6.6 | 7.1 |
| France | 26.8 | 18.8 | 16.0 | 14.0 | 12.1 | 10.7 | 10.3 | 10.0 | 13.1 | 10.0 | 9.4 | 9.3 |
| Germany | 27.4 | 19.5 | 15.3 | | 11.9 | 10.8 | 10.0 | | 11.2 | 9.1 | 8.3 | |
| Greece | 17.6 | 13.5 | 9.8 | 6.5 | 6.5 | 5.9 | 5.1 | 4.0 | 7.8 | 4.3 | 4.4 | 2.4 |
| Ireland | 27.4 | 21.8 | 13.9 | 10.8 | 8.1 | 8.5 | 6.8 | 6.1 | 8.1 | 6.2 | 5.0 | 5.2 |
| Italy | 20.5 | 17.6 | 13.3 | 12.5 | 7.6 | 7.5 | 7.3 | 7.1 | 10.0 | 7.3 | 5.9 | 5.9 |
| Luxembourg | 44.2 | 28.5 | 25.9 | 24.7 | 17.8 | 16.7 | 15.5 | 16.7 | 18.3 | 17.2 | 14.6 | 21.5 |
| Netherlands | 25.6 | 19.1 | 15.3 | 11.7 | 10.9 | 10.9 | 9.8 | 8.4 | 12.3 | 8.9 | 8.8 | 7.7 |
| Portugal | 13.6 | 10.1 | 6.3 | 4.9 | 4.9 | 4.4 | 3.7 | 3.0 | 4.3 | 2.8 | 2.7 | 2.7 |
| Spain | 19.3 | 15.8 | 11.6 | 10.9 | 6.1 | 6.4 | 6.3 | 5.8 | 5.8 | 5.0 | 5.8 | 5.4 |
| UK | 26.9 | 19.5 | 12.3 | 9.9 | 11.6 | 10.6 | 8.0 | 7.1 | 11.1 | 9.2 | 7.1 | 6.7 |
| Interquartile range | | | | | | | | | | | | |
| Austria | 20.6 | 16.9 | 17.9 | 14.2 | 7.9 | 5.9 | 6.8 | 6.7 | 16.4 | 11.3 | 10.8 | 6.4 |
| Belgium | 19.7 | 15.7 | 13.4 | 9.4 | 7.3 | 6.7 | 7.1 | 5.7 | 13.7 | 11.1 | 12.1 | 8.3 |
| Denmark | 14.6 | 13.4 | 7.7 | 10.7 | 6.1 | 5.8 | 4.4 | 7.4 | 6.6 | 6.6 | 6.1 | 7.2 |
| Finland | 14.8 | 11.7 | 11.7 | 7.6 | 5.3 | 6.7 | 3.8 | 4.1 | 8.3 | 6.3 | 3.1 | 3.9 |
| France | 20.2 | 17.9 | 13.6 | 15.1 | 9.0 | 9.5 | 7.0 | 7.7 | 16.2 | 12.6 | 9.9 | 9.4 |
| Germany | 21.0 | 16.7 | 12.1 | | 8.0 | 7.4 | 6.0 | | 14.4 | 10.9 | 9.4 | |
| Greece | 14.0 | 13.7 | 11.2 | 9.0 | 5.2 | 5.5 | 4.6 | 3.6 | 13.4 | 11.1 | 6.0 | 4.1 |
| Ireland | 20.1 | 23.2 | 15.5 | 8.9 | 6.1 | 7.2 | 5.9 | 3.6 | 16.7 | 13.4 | 6.0 | 2.7 |
| Italy | 15.7 | 15.5 | 12.9 | 10.7 | 6.0 | 5.6 | 4.9 | 5.1 | 14.9 | 11.1 | 5.1 | 5.1 |
| Luxembourg | 29.7 | 20.1 | 22.4 | 17.8 | 12.5 | 11.6 | 7.7 | 11.7 | 35.5 | 23.1 | 16.9 | 11.1 |
| Netherlands | 13.9 | 15.9 | 8.8 | 8.7 | 6.5 | 7.9 | 5.5 | 3.6 | 15.3 | 17.2 | 7.7 | 3.9 |
| Portugal | 13.6 | 11.0 | 7.7 | 5.0 | 4.9 | 3.9 | 3.0 | 2.0 | 9.2 | 5.5 | 2.5 | 1.3 |
| Spain | 16.5 | 14.3 | 11.0 | 13.6 | 5.6 | 5.2 | 3.8 | 3.5 | 14.2 | 11.3 | 4.8 | 2.0 |
| UK | 20.6 | 17.0 | 10.7 | 7.6 | 8.9 | 8.6 | 5.9 | 4.3 | 12.9 | 10.9 | 6.8 | 4.8 |

Information on income dispersion is provided in the bottom half of Table 3 that presents the interquartile range of the three income measures considered at ages 50, 60, 70 and 80. The variability of all income measures tends to fall with age. This decline is particularly strong for personal income. In some countries (most notably in Greece, Italy, the Netherlands, Spain), the drop in the variability of personal income is quite sharp and concentrated in the age range where the bulk of retirement occurs.

Figure 3 shows the distribution of current activity status by country and age. We follow the convention of classifying people aged 65+ as inactive if they report themselves as unemployed. The figures show the steady decline of the share of employed people and the corresponding increase in the share of inactive people. The various countries differ in the initial level of the two profiles, and in their subsequent slope. Unemployment tends to be high before age 60 in Finland, France, Germany and Spain. This largely reflects the role played by unemployment insurance as one of the pathways of exit from the labour force. In fact, the share of unemployment in these countries drops to almost zero around the age of eligibility for early retirement benefits.

Parallel to the changes in the distribution by activity status, we observe substantial changes in the composition of personal income by income source (Figure 4). The age profile of the structure of personal income very closely follows the profile of labour force participation. As the latter falls and the fraction of people out of the labour force rises, the fraction of earnings on total income also falls and the fraction of pension income rises. Except for Greece and Italy, other types of social insurance benefits (unemployment insurance and sickness/invalidity benefits) play an important role during the transitional period from activity to inactivity, but become negligible afterwards (except in Luxembourg and the UK). The role played by other types of private income, such as asset income and private transfers received, is instead negligible.

The changes in household and personal income are likely to have an impact on wealth holding. Unfortunately, the ECHP contains some information on housing and durables at the household level but no information on other forms of wealth, especially financial wealth. In particular, the survey provides information on home ownership (including possession of a second home) and tenure, along with information on the characteristics of the dwelling and the area where it is located.

Figure 5 shows, for each age, the fraction of people living in a home owned by the household, along with the fraction of those living in a rented home and those for whom the accommodation is provided rent-free. The percentage of homeowners varies widely by country. It tends to be lower in Germany and the Netherlands, and higher in Finland, Ireland and the Southern European countries. In some countries (most notably Denmark, the Netherlands and the UK), we observe a steady decline in home ownership with age and a parallel increase in the fraction of elderly people living in rented homes. In no country do we see a trend towards increasing home ownership with age. This evidence may be viewed as lending support to the life cycle hypothesis, which predicts some form of asset decumulation at older ages.

To summarise, in all countries considered, ageing is associated with a substantial reduction in the size of a household and with changes in its composition. These phenomena partly offset the observed fall of household income, causing only a modest decline in median equivalised household income. While ageing increases the differences in household income with respect to people of younger ages, it does reduce household income differentials within the various age groups.

In all countries, ageing is accompanied by a steady deterioration of health status, as measured by a variety of indicators. Over the age range considered, however, we see no evidence that this deterioration accelerates with age.

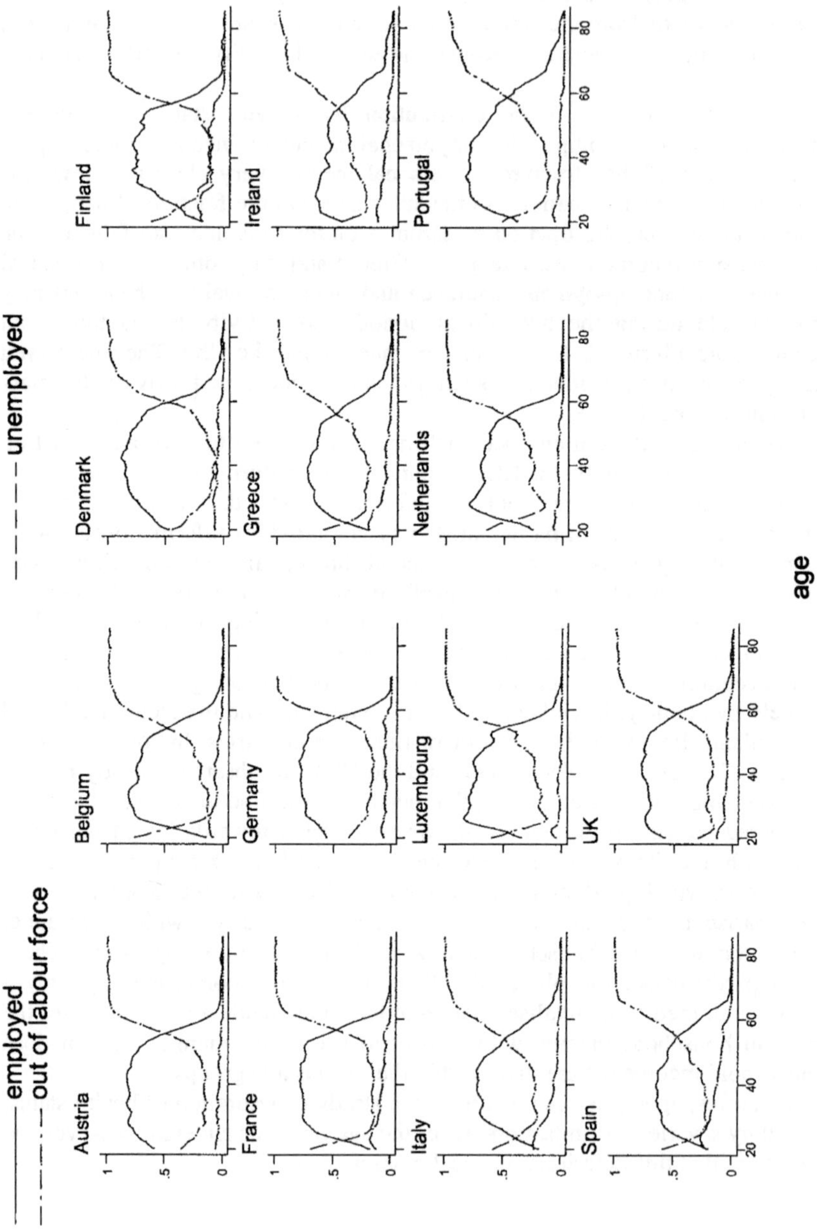


*Figure 3. Distribution of labour force status by country and age.*

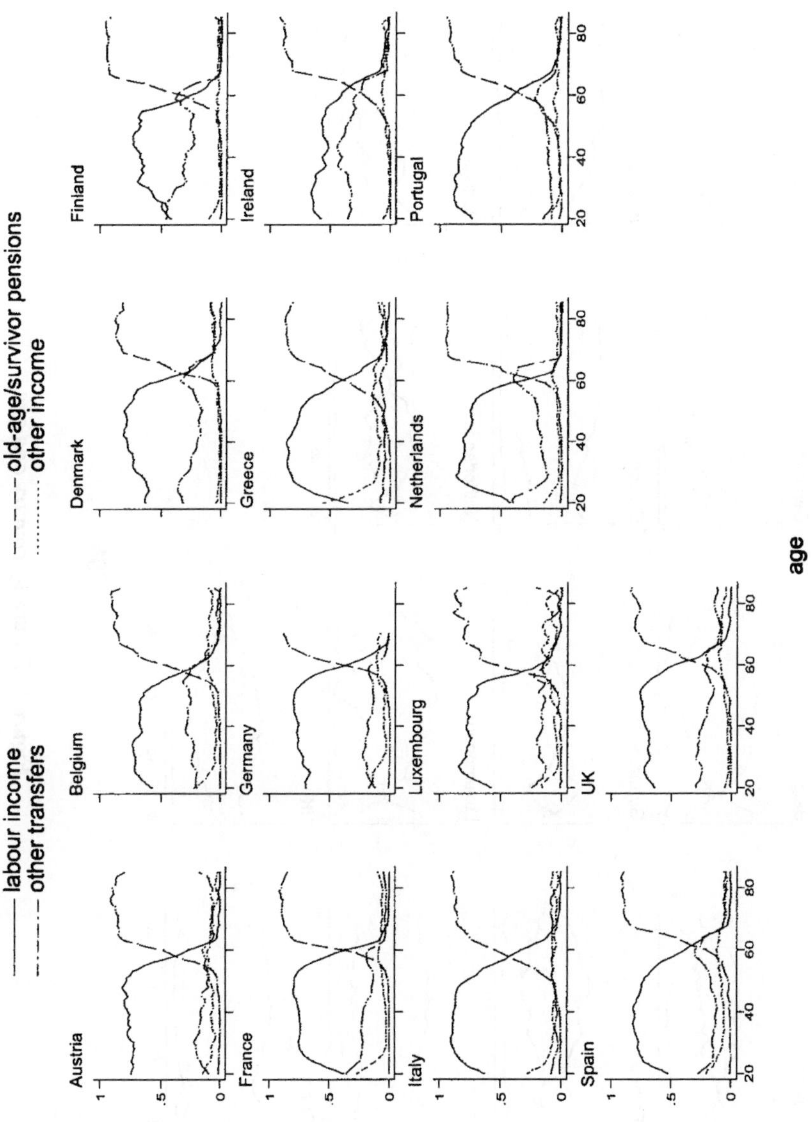


*Figure 4. Composition of personal income by country and age.*

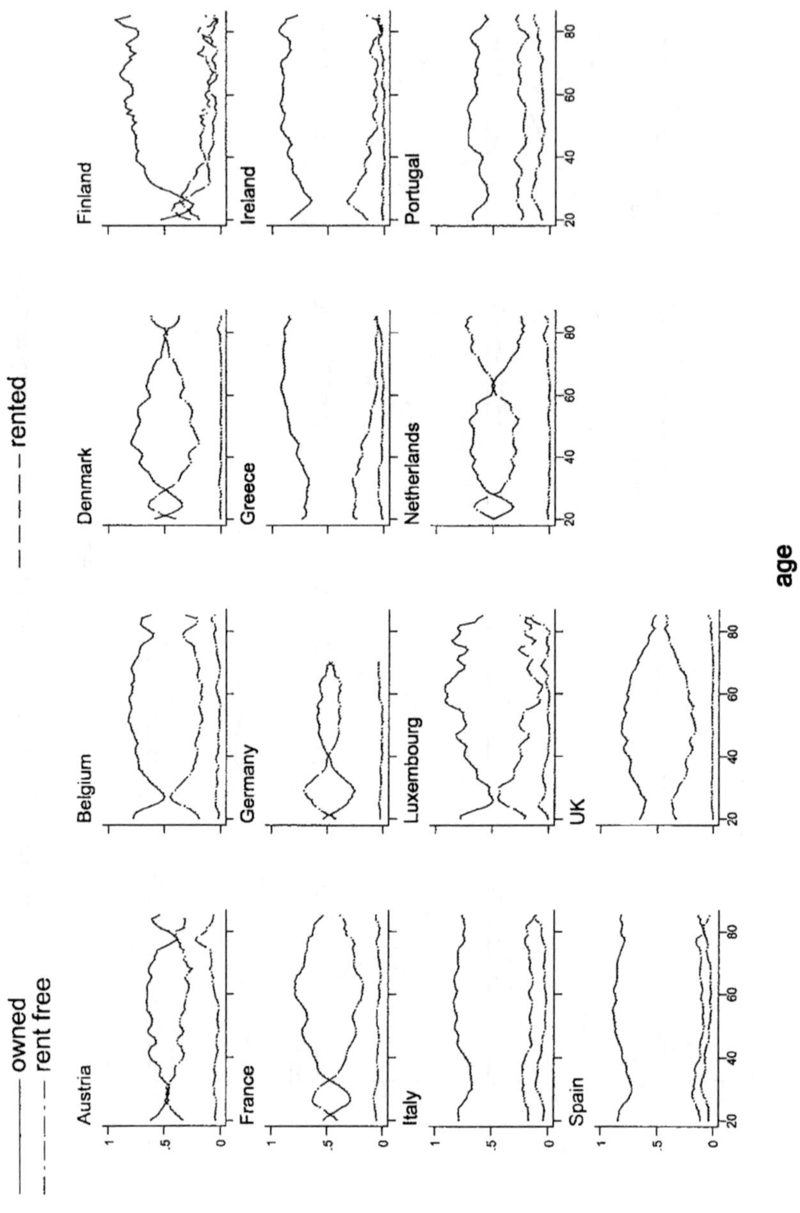


*Figure 5. Tenure by country and age.*

In terms of labour market outcomes, ageing is characterised by a drop in labour force participation and a parallel loss of importance of labour earnings as a source of personal income. After age 70, labour earnings are negligible and personal income is made up almost entirely of old-age pensions. In most countries, other types of social insurance benefits play an important role during the transitional period from activity to inactivity, but become negligible afterwards. The role played by other types of private income is always negligible.

Although the ECHP contains little information on wealth, the decline in home ownership with age and the parallel increase in the fraction of elderly people living in rented homes lends support to the life cycle hypothesis, which predicts some form of asset decumulation at older ages.

In the remainder of the paper we focus on some of the trends outlined in this section by looking in more detail at cross-country differences and the role played by other observed individual characteristics, such as sex, education and marital status. To fully appreciate the role played by these variables, Table 4 shows the differences by country, sex and age group in the distribution of the sample by educational attainments and marital status. As we shall see, these compositional effects help explain some of the trends outlined in this section. Note that missing information on key covariates, such as education, is a problem in some countries.

*Table 4: Distribution of the sample by highest level of education completed and marital status.*

| Country | Education completed | | | | | | | | Marital status | | | |
|---|---|---|---|---|---|---|---|---|---|---|---|---|
| | Tertiary | | Secondary | | Primary | | Missing | | No spouse | | Missing | |
| | 50-69 | 70+ | 50-69 | 70+ | 50-69 | 70+ | 50-69 | 70+ | 50-69 | 70+ | 50-69 | 70+ |
| **Men** | | | | | | | | | | | | |
| Austria | .050 | .054 | .643 | .481 | .306 | .465 | .001 | .000 | .133 | .204 | .000 | .000 |
| Belgium | .256 | .165 | .266 | .248 | .446 | .563 | .032 | .024 | .198 | .289 | .007 | .004 |
| Denmark | .334 | .144 | .351 | .358 | .313 | .498 | .001 | .000 | .236 | .373 | .001 | .000 |
| Finland | .217 | .158 | .291 | .200 | .492 | .642 | .000 | .000 | .179 | .215 | .000 | .000 |
| France | .151 | .089 | .304 | .175 | .541 | .732 | .005 | .004 | .160 | .281 | .003 | .003 |
| Germany | .334 | .261 | .453 | .475 | .213 | .264 | .000 | .000 | .125 | .197 | .000 | .000 |
| Greece | .112 | .074 | .147 | .099 | .739 | .825 | .001 | .003 | .071 | .191 | .001 | .001 |
| Ireland | .113 | .053 | .241 | .102 | .641 | .828 | .006 | .016 | .176 | .361 | .000 | .000 |
| Italy | .062 | .049 | .177 | .106 | .694 | .620 | .066 | .225 | .108 | .217 | .000 | .000 |
| Luxembourg | .157 | .112 | .279 | .283 | .564 | .599 | .000 | .005 | .198 | .193 | .000 | .000 |
| Netherlands | .202 | .136 | .569 | .546 | .213 | .297 | .016 | .021 | .147 | .240 | .000 | .000 |
| Portugal | .032 | .015 | .028 | .018 | .929 | .963 | .011 | .004 | .111 | .248 | .001 | .001 |
| Spain | .106 | .056 | .069 | .051 | .825 | .892 | .000 | .000 | .124 | .242 | .000 | .000 |
| UK | .215 | .133 | .267 | .206 | .515 | .661 | .002 | .001 | .190 | .329 | .020 | .013 |
| **Women** | | | | | | | | | | | | |
| Austria | .026 | .020 | .426 | .245 | .546 | .733 | .001 | .002 | .279 | .680 | .000 | .000 |
| Belgium | .171 | .103 | .238 | .193 | .546 | .676 | .044 | .028 | .303 | .641 | .006 | .005 |
| Denmark | .238 | .098 | .258 | .185 | .503 | .718 | .000 | .000 | .317 | .657 | .000 | .000 |
| Finland | .241 | .102 | .254 | .192 | .505 | .706 | .000 | .000 | .228 | .586 | .000 | .000 |
| France | .106 | .044 | .231 | .110 | .656 | .837 | .006 | .010 | .292 | .644 | .005 | .002 |
| Germany | .077 | .045 | .440 | .318 | .481 | .634 | .002 | .002 | .225 | .611 | .000 | .001 |
| Greece | .043 | .016 | .109 | .057 | .847 | .927 | .001 | .000 | .242 | .674 | .001 | .001 |
| Ireland | .085 | .048 | .264 | .123 | .642 | .818 | .008 | .011 | .216 | .667 | .000 | .000 |
| Italy | .025 | .009 | .126 | .068 | .713 | .586 | .136 | .337 | .233 | .654 | .000 | .000 |
| Luxembourg | .049 | .000 | .217 | .166 | .732 | .818 | .003 | .016 | .271 | .693 | .001 | .000 |
| Netherlands | .110 | .063 | .471 | .298 | .394 | .599 | .025 | .039 | .265 | .569 | .000 | .000 |
| Portugal | .017 | .005 | .015 | .012 | .948 | .980 | .019 | .004 | .264 | .624 | .001 | .000 |
| Spain | .047 | .018 | .050 | .022 | .903 | .959 | .000 | .001 | .242 | .651 | .000 | .000 |
| UK | .150 | .092 | .234 | .168 | .613 | .739 | .002 | .001 | .278 | .662 | .008 | .007 |

## 4. HEALTH STATUS

The remainder of this paper looks in more detail at the health status, labour market activity, income and wealth of the elderly. We begin with health status because of the important role played by this variable in determining labour market outcomes for the elderly.[8] Our measure of health status is the binary indicator for being severely hampered in daily activities by any physical or mental health problem, illness or disability. We do not use the information on chronic physical or mental health problems because of the high nonresponse rates.

We estimate a simple model for the conditional probability of being in bad health as a function of observable personal characteristics. The model is a standard logit model of the form $p(X) = \exp(\alpha + \beta'X)/[1 + \exp(\alpha + \beta'X)]$, where $\alpha$ and $\beta$ are parameters to be estimated and $X$ is a vector of covariates which includes age, age squared, indicators for the highest level of education completed (2 dummies, one for college and one for secondary education), an indicator for people without spouse, the level of equivalised household income, and indicators for the first two waves of the ECHP. The intercept $\alpha$ corresponds to the log-odds of being severely hampered in daily activities in 1996 for a person aged 60, married, with only primary education completed and equivalised household income equal to the country median for people aged 50+.

Table 5 reports the estimates obtained by fitting the model, separately by country and sex, to the subsample of people aged 50+. Although the goodness of fit is rather low, indicating the importance of factors that our model does not control for, the estimates confirm the worsening of health status with age. We also find that good health is strongly positively related with educational attainments, especially for men, and with being married. Household income is found to have an important effect, even after controlling for education and marital status. In fact, the probability of being in bad health falls significantly with equivalised household income, especially for men. A comparison of the estimated intercepts shows that the baseline odds of being in bad health are lowest in Ireland and Italy for both men and women, and highest in Austria and the UK for men and in Finland, the Netherlands and Portugal for women.

*Table 5: Estimated logit models for the probability of being in bad health (** denotes an observed significance level below 5%, * denotes an observed significance level between 5% and 10%).*

| Country | Intercept | Age | $Age^2$ | Tertiary | Second. | No spouse | Hh. income | *n* | $R^2$ |
|---|---|---|---|---|---|---|---|---|---|
| | | | | Men | | | | | |
| Austria | -1.860 ** | -.011 | .001 * | -.813 ** | -.783 ** | .029 | -.002 | 2534 | .042 |
| Belgium | -2.421 ** | .028 | .000 | -.434 ** | -.043 | .331 ** | -.058 ** | 3083 | .044 |
| Denmark | -2.757 ** | .056 ** | -.001 | -.353 * | .058 | .355 ** | -.072 ** | 2814 | .059 |
| Finland | -2.200 ** | .062 ** | .000 | -1.472 ** | .121 | .398 ** | -.039 ** | 1400 | .116 |
| France | -2.137 ** | .044 ** | .000 | -.948 ** | -.256 ** | .386 ** | -.024 ** | 6614 | .059 |
| Germany | -2.091 ** | .093 ** | -.003 * | -.926 ** | -.540 ** | .200 | -.040 ** | 4342 | .041 |
| Greece | -2.736 ** | .046 ** | -.000 | -.866 ** | -.094 | .270 ** | -.069 ** | 7050 | .050 |
| Ireland | -3.007 ** | .008 | .001 | -1.476 ** | -.384 ** | -.197 | -.079 ** | 4377 | .063 |
| Italy | -3.072 ** | .031 ** | .001 * | -.441 ** | -.813 ** | .479 ** | -.050 ** | 9098 | .069 |
| Luxembourg | -2.095 ** | -.035 | .002 * | -.700 | -.933 ** | .650 ** | -.051 ** | 986 | .086 |
| Netherlands | -2.360 ** | .041 ** | -.000 | -.435 ** | -.263 ** | .121 | -.043 ** | 4389 | .034 |
| Portugal | -2.303 ** | .062 ** | -.001 | -.500 | -.466 | -.044 | -.058 ** | 6793 | .037 |
| Spain | -2.792 ** | .061 ** | -.001 ** | -.705 ** | -.555 ** | .222 ** | -.057 ** | 8631 | .032 |
| UK | -1.927 ** | .004 | .000 | -1.062 ** | -.260 ** | .527 ** | -.053 ** | 4364 | .057 |
| | | | | Women | | | | | |
| Austria | -2.450 ** | -.027 | .002 ** | -1.136 * | -.289 ** | .363 ** | -.013 | 3050 | .062 |
| Belgium | -2.611 ** | .029 | .001 | -.898 ** | -.284 ** | .320 ** | -.015 * | 3639 | .054 |
| Denmark | -2.557 ** | .058 ** | -.001 | -.232 | -.378 ** | .172 | -.014 | 3148 | .037 |
| Finland | -2.038 ** | .017 | .001 * | -1.153 ** | -.150 | .073 | -.024 | 1448 | .102 |
| France | -2.137 ** | .045 ** | -.000 | -.737 ** | -.262 ** | .275 ** | -.017 ** | 7618 | .040 |
| Germany | -2.975 ** | .110 ** | -.004 ** | -.141 | -.225 ** | .700 ** | -.018 ** | 4431 | .025 |
| Greece | -2.761 ** | .032 ** | .000 | -.429 | -.361 ** | .182 ** | -.027 ** | 8016 | .035 |
| Ireland | -3.536 ** | .059 ** | .000 | -.782 ** | -.167 | .312 ** | -.020 | 4445 | .066 |
| Italy | -3.163 ** | .055 ** | .000 | -.340 | -.494 ** | .127 * | -.029 ** | 9825 | .078 |
| Luxembourg | -2.370 ** | .021 | -.001 | .975 ** | .255 | .239 | -.026 ** | 1031 | .017 |
| Netherlands | -2.069 ** | .004 | .001 * | -.261 | -.309 ** | .166 * | -.009 | 4958 | .026 |
| Portugal | -2.067 ** | .032 ** | .000 | -.111 | -2.820 ** | .015 | -.021 ** | 8039 | .032 |
| Spain | -2.696 ** | .025 ** | .001 * | -.278 | -.801 ** | .080 | -.044 ** | 10203 | .043 |
| UK | -2.600 ** | .061 ** | -.001 | -.358 ** | -.094 | .298 ** | -.038 ** | 5231 | .049 |

## 5. LABOUR MARKET ACTIVITY

This section focuses on people in the 50-69 age range and analyses labour force participation and exit from the labour force. We are mainly interested in documenting cross-country differences in the characteristics of the retirement process and how they depend on observable individual characteristics.

### *5.1. Labour force participation*

The ECHP collects information on both current activity and main activity in the year before the survey. For current activity, the survey lacks a precise period or date of reference. After a filter question ("Are you at present working in a job or business for at least 15 hours a week?") used to separate the active and the inactive people, the active people are asked to self-define their main activity status by choosing from among four professional positions (paid employment, training under special schemes related to employment, self-employment, unpaid family work), while the inactive people (excluding those temporarily inactive) are asked to self-define their main activity. For main activity in the year before the survey there is instead no misunderstanding concerning the period of reference. In fact, the survey asks people to self-define their main activity status in each month of the previous year.

In this section we adopt the standard International Labour Office (ILO) classification of labour force status in three categories: employed, unemployed, and inactive or out of the labour force. The employed are those whose current activity is paid employment, paid apprenticeship, or training under special schemes related to employment or self-employment. This definition of employment excludes those currently working less than 15 hours per week. Following the ILO definition, the unemployed are those who are looking for a job, are ready to work and have carried out some active search activity in the last month.[9] The inactive are those who are neither employed nor unemployed.

To control for the effect of observable individual characteristics, Table 6 shows the estimates of a simple logit model for the probability of employment. The model, fitted separately by country and sex, includes among the covariates a cubic polynomial in age, indicators for the highest level of education completed (2 dummies, one for college and one for secondary education), and indicators for people without spouse, bad health, and each of the first two waves of the survey. The intercept of the model corresponds to the log-odds of being employed in wave 3 (1996) for a person aged 60, married, in good health, and with only primary education completed.

*Table 6: Estimated logit models for the probability of being employed (** denotes an observed significance level below 5%, * denotes an observed significance level between 5% and 10%).*

| Country | Intercept | $Age^1$ | $Age^2$ | $Age^3$ | Tertiary | Second. | No spouse | Bad health | $n$ | $R^2$ |
|---|---|---|---|---|---|---|---|---|---|---|
| **Men** | | | | | | | | | | |
| Austria | -1.468 ** | -.509 ** | .008 ** | .003 ** | 1.118 ** | .386 ** | -.510 ** | -1.529 ** | 1972 | .417 |
| Belgium | -.899 ** | -.356 ** | .000 | .001 * | .791 ** | .659 ** | -.485 ** | -2.711 ** | 2189 | .383 |
| Denmark | .521 ** | -.312 ** | -.003 | .001 ** | .612 ** | -.106 | -.855 ** | -1.635 ** | 2044 | .309 |
| Finland | -.247 * | -.277 ** | -.003 | .000 | .325 | .135 | -.580 ** | -1.047 ** | 1075 | .272 |
| France | -.762 ** | -.484 ** | -.001 | .001 ** | 1.001 ** | .131 | -.386 ** | -1.387 ** | 4927 | .467 |
| Germany | -.67 ** | -.463 ** | -.006 ** | .001 ** | .903 ** | .433 ** | -.355 ** | -1.313 ** | 4240 | .406 |
| Greece | .475 ** | -.289 ** | .000 | .001 ** | -.209 * | -.599 ** | -.404 ** | -1.704 ** | 5356 | .275 |
| Ireland | .633 ** | -.181 ** | -.007 ** | .000 | .629 ** | -.135 | -.503 ** | -2.547 ** | 3277 | .190 |
| Italy | -.294 ** | -.227 ** | -.003 ** | .000 | 1.703 ** | .427 ** | -.289 ** | -1.009 ** | 7254 | .236 |
| Luxembourg | -1.771 ** | -.457 ** | .015 ** | .003 ** | 1.247 ** | .237 | -.333 | -2.182 ** | 809 | .431 |
| Netherlands | -1.549 ** | -.515 ** | .005 ** | .003 ** | 1.052 ** | .903 ** | -.566 ** | -1.874 ** | 3263 | .441 |
| Portugal | 1.066 * | -.121 * | -.005 * | .001 * | .557 * | -.329 | -.278 * | -1.47 * | 4962 | .204 |
| Spain | -.013 | -.269 ** | -.017 ** | -.001 ** | .946 ** | .390 ** | -.501 ** | -1.432 ** | 6388 | .318 |
| UK | .626 ** | -.240 ** | -.012 ** | .000 | .229 ** | .043 | -.640 ** | -2.835 ** | 3184 | .298 |
| **Women** | | | | | | | | | | |
| Austria | -2.409 ** | -.333 ** | -.009 | .000 | 1.318 ** | .453 ** | .153 | -.617 ** | 2111 | .255 |
| Belgium | -2.611 ** | -.314 ** | -.001 | .001 * | 1.129 ** | .663 ** | .346 ** | -1.134 ** | 2481 | .265 |
| Denmark | -.859 ** | -.281 ** | -.007 ** | .001 | .915 ** | .594 ** | -.104 | -1.751 ** | 2153 | .282 |
| Finland | -.541 ** | -.332 ** | -.014 ** | .000 | .680 ** | .285 | -.172 | -1.233 ** | 1095 | .306 |
| France | -1.624 ** | -.371 ** | -.007 ** | .001 ** | .548 ** | .163 * | .684 ** | -1.176 ** | 5402 | .291 |
| Germany | -1.987 ** | -.481 ** | -.019 ** | .001 | .905 ** | .158 * | .680 ** | -1.070 ** | 4315 | .289 |
| Greece | -1.283 ** | -.155 ** | -.006 ** | .000 | .047 | -.690 ** | .067 | -1.155 ** | 5706 | .122 |
| Ireland | -2.271 ** | -.145 ** | -.009 ** | -.001 | 2.042 ** | .698 ** | .335 ** | -2.075 ** | 3308 | .162 |
| Italy | -2.372 ** | -.267 ** | -.002 | .001 ** | 2.029 ** | 1.258 ** | .708 ** | -.439 ** | 7418 | .181 |
| Luxembourg | -3.269 ** | -.415 ** | -.004 | .002 | 1.895 ** | 1.046 ** | .860 ** | -.737 * | 756 | .267 |
| Netherlands | -2.994 ** | -.335 ** | -.021 ** | -.001 | 1.872 ** | .780 ** | 1.032 ** | -1.227 ** | 3616 | .296 |
| Portugal | -.397 ** | -.128 ** | -.011 ** | .000 | 1.650 ** | -.020 | .319 ** | -.856 ** | 5743 | .124 |
| Spain | -2.092 ** | -.155 ** | -.017 ** | -.001 ** | 1.673 ** | .709 ** | .997 ** | -.299 ** | 6968 | .162 |
| UK | -1.194 ** | -.307 ** | -.007 ** | .001 * | .493 ** | .215 ** | .311 ** | -1.757 ** | 3599 | .269 |

The behaviour by sex and age agrees with the nonparametric estimates in Figure 3. In all countries except Greece, employment probabilities increase with schooling attainments and are significantly higher for people with tertiary education (college degree). They are also lower for people in bad health. Another common feature is the different effect of marital status on the employment probabilities of men and women: not having a spouse tends to reduce employment probabilities for men, whereas for women the effect is just the opposite.

### *5.2. Exit from the labour force*

The availability of only three waves of ECHP data only enables us to analyse short-run dynamics. Thus we can study transitions between labour force states or income dynamics between two consecutive years but it is impossible, without strong assumptions, to reconstruct work careers or lifetime earnings profiles.

We now use the longitudinal nature of the ECHP to study cross-country differences in the exit rates from employment over a one-year period for individuals in the 50-69 age range as a function of sex, age and other personal characteristics. Finland is excluded because only one wave of the ECHP is available.

Figure 6 shows the exit rates from employment by sex and age estimated by pooling the two available pairs of waves (1994-95 and 1995-96). Despite the noise due to the limited sample size, these non-parametric estimates reveal the presence of peaks in the retirement hazards at certain ages (typically age 60 and age 65). These peaks are commonly explained as the result of Social Security rules, which induce concentration of exit at certain ages.[10]

We do not show exit rates from inactivity because in all countries this state is absorbing, with exit rates that are rapidly declining with age and become negligible for both men and women after age 55.

To control for the effect of observable individual characteristics, Table 7 shows the estimates of a simple logit model for the probability of leaving employment. The model, fitted separately by sex and country, is similar to the one discussed in the previous section, except that now the covariate vector $X$ contains a linear trend in age, indicators for age 50 and age 65, indicators for the highest level of education completed (2 dummies, one for college and one for secondary education), and indicators for people without spouse, bad health and exit between the first and the second wave of the survey. The intercept of the model corresponds to the log-odds of leaving employment between the second and the third wave for a person aged 50, married, in good health and with only primary education completed.

Qualitatively, the behaviour of the estimates by sex and age agrees with the nonparametric estimates in Figure 6. In particular, exit rates from employment at age 50 are highest in Ireland, Italy and Spain, and lowest in the UK. Exit rates increase with age and the dummies for age 60 or age 65 are strongly significant in many countries. In most countries, exit rates decrease with schooling attainments and are significantly lower for people with college degree. With some exceptions, they are also lower for people without spouse. Finally, as already found for the ECHP by Jiménez, Labeaga and Martinez (1999), bad health significantly increases the probability of leaving employment over a one-year period.

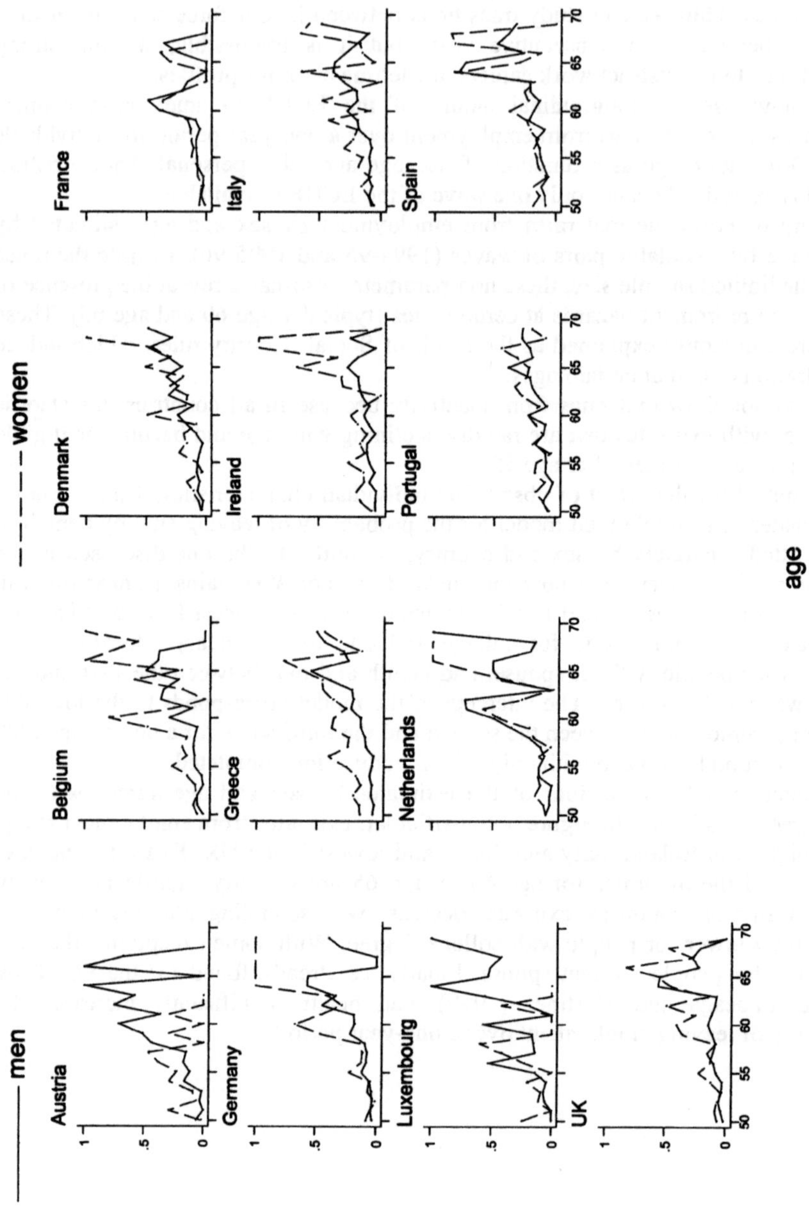


*Figure 6. Age profiles of exit rates from employment.*

*Table 7: Estimated logit models for the probability of leaving employment (** denotes an observed significance level below 5%, * denotes an observed significance level between 5% and 10%).*

| Country | Intercept | Age | Age 60 | Age 65 | Tertiary | Second. | No spouse | Bad health | $n$ | $R^2$ |
|---|---|---|---|---|---|---|---|---|---|---|
| **Men** | | | | | | | | | | |
| Austria | -3.555 ** | .325 ** | 1.308 * | . | -.933 | -.224 | .428 | 1.937 ** | 392 | .245 |
| Belgium | -3.164 ** | .168 ** | .849 * | .596 | -1.065 ** | -.297 | -.426 | .839 | 570 | .135 |
| Denmark | -3.549 ** | .180 ** | .721 * | -.588 | -.451 | .049 | .420 | 1.659 ** | 769 | .151 |
| France | -2.903 ** | .181 ** | 1.127 ** | . | -1.150 ** | -.276 | -.816 ** | 1.166 ** | 1243 | .196 |
| Germany | -3.797 ** | .207 ** | -.082 | 1.036 | -.092 | .357 | -.296 | 1.427 ** | 1402 | .123 |
| Greece | -3.443 ** | .172 ** | -.098 | .862 ** | -.534 * | .112 | .796 ** | .651 ** | 1845 | .142 |
| Ireland | -2.807 ** | .076 ** | .547 | .952 ** | -.647 * | .090 | -.171 | 1.180 ** | 1221 | .049 |
| Italy | -2.727 ** | .112 ** | .438 ** | 1.167 ** | -.826 ** | -.510 ** | .079 | .829 ** | 2263 | .080 |
| Luxembourg | -3.241 ** | .281 ** | .695 | -.264 | -.351 | -.591 | -.702 | 2.934 ** | 210 | .299 |
| Netherlands | -3.252 ** | .231 ** | .770 | .375 | -.440 | -.392 | -.022 | 1.784 ** | 898 | .176 |
| Portugal | -3.424 ** | .108 ** | .426 | .873 ** | -.223 | .014 | -.328 | 1.044 ** | 1926 | .093 |
| Spain | -2.773 ** | .145 ** | -.298 | 1.901 ** | -.669 ** | -.443 | .364 | 1.026 ** | 1719 | .102 |
| UK | -4.058 ** | .164 ** | .151 | 1.18 ** | .590 ** | .699 ** | .263 | 1.443 ** | 985 | .120 |
| **Women** | | | | | | | | | | |
| Austria | -1.775 ** | .107 * | . | . | -1.272 | -.474 | -.121 | 1.996 ** | 197 | .091 |
| Belgium | -2.763 ** | .168 ** | 2.431 ** | -.768 | .338 | .045 | -.209 | 1.051 | 303 | .145 |
| Denmark | -2.728 ** | .128 ** | 1.347 ** | .706 | -.391 | -.324 | -.058 | 1.694 ** | 565 | .114 |
| France | -2.453 ** | .107 ** | 1.043 ** | .648 | -.055 | -.280 | -.369 | .308 | 856 | .071 |
| Germany | -3.24 ** | .252 ** | 1.650 ** | . | -.452 | .256 | -.409 | 1.006 ** | 775 | .148 |
| Greece | -1.974 ** | .113 ** | -.057 | .683 * | .150 | .188 | -.197 | .059 | 822 | .065 |
| Ireland | -1.864 ** | .077 ** | .426 | 2.248 ** | -3.320 ** | .065 | -.458 | 4.026 ** | 318 | .164 |
| Italy | -1.837 ** | .104 ** | -.680 | -1.332 | -.405 | -.867 ** | .016 | .305 | 864 | .053 |
| Luxembourg | -2.341 ** | .150 | . | . | .579 | .319 | -1.195 | 1.429 | 76 | .091 |
| Netherlands | -1.982 ** | .122 ** | .519 | . | -.396 | -.295 | -1.081 ** | . | 354 | .066 |
| Portugal | -2.172 ** | .090 ** | .177 | -.354 | -1.930 * | .313 | -.224 | .227 | 1139 | .043 |
| Spain | -1.689 ** | .097 ** | .282 | .476 | -.766 ** | -.676 | -.646 ** | .669 ** | 638 | .088 |
| UK | -2.981 ** | .166 ** | .308 | .232 | .498 * | -.184 | .023 | 1.469 ** | 663 | .097 |

## 6. INCOME

**This section looks at the two main sources of income of the elderly: wage and salary earnings and old-age and survivor pensions. We present evidence on cross-country differences in the structure of these income components, that is, on differentials by sex, age and other observable individual characteristics, and on replacement rates by sex, age and education.**

### *6.1. Structure of earnings*

**Table 8 presents the estimates of a simple median regression model for the logarithm ln *W* of monthly current wage and salary earnings, net of taxes and social**

security contributions and converted to a common scale by using purchasing power parities. The model specifies the conditional median of ln *W* given a vector *X* of observable individual characteristics as $m(X) = \alpha + \beta' X$, where $\alpha$ and $\beta$ are parameters to be estimated and the vector *X* includes age, potential labour market experience (defined as the difference between the current age and the one at which the person started her/his working life), indicators for education completed (2 dummies, one for college and one for secondary education), and indicators for people without spouse, bad health and each of the first two waves of the survey. The intercept $\alpha$ corresponds to the logarithm of median monthly earnings in 1996 for a worker aged 60, married, with 30 years of labour market experience and only primary education completed.

The model has been fitted separately by country and sex using the subsample of full-time non-agricultural employees aged 50-69, with full-time defined as working at least 30 hours per week. The estimated standard errors have been computed under the homoskedasticity assumption. The table also reports a measure of goodness of fit ($R^2$) computed, by analogy with ordinary least squares, as the complement to 1 of the ratio between the mean absolute regression residual and the mean absolute deviation of log earnings from the median.

Most of the estimated coefficients have the expected sign. In particular, earnings increase with educational attainments (often substantially, as in France, Ireland and Portugal) and tend to increase with age. They also tend to be lower for people in bad health and, in the case of men (but not of women), for people without spouse. As expected, the intercept is always smaller for women than for men, although the coefficients on age, experience and the education dummies do not differ systematically between men and women. The only variable that does not seem to have the expected sign is labour market experience, whose coefficient is mostly negative.

As in the case of employment probabilities and exit rates from the labour force, cross-country differences in the estimated coefficients are very large. For example, the estimated baseline "gender gap" ranges from a minimum of about 15% in the Netherlands to a maximum of 50% in the UK, whereas the variability in the size of the education dummies is even larger. What accounts for these large differences across countries, in particular the relative importance of market forces, institutional settings and measurement problems, is an open issue.

*Table 8: Estimated median regression models for the logarithm of net monthly wage and salary earnings (** denotes an observed significance level below 5%, * denotes an observed significance level between 5% and 10%).*

| Country | Intercept | Age | Experience | Tertiary | Second. | No spouse | Bad health | *n* | $R^2$ |
|---|---|---|---|---|---|---|---|---|---|
| | | | | Men | | | | | |
| Austria | 7.107 ** | .010 | -.013 ** | .523 ** | .208 ** | -.129 ** | -.112 * | 571 | .095 |
| Belgium | 7.312 ** | .027 ** | -.021 ** | .198 ** | .028 | -.112 ** | -.122 | 601 | .171 |
| Denmark | 7.064 ** | .000 | -.005 | .282 ** | .045 | -.020 | -.055 | 963 | .150 |
| Finland | 6.904 ** | .012 * | -.011 ** | .382 ** | .134 ** | -.003 | -.042 | 300 | .217 |
| France | 7.201 ** | .034 ** | -.035 ** | .684 ** | .140 ** | -.055 * | -.065 | 1083 | .255 |
| Germany | 7.365 ** | .033 ** | -.037 ** | .290 ** | .078 ** | -.178 ** | -.078 ** | 1803 | .107 |
| Greece | 6.579 ** | -.002 | -.006 ** | .460 ** | .256 ** | .031 | -.115 | 910 | .151 |
| Ireland | 7.173 ** | -.005 | .000 | .710 ** | .274 ** | -.246 ** | -.203 * | 874 | .228 |
| Italy | 6.908 ** | -.006 ** | .000 | .559 ** | .219 ** | -.054 * | -.094 ** | 1776 | .157 |
| Luxembourg | 7.763 ** | .037 ** | -.041 ** | .485 ** | .327 ** | -.130 ** | -.398 ** | 251 | .305 |
| Netherlands | 7.172 ** | .007 | -.006 ** | .433 ** | .122 ** | -.126 ** | -.016 | 998 | .145 |
| Portugal | 6.431 ** | .005 | -.011 ** | 1.079 ** | .486 ** | -.110 ** | -.108 ** | 1240 | .193 |
| Spain | 6.999 ** | -.003 | -.005 ** | .629 ** | .314 ** | -.044 | -.135 ** | 1712 | .217 |
| UK | 7.209 ** | .019 ** | -.042 ** | .411 ** | .039 | -.032 | -.248 ** | 1047 | .196 |
| | | | | Women | | | | | |
| Austria | 6.683 ** | .021 * | -.005 | .742 ** | .385 ** | .074 | -.089 | 194 | .160 |
| Belgium | 6.911 ** | .007 | -.002 | .445 ** | .240 ** | .047 | -.152 | 273 | .194 |
| Denmark | 6.905 ** | .019 ** | -.016 ** | .232 ** | .158 * | .026 | -.072 | 596 | .191 |
| Finland | 6.602 ** | .002 | -.005 ** | .284 ** | .088 ** | .085 ** | -.015 | 344 | .166 |
| France | 6.678 ** | -.015 * | .003 | .670 ** | .233 ** | .018 | -.073 | 575 | .124 |
| Germany | 6.769 ** | .004 | -.008 ** | .237 ** | .088 ** | .212 * | .062 | 676 | .080 |
| Greece | 6.375 ** | -.007 | .007 ** | .488 ** | .205 ** | -.033 | -.001 | 238 | .192 |
| Ireland | 6.903 ** | .006 | -.002 | .666 ** | .139 * | -.114 | -.131 | 230 | .216 |
| Italy | 6.764 ** | .002 | -.001 | .401 ** | .225 ** | -.005 | -.048 | 540 | .181 |
| Luxembourg | 6.945 ** | -.018 | -.020 | -.040 | .523 ** | .140 | -.399 | 67 | .166 |
| Netherlands | 6.952 ** | .023 ** | -.029 ** | .297 ** | .068 | .029 | .188 | 222 | .170 |
| Portugal | 6.077 ** | -.015 ** | .002 | 1.095 ** | .668 ** | .140 ** | -.055 * | 637 | .217 |
| Spain | 6.724 ** | .001 | -.001 | .662 ** | .389 ** | .022 | -.020 | 492 | .264 |
| UK | 6.721 ** | .006 | -.013 ** | .707 ** | .236 ** | -.033 | -.067 | 623 | .237 |

## *6.2. Structure of pensions*

Table 9 presents the estimates of a simple median regression model for the logarithm ln *P* of net monthly old-age and survivor pension benefits, defined as annual benefits divided by 12 and converted to a common scale by using purchasing power parities. We consider this coarse aggregate because separate data on old-age and survivor pensions are not available for Germany.

*Table 9: Estimated median regression models for the logarithm of net monthly old-age and survivor pension benefits (** denotes an observed significance level below 5%, * denotes an observed significance level between 5% and 10%).*

| Country | Intercept | Yrs from ret. | Work career | Tertiary | Secondary | No spouse | *n* | $R^2$ |
|---|---|---|---|---|---|---|---|---|
| **Men** | | | | | | | | |
| Austria | 6.780 ** | .002 | -.007 ** | 1.021 ** | .255 ** | -.106 ** | 1068 | .083 |
| Belgium | 6.742 ** | .007 ** | -.008 ** | .304 ** | .184 ** | -.095 ** | 1155 | .081 |
| Denmark | 6.336 ** | -.006 * | -.006 ** | .624 ** | .064 ** | .074 ** | 987 | .104 |
| Finland | 6.178 ** | .011 * | .002 | .679 ** | .165 ** | .004 | 434 | .128 |
| France | 6.756 ** | .012 ** | -.020 ** | .720 ** | .332 ** | -.156 ** | 3210 | .121 |
| Germany | 6.717 ** | .021 ** | .005 | .125 ** | .060 | -.047 | 1969 | .02 |
| Greece | 6.148 ** | .001 | -.019 ** | .809 ** | .623 ** | -.056 | 2500 | .179 |
| Ireland | 6.475 ** | -.001 | -.008 ** | .747 ** | .396 ** | -.301 ** | 1416 | .177 |
| Italy | 6.634 ** | -.001 | -.015 ** | .680 ** | .335 ** | -.188 ** | 2938 | .106 |
| Luxembourg | 7.454 ** | .001 | .000 | .408 ** | .137 ** | -.164 ** | 419 | .062 |
| Netherlands | 6.996 ** | -.026 ** | -.004 ** | .778 ** | .256 ** | -.093 ** | 1619 | .145 |
| Portugal | 6.049 ** | -.019 ** | -.030 ** | 1.212 ** | 1.08 ** | -.025 | 2050 | .134 |
| Spain | 6.498 * | .009 ** | -.017 * | .793 ** | .441 ** | -.126 ** | 3164 | .130 |
| UK | 6.407 ** | -.001 | -.006 ** | .608 ** | .153 ** | -.145 ** | 1835 | .084 |
| **Women** | | | | | | | | |
| Austria | 6.016 ** | .005 | .002 | .919 ** | .471 ** | .362 ** | 688 | .129 |
| Belgium | 6.515 ** | -.010 ** | -.005 ** | .432 ** | -.038 | .144 ** | 469 | .109 |
| Denmark | 6.213 ** | .003 | -.002 | .210 ** | .034 | .188 ** | 866 | .04 |
| Finland | 6.013 ** | .005 | -.001 | .438 ** | .130 ** | .189 ** | 460 | .082 |
| France | 6.027 ** | .005 | -.005 * | .870 ** | .540 ** | .431 ** | 2224 | .143 |
| Germany | 6.156 ** | -.002 | .003 | .327 ** | .119 ** | .383 ** | 1339 | .097 |
| Greece | 5.406 ** | -.018 ** | -.045 ** | .928 ** | .842 ** | .138 ** | 1325 | .378 |
| Ireland | 6.019 ** | .005 ** | .002 * | .735 ** | .345 ** | .016 | 455 | .169 |
| Italy | 6.068 ** | -.003 | -.003 ** | .936 ** | .725 ** | .223 ** | 1365 | .204 |
| Luxembourg | 5.821 ** | .031 ** | .020 ** | 1.588 ** | .251 ** | .807 ** | 108 | .244 |
| Netherlands | 6.056 ** | .000 | .002 ** | .653 ** | .002 | .478 ** | 519 | .169 |
| Portugal | 5.448 ** | -.001 ** | -.002 ** | 1.641 ** | 1.351 ** | .046 ** | 1466 | .097 |
| Spain | 6.128 ** | .000 | .000 | 1.107 ** | .487 ** | .020 ** | 979 | .134 |
| UK | 5.314 ** | .002 | .003 ** | .631 ** | .152 ** | .701 ** | 1579 | .227 |

The model for $\ln P$ is similar to the one discussed in the previous section for the logarithm of earnings except that now the covariate vector $X$ contains the number of years since retirement (defined as the difference between the current year and the year the person stopped working in the last job), the length of the work career and indicators for education completed (2 dummies, one for college and one for secondary education), people without spouse, and each of the first two waves of the ECHP. The intercept of the model corresponds to the logarithm of median monthly benefits in 1995 for a new retiree, married, with a work career of 40 years and only primary education completed.

The model has been fitted separately by country and sex using the subsample of people aged 50+ who have been retired for at least one year. As before, the estimated standard errors have been computed under the homoskedasticity assumption.

Most of the estimated coefficients have the sign that one would expect if pension benefits were roughly proportional to lifetime earnings, as is the case for most of the countries considered. In particular, pension benefits increase with educational attainments and are higher for men than for women. Notice that, despite the progressive nature of most benefit formulae, the differences by education tend to be larger for pensions than for earnings. This means that, at least along the educational dimension, pre-retirement inequalities in the distribution of earnings are actually accentuated after retirement.

Also notice that the coefficient on the number of years since retirement tends to be positive. For the countries where it is positive and statistically significant (Finland, France, Germany and Spain), its order of magnitude (between 1% and 2% per year) appears to be consistent with indexation of outstanding pensions to real productivity growth. The only puzzling result is the tendency for the coefficient on the length of the work career to be negative.

Finally, men with a spouse tend to have higher pensions than those without a spouse, whereas the opposite tends to be true for women. Because most men without a spouse are single but most women without a spouse are widows, this is likely to reflect the fact that our definition of pension benefits includes survivor's benefits which, in most countries, can be added to the own old-age pension.

### *6.3. Replacement rates*

The analysis of earnings and pensions in the previous sections could have been carried out by just using one or more cross-sections of the population, without any need for longitudinal data. We now exploit the longitudinal nature of the ECHP in order to study to what extent pensions of retirees replace pre-retirement earnings. Replacement rates, defined as the ratio of post-retirement pension benefits to pre-retirement earnings, play a very important role in the public policy debate because they provide a simple and easily understandable measure of the income-smoothing role of pensions.

Table 10 shows the estimates of a median regression model for the logarithm of the replacement rate fitted separately by country. We compute the replacement rate for all people that were employed in January 1993 and moved permanently to retirement in some month between February 1993 and December 1995. For people who retired in 1994, we define the replacement rate as the ratio of annual pension benefits in 1995 to annual labour income in 1993. For people who retired in 1993, we compute the replacement rate as the ratio between monthly pension income in 1994 (annual pension income divided by 12) and monthly labour income in 1993 (annual labour income in 1993 divided by the number of months during which the person was employed). By analogy, for people who retired in 1995, we define the replacement rate as the ratio between monthly pension income in 1995 (annual pension income divided by the number of months during which the person was retired) and monthly labour income in 1994 (annual income in 1994 divided by 12). The replacement rate for the Netherlands is missing because the monthly information on activity status is not available in the UDB for this country.

*Table 10: Estimated median regression models for the logarithm of the replacement rate (** denotes an observed significance level below 5%, * denotes an observed significance level between 5% and 10 %).*

| Country | Intercept | Exponential of intercept | Earnings | Age | Work career | Sex | No spouse | Tertiary | Secondary | $n$ | $R^2$ |
|---|---|---|---|---|---|---|---|---|---|---|---|
| Belgium | -.254 ** | 0.776 | -.341 ** | .022 ** | -.004 | -.085 | -.004 | .123 | -.116 | 71 | .172 |
| Denmark | -.156 | 0.856 | -.402 ** | .051 ** | -.032 ** | -.088 | -.103 | .161 | -.104 | 73 | .194 |
| France | -.267 ** | 0.765 | -.158 ** | .006 | -.001 | .110 * | .048 | .147 * | -.005 | 225 | .125 |
| Germany | -.143 * | 0.867 | -.173 ** | .017 | .001 | .038 | .005 | .047 | -.049 | 131 | .133 |
| Greece | -.232 ** | 0.793 | -.285 ** | -.036 * | -.012 | -.310 * | -.005 | .229 | .277 | 135 | .133 |
| Ireland | -.399 ** | 0.671 | -.821 ** | -.014 | -.016 | -.313 | -.089 | .773 ** | .056 | 70 | .252 |
| Italy | -.155 ** | 0.857 | -.502 ** | -.006 | .001 | .079 | -.033 | .208 * | .191 ** | 283 | .142 |
| Luxembourg | -.217 | 0.805 | -.032 | -.013 | .008 | 2.105 ** | -1.524 ** | .061 | .028 | 34 | .083 |
| Portugal | -.094 | 0.911 | -.176 ** | -.027 | .011 | -.058 | .415 | .138 | .334 | 115 | .098 |
| Spain | -.065 | 0.937 | -.274 ** | .004 | -.003 | .105 | -.021 | .155 | .084 | 122 | .160 |
| UK | -1.027 ** | 0.358 | -.141 ** | -.047 | .062 | .118 | .010 | .348 * | .078 | 93 | .144 |

Pension benefits are the sum of old-age and survival pensions, while labour income is the sum of wage and salary earnings and self-employment income. All income amounts are net of taxes and social security contributions, and have been converted to a common scale by using purchasing power parities. The covariate vector contains age, the length of the work career (defined as the difference between the age at which the person stopped working in the last job and the age at which the person started her/his working life), and indicators for sex, people without spouse, college and secondary education. We also consider a model that contains the annual earnings before retirement as an additional covariate.

The intercept of the model corresponds to the logarithm of the median replacement rate for a married man aged 60 in 1993, with pre-retirement earnings equal to the median for a worker aged 50+, a work career of 40 years and only primary education completed. The exponential of this intercept, that is the estimated baseline replacement rate, ranges between a minimum of 36% in the UK and over 90% in Portugal and Spain. Our results also show that the logarithm of the replacement rate depends negatively on the level of pre-retirement earnings, that is, inequalities in pre-retirement earnings tend to shrink after retirement. Everything else equal, people with higher education tend to have higher replacement rates. On the other hand, the coefficients on age, length of the work career, sex and people without spouse, although quite different across countries, are not statistically significant in general.

# 7. WEALTH

The ECHP contains information on housing and durables at the household level but no information on financial wealth. Here we look at the probability of home ownership as a function of observable personal characteristics, and to ownership of several types of durables for households with and without an elderly (aged 50+) member.

## *7.1. Home ownership*

We define home ownership in a broad sense by also including the case when the dwelling is provided for free. The model for the probability of observing such event is a standard logit model with a covariate vector consisting of age, age squared, and indicators for educational attainments, not having a spouse, bad health and the first two waves of the survey. The intercept of the model corresponds to the log-odds of home ownership in 1996 for a person aged 60, married, in good health and with only primary education completed.

Table 11 reports the estimates obtained by fitting the model, separately by country and sex, to the subsample of people aged 50+. The estimates confirm the negative age trend in home ownership in Denmark, the Netherlands and the UK. Not having a spouse or being in bad health negatively affect the probability of home ownership, whereas the effects of educational attainments are mixed. In Austria, Germany, Greece, Portugal and Spain home ownership is less common among people with higher education, while the opposite is true in all other countries.

## *7.2. Durables*

The household questionnaire of the ECHP also collects information on ownership of certain types of durables, namely car, colour TV, video recorder (VCR), microwave, dishwasher, telephone and home personal computer (PC).

Figure 7 shows the fraction of households that own such durables. The figure reports ownership separately for households with and without an elderly (aged 50+) member and plots, separately by country and type of durable, the fraction of owners among the two types of household. For countries near the 45° line, ownership does not change much with the household type.

Ownership of a telephone, and especially of a colour TV, shows little differences across countries and household types. On the other hand, cross-country differences and differences across households are large for all other durables, in particular the microwave, the dishwasher and the home PC. These three types of durables are much less common in Southern European countries and among households with an elderly member. Qualitatively, these conclusions do not change if we instead compare households with and without a member aged 70+.

*Table 11: Estimated logit models for the probability of home ownership (** denotes an observed significance level below 5%, * denotes an observed significance level between 5% and 10%).*

| Country | Intercept | Age | $Age^2$ | Tertiary | Secondary | No spouse | Bad health | *n* | $R^2$ |
|---|---|---|---|---|---|---|---|---|---|
| **Men** | | | | | | | | | |
| Austria | 2.205 ** | .017 ** | -.001 * | -1.412 ** | -1.130 ** | -.750 ** | -.259 * | 2544 | .054 |
| Belgium | 1.643 ** | -.022 ** | .002 ** | .786 ** | .298 ** | -1.315 ** | -.481 ** | 312 | .078 |
| Denmark | 1.945 ** | -.029 ** | .001 ** | .488 ** | -.376 ** | -1.319 ** | -1.016 ** | 2816 | .107 |
| Finland | 4.458 ** | .063 ** | -.003 | 1.567 ** | 1.015 ** | -2.246 ** | -.874 ** | 1297 | .184 |
| France | 1.603 ** | .038 ** | -.002 ** | .442 ** | .366 ** | -1.015 ** | -.368 ** | 6649 | .046 |
| Germany | .755 ** | -.001 | .001 | -.266 ** | -.192 ** | -.727 ** | -.371 ** | 4367 | .014 |
| Greece | 2.589 ** | .050 ** | .000 | -.589 ** | -.588 ** | -.291 ** | -.209 | 7081 | .035 |
| Ireland | 3.027 ** | .027 ** | .001 | . | .514 ** | -1.009 ** | -.844 ** | 3979 | .047 |
| Italy | 1.910 ** | .018 ** | -.001 ** | .702 ** | .219 ** | -.523 ** | -.065 | 9273 | .013 |
| Luxembourg | 2.052 ** | .070 ** | -.003 ** | 1.194 ** | 1.280 ** | -1.796 ** | -.405 | 987 | .168 |
| Netherlands | -.390 ** | -.065 ** | .002 ** | 2.005 ** | .936 ** | -.828 ** | -.380 ** | 4414 | .127 |
| Portugal | 1.594 ** | .014 ** | .000 | -.369 ** | .010 | .011 | -.049 | 6882 | .002 |
| Spain | 2.511 ** | -.012 | .001 | -.467 ** | -.576 ** | -.323 ** | -.048 | 865 | .008 |
| UK | 1.374 ** | -.009 | -.001 | 1.727 ** | .783 ** | -1.066 ** | -.908 ** | 450 | .131 |
| **Women** | | | | | | | | | |
| Austria | 1.790 ** | .010 | .000 | -1.192 ** | -.692 ** | -.619 ** | -.450 ** | 3058 | .039 |
| Belgium | 1.922 ** | .012 | -.001 | .362 ** | .132 | -1.303 ** | -.579 ** | 3714 | .074 |
| Denmark | 1.542 ** | .000 | .000 | .613 ** | .304 ** | -1.816 ** | -.658 ** | 3152 | .149 |
| Finland | 4.844 ** | .001 | .002 | . | .540 | -2.826 ** | -1.226 ** | 1089 | .211 |
| France | 1.712 ** | .012 ** | -.001 ** | .632 ** | .192 ** | -1.128 ** | -.243 ** | 7687 | .060 |
| Germany | .677 ** | -.006 | .001 | -.603 ** | -.107 | -.767 ** | -.560 ** | 4487 | .031 |
| Greece | 2.770 ** | .037 ** | -.001 ** | -.138 | -.427 ** | -.672 ** | -.257 ** | 8056 | .021 |
| Ireland | 3.061 ** | .031 ** | .001 | 1.147 ** | 1.170 ** | -1.444 ** | -.228 | 4521 | .080 |
| Italy | 1.932 ** | .001 | .000 | .816 ** | .415 ** | -.478 ** | -.223 ** | 10005 | .017 |
| Luxembourg | 2.791 ** | .054 ** | -.003 ** | -.220 | .503 | -1.332 ** | -1.076 ** | 1034 | .091 |
| Netherlands | -.023 | -.053 ** | .001 * | 1.890 ** | .579 ** | -.955 ** | -.672 ** | 506 | .134 |
| Portugal | 1.575 ** | -.005 | .001 ** | -.124 | -.533 ** | -.377 ** | -.059 | 8149 | .006 |
| Spain | 2.407 ** | -.015 ** | .001 ** | .020 | -.175 | -.424 ** | -.100 | 10258 | .008 |
| UK | 1.320 ** | -.026 ** | .001 | 1.788 ** | 1.065 ** | -1.101 ** | -.709 ** | 5332 | .134 |

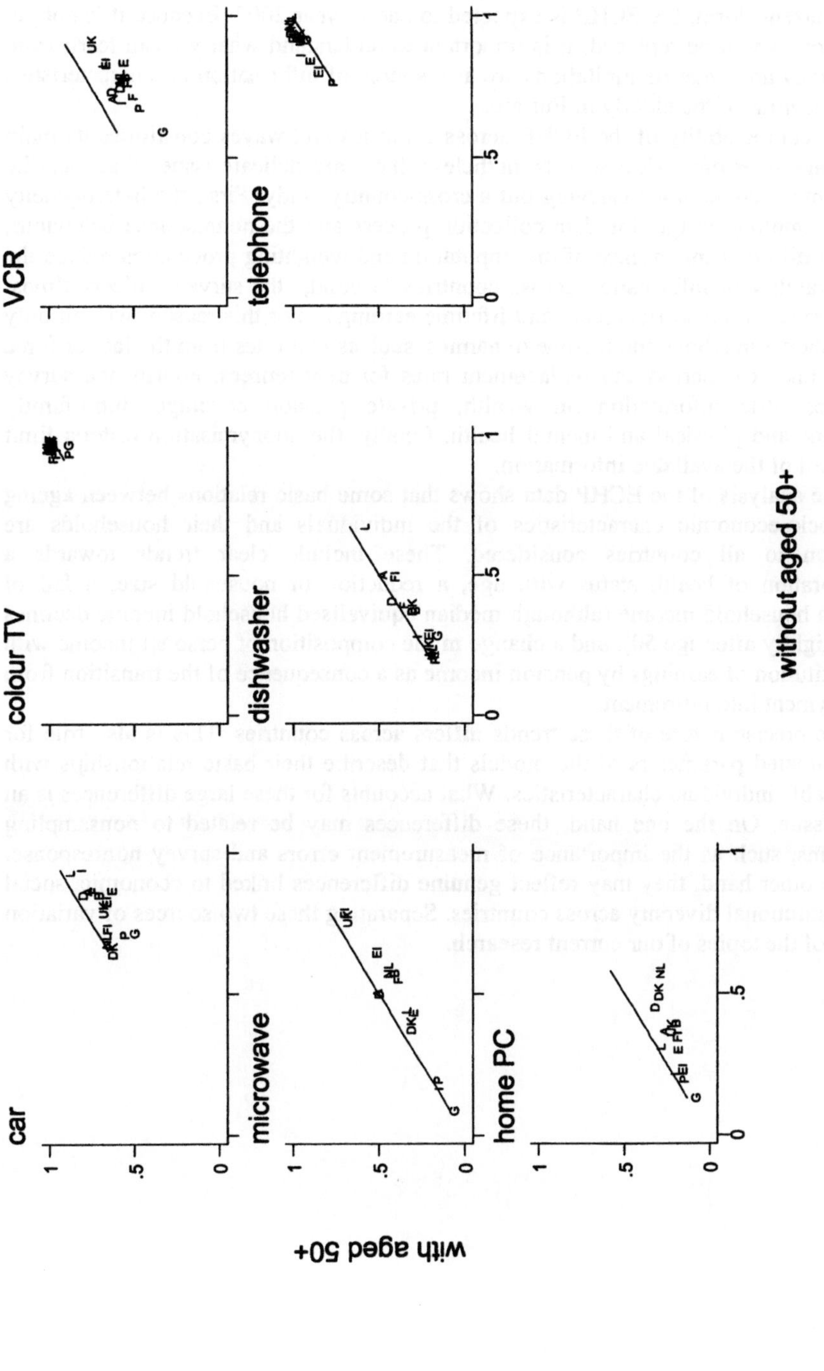


*Figure 7. Ownership of durables by type of household and durable.*

## 8. CONCLUSIONS

In its current form, the ECHP is expected to end in year 2002. Because it is not yet clear how it will be replaced, it is important to understand what we can learn from this survey and what its limitations are as a source of information on characteristics and behaviour of the elderly in Europe.

The comparability of the ECHP across countries and waves constitutes its main advantage over other data sets. Nonetheless, there are delicate issues that must be taken into account when carrying out a cross-country study. First, the heterogeneity in the sampling design, the data collection process and the nonresponse behaviour, and the different importance of the imputation and weighting procedures reduce the comparability of information across countries. Second, the survey collects almost no information on work careers and lifetime earnings. For this reason, we can only study short-run labour and income dynamics, such as exit rates from the labour force over a one-year period and replacement rates for new retirees. Fourth, the survey provides little information on wealth, private pension coverage, intra-family transfers, and physical and mental health. Finally, the anonymisation criteria limit the detail of the available information.

The analysis of the ECHP data shows that some basic relations between ageing and socio-economic characteristics of the individuals and their households are common to all countries considered. These include clear trends towards a deterioration of health status with age, a reduction of household size, a fall of median household income (although median equivalised household income declines only slightly after age 50), and a change in the composition of personal income with a substitution of earnings by pension income as a consequence of the transition from employment into retirement.

The precise nature of these trends differs across countries. This is also true for the estimated parameters of the models that describe their basic relationships with observable individual characteristics. What accounts for these large differences is an open issue. On the one hand, these differences may be related to nonsampling problems, such as the importance of measurement errors and survey nonresponse. On the other hand, they may reflect genuine differences linked to economic, social and institutional diversity across countries. Separating these two sources of variation is one of the topics of our current research.

## NOTES

1. For a more detailed description of the ECHP and the statistical problems arising from these data see Eurostat (1999) and Peracchi (2001).
2. By achieved sample size we mean the number of people who returned the personal questionnaire.
3. If the interviewer neither succeeds in contacting a person nor obtains information from relatives, neighbours or other sources, then the ECHP treats the person as eligible. Thus, the category data collection problems may also include cases of absence of contact of ineligible persons.
4. Detailed tabulations are available from the authors upon request.
5. For more details on the computation of the weights see Eurostat (1998, 2000a, 2000b).
6. We refer to Little and Rubin (1987) and Schafer (1997) for a description of estimation with incomplete data using the EM algorithm.
7. For further details see Raghunathan, Solenberger and Hoewyk (1999) and Eurostat (2000a).
8. See for example Sickles and Taubman (1986).
9. On the arbitrariness and ambiguity of this definition, see Jones and Riddell (1999).
10. See Gruber and Wise (1999) for details.

## REFERENCES

EUROSTAT (1998), "Weighting for wave 3: technical specifications", PAN 109/98, Eurostat, Luxembourg.

EUROSTAT (1999), *ECHP UDB Manual. Waves 1, 2 and 3*, Eurostat, Luxembourg.

EUROSTAT (2000a), "Imputation of income in the ECHP", PAN 164/00, Eurostat, Luxembourg.

EUROSTAT (2000b), "Construction of the weights in the ECHP", PAN 165/00, Eurostat, Luxembourg.

GRUBER J. and WISE D. A. (1999), *Social Security and Retirement Around the World*, University of Chicago Press, Chicago.

HOROWITZ J. L. and MANSKI C. F. (1998), "Censoring of outcomes and regressors due to survey nonresponse: Identification and estimation using weights and imputation", *Journal of Econometrics*, 84:37-58.

JIMÉNEZ S., LABEAGA J.M. and MARTÌNEZ M. (1999), "Health status and retirement decisions for older European couples", mimeo.

JONES S. R. G., and RIDDELL W. C. (1999), "The measurement of unemployment: An empirical approach", *Econometrica*, 67:147-162.

LITTLE J. A. and RUBIN D. B. (1987), *Statistical Analysis with Missing Data*, Wiley, New York.

PERACCHI F. (2001), "The European Community Household Panel: A review", *Empirical Economics*, forthcoming.

RAGHUNATHAN T. E., SOLENBERGER P. W. and HOEWYK J. V. (1999), *IVEware: Imputation and Variance Estimation Software. Installation Instructions and User Guide. Survey Methodology Program.* Survey Research Center, Institute for Social Research, University of Michigan.

SCHAFER J. L. (1997), *Analysis of Incomplete Multivariate Data*, Chapman and Hall, London.

SICKLES R. C. and TAUBMAN P. (1986), "An analysis of the health and retirement status of the elderly", *Econometrica*, 54:1339-1356.

# ANNEX

# THE EC SHOULD MAKE SURE THAT EUROPEAN CITIZENS ARE INFORMED ABOUT THE LONG-TERM SUSTAINABILITY OF THEIR PENSION SYSTEMS

*An appeal to President Prodi*

**Europeans are living longer, and fewer now remain in the labour force as they grow older. Many European countries have responded to these pressures by reforming their public pension systems. There is considerable uncertainty as to the effects of these reforms – as they typically do not alter the unfunded nature of public pension arrangements – and this uncertainty is itself costly. Not only does it undermine the credibility of public pension programmes inducing people to retire early, but it also distorts savings behaviour and capital accumulation.**

**In order to restore the credibility of public pension programmes and induce Governments to make the right decisions, European citizens need to be informed about the *long-term* sustainability of their pension systems. A well-informed and open debate on the true dynamics of public pension outlays and on the long-term commitments implicit in pension programmes will force governments to make forward-looking choices. It will also help in gaining support for the reforms which are required to cope with the demographic transition by making public opinion aware of the intergenerational transfers implied by pension systems as currently designed.**

**The European Commission has a key role to play in this context. Although it cannot substitute for Governments in reforming national pension systems, it can play a unique role in imposing basic standards in the collection, use and dissemination of information on public pension arrangements.**

**Moreover, the single market principles and the mobility of workers across national borders require that *all* European citizens have access to information on the state of *all* public pension programmes offered within the EU. Current efforts to develop better systems to monitor and forecast pension expenditure need to be *coordinated* across the EU Members, otherwise it will not be possible to compare the progress being made in the various countries and hence to learn from the experience of individual countries.**



*T.Boeri, A.Börsch-Supan, A.Brugiavini, R.Disney, A.Kapteyn and F.Peracchi (eds.), Pensions: More Information, Less Ideology, 189—194.*

In three areas, in particular, an urgent initiative of the Commission is warranted:

1. the *harmonisation of methodologies* used in the various countries to report pension outlays and forecast future pension liabilities;
2. a *definition of common standards* as to the frequency of expenditure forecasts and the length of the forecast horizons;
3. the development of a *European household panel survey*, if possible linked to administrative data, providing timely information on trends in contributors to the pension system, and on the determinants of retirement decisions.

## MOTIVATIONS OF THESE PROPOSALS

*A European household panel is indispensable to monitor progress made in reforming European pensions.*

Many ongoing reforms make it essential to gather information on work histories and longitudinal data on earnings, marital status, health status and disability. While long earnings histories were not needed under the old defined-benefit regimes (which were often based on the last few years of wages), many recent reforms go in the direction of defining pension amounts on the basis of the working history of individuals or on their payroll tax payments over the life cycle. Private pension funds are also experiencing a switch from final-salary benefits to average-salary benefits or even to defined contributions schemes.

The reforms also tend to allow more freedom in deciding upon the retirement age. Thus, in order to develop sensible forecasts of pension outlays, one should carefully model retirement decisions. This requires having access to reliable and timely information on inflows to the pension system at least by sex, age and marital status.

The comparable data available at the European level unfortunately cannot cope with all such needs at once. To give a few examples, the new European Community Household Panel (ECHP), while enhancing the information available on household and personal income, does not contain information on consumption. Neither is information on flows from and to participation and on the length of employment records provided by the ECHP. The harmonised European Labour Force Survey (ELFS) provides such transitions, but does not allow researchers to identify the retirees and the kind of pension that they receive. More broadly, none of these surveys is designed in such a way as to gather information on the problems of the retirees and those of the age of retirement, e.g., on issues like health status, the provision of social support and services to the elderly, etc.

A complete European survey would also make it possible to develop generational social policy accounting which is essential to highlight the redistribution involved in different pension reform options. In many European countries, public pensions indeed play an important role in providing income support to non-employed individuals in working age. A standard argument used to downplay concerns about the dynamics of pension expenditure is that pensions are improperly used as unemployment benefits. By developing consolidated social policy expenditure accounts by age, the different roles played by pensions (and other cash transfer systems) can be better isolated and assessed.

Thus, a comprehensive household panel survey carried out on the European scale is essential for better policy-making in this area. Such a survey should provide information on the household and its members, economic variables (especially current work activity and job characteristics, education, employment history, private pension coverage and characteristics, sources and composition of current income, wealth), health, social networks and social support. It would also be important to be able to link the survey information to administrative records. This is the task accomplished by surveys like the HRS (Health and Retirement Survey) in the US. The HRS has a long-standing history in providing essential information to understand the economic behaviour of the elderly, monitor changes in the socio-economic structure of the aged and forecast social security expenditures.

*Learning from experience requires more frequent projections and the harmonisation of forecasting techniques.*

There are three principles to be followed in this respect.

It is, first of all, indispensable to state explicitly the assumptions used in projecting public pension outlays and try as much as possible to harmonise them. In particular, underlying economic assumptions should be consistent across countries and an effort should be made to take account of cohort profiles of participation rates, earnings, unemployment rates etc. This is because simulations based on cross sections or 'snapshots' of individuals at a point in time give a highly misleading account of the evolution of public budgetary costs over time.

Second, some basic standards should be defined in terms of the length of the forecasting horizon (which should be at least 50 years, that is, the residual life expectancy of an individual starting to contribute to the system) and as to the frequency of forecasts, which cannot be less than 2 years. This also requires that some of the ingredients of the forecast, such as mortality tables, should be revised at much more frequently.

Third, forecasting techniques should be based on stochastic forecasting models of demography and the main economic variables rather than on *ad hoc* assumptions as to likely outcomes along with arbitrary 'high fertility' and 'low fertility' assumptions (for example). In particular, further refinement is required in estimating survival probabilities for those aged 80 and more as current techniques do not seem to take duly into account the effects of selection of survival probabilities and hence tend to overestimate mortality rates for this age group. Current methods giving point estimates based on the 'best estimates' of official actuaries have been shown systematically to understate growing longevity in many OECD countries. There will inevitably be errors in forecasting the future, but statistical methods exist which permit the estimation of confidence intervals around projections, and such models ought to be implemented on a consistent basis.

*Promoters:*

Fondazione RODOLFO DEBENEDETTI, Tito Boeri (Bocconi University), Axel Boersch-Supan (Director, Institute for Economics and Statistics - Universität Mannheim), Agar Brugiavini (University of Venice), Richard Disney (University of Nottingham), Franco Peracchi (University of Rome, Tor Vergata).

*The following have endorsed the appeal:*

Orazio Attanasio (University College of London)
André Babeau (University of Paris-Dauphine)
James Banks (Institute for Fiscal Studies, London)
Charles Bean (London School of Economics)
Samuel Bentolila (CEMFI – Centre for Monetary and Financial Studies)
Giuseppe Bertola (European University Institute and University of Turin)
David Blake (Director, Pensions Institute, Birkbeck College)
Richard Blundell (University College of London)
Michele Boldrin (University of Minnesota and Universidad Carlos III de Madrid)
Alison Booth (Institute for Social and Economic Research, University of Essex)
Paolo Bosi (University of Modena)
Martin Browning (University of Copenhagen)
Michael Burda (Institut für Wirtschaftstheorie, Humboldt-Universität zu Berlin)
Onorato Castellino (University of Turin and CeRP)
CeRP (Center for Research on Pension and Welfare Policies)
Riccardo Cesari (University of Bologna)
CESifo (Centre for Economic Studies and Institute for Economic Research, Munich)
Pierre-André Chiappori (University of Chicago)
Gordon L. Clark (University of Oxford)
Frank A. Cowell (London School of Economics and Political Science)
Hugh Davies (Centre for Pensions and Social Insurance, Birkbeck College)
E. Philip Davis (Bank of England)
Didier Davydoff (Director, Observatoire de l'Epargne Européenne)
Daniela Del Boca (University of Turin)
Juan Dolado (Universidad Carlos III de Madrid)
Gosta Esping-Andersen (University of Trento and Universitat Pompeu Fabra)
Christopher Flinn (New York University)
Elsa Fornero (University of Turin and CeRP)
Michael Forster (Head of Programme, "Incomes, Poverty and Social Policy", European Centre for Social Welfare Policy and Research, Vienna)
Vincenzo Galasso (Universidad Carlos III, Madrid)
Francesco Giavazzi (Bocconi University)
Marek Gora ("Security through Diversity" Pension Reform Leader, Poland)
Jonathan Gruber (MIT)
Luigi Guiso (Ente Einaudi)
Michael Haliassos (University of Cyprus)

Stephen Hall (Imperial College)
Georges Heinrich (CEPS/Instead)
Pierre Hausman (CEPS/Instead)
Jose A. Herce (FEDEA and Universidad Complutense of Madrid)
Alberto Holly (DEEP, University of Lausanne)
Robert Holzmann (Director, Social Protection, The World Bank, and University of Saarland)
Andrew Hughes Hallett (University of Strathclyde)
Andrea Ichino (European University Institute)
Institute of Economics at the University of Copenhagen
Tullio Jappelli (CSEF, University of Salerno)
Juan F. Jimeno (Universidad de Alcalà and FEDEA)
Heather Joshi (Centre for Longitudinal Studies, Institute of Education, London)
Arie Kapteyn (Tilburg University)
Ramon Marimon (European University Institute)
Bernd Marin (Executive Director, European Centre for Social Welfare Policy and Research, Vienna)
Franco Modigliani (MIT)
Paolo Onofri (University of Bologna)
Mike Orszag (Centre for Pensions and Social Insurance - Birkbeck College)
Marco Pagano (CSEF, University of Salerno)
Marten Palme (Stockholm School of Economics)
Pierre Pestieau (CREPP,Université de Liège)
Christopher Pissarides (London School of Economics)
Luigi Pistaferri (Stanford University)
Christopher Prinz (Head of Programme "Social Welfare Modelling", European Centre for Social Welfare Policy and Research, Vienna)
Rafael Repullo (CEMFI, Centre for Monetary and Financial Studies)
Jean-Marie Robine (INSERM, Demography and Health, University of Montpellier 1)
Gerard Roland (Université Libre de Bruxelles and ECARE)
Michal Rutkowski (The World Bank, Head of Social Protection Group, Europe and Central Asia Region)
Gaston Schaber (CEPS/Instead)
Günter Schmaus (CEPS/Instead)
Hans-Werner Sinn (CESifo, Munich)
Peter B. Sorensen (University of Copenhagen)
Peter Sturm (IMF, Research Department)
Salvador Valdés-Prieto (Catholic University of Chile)
Thierry Verdier (CERAS, Ecole des Ponts et Chaussées and DELTA, Ecole Normale)
Juergen von Hagen (Director, Center for European Integration Studies, University of Bonn)
Gert G. Wagner (DIW, Berlin, European University Viadrina and CEPS/Instead)
Sue Ward (Freelance Journalist)
Guglielmo Weber (University of Padua)

Edward Whitehouse (Director, Axia Economics, London, and Consultant Economist, The World Bank)
Charles Wyplosz (Graduate Institute of International Studies)
Stephen Yeo (CEO of CEPR)
Geneviève Zdrojewski (European Commission)

# SUBJECT INDEX

MIX
Papier aus verantwortungsvollen Quellen
Paper from responsible sources
FSC® C105338

If you have any concerns about our products,
you can contact us on
**ProductSafety@springernature.com**

In case Publisher is established outside the EU,
the EU authorized representative is:
**Springer Nature Customer Service Center GmbH**
**Europaplatz 3, 69115 Heidelberg, Germany**

Printed by Libri Plureos GmbH
in Hamburg, Germany